COURTS, PROSECUTION, AND CONVICTION

Courts, Prosecution, and Conviction

by
Michael McConville
and
John Baldwin

CLARENDON PRESS · OXFORD
1981

Oxford University Press, Walton Street, Oxford OX2 6DP

LONDON GLASGOW NEW YORK TORONTO
DELHI BOMBAY CALCUTTA MADRAS KARACHI
KUALA LUMPUR SINGAPORE HONG KONG TOKYO
NAIROBI DAR ES SALAAM CAPE TOWN
MELBOURNE AUCKLAND
AND ASSOCIATE COMPANIES IN
BEIRUT BERLIN IBADAN MEXICO CITY

Published in the United States by
Oxford University Press, New York

British Library Cataloguing in Publication Data
Baldwin, John
Courts, prosecution and conviction.
1. Prosecution—England
I. Title II. McConville, Michael
344.205′75 KD8220
ISBN 0–19–825355–9

Typeset by Butler and Tanner Ltd., Frome
Printed in Great Britain
at the University Press, Oxford
by Eric Buckley
Printer to the University

ACKNOWLEDGEMENTS

We owe a debt of gratitude to a number of people in preparing this book. The Home Office and the Royal Commission on Criminal Procedure have generously funded different parts of our research and members of those organizations have commented helpfully on the manuscript. We are particularly grateful to the secretary of the Royal Commission, Mr C. T. Train, for smoothing out various difficulties we encountered, and to Mr C. W. Pratley of the Lord Chancellor's Department and Mr R. Steventon of the Metropolitan Police for allowing access to a great number of Crown Court papers and for facilitating our research in many other ways. Gordon Borrie, despite heavy commitments as Director General of Fair Trading, has maintained a close interest in our work and has given us the benefit of his advice on every occasion on which we have sought it. Professor W. R. Cornish, Mrs S. McCabe, Professor W. E. Cavenagh, and His Honour Judge Skinner have similarly made helpful comments on earlier drafts of the manuscript. Our friends, Mr A. F. Wilcox and Dr J. P. Wilson, who have been closely associated with our research from the outset, have displayed a loyalty and commitment to the research that we had no right to expect. As will be apparent throughout this book, they have carried out an enormous amount of work on our behalf with great efficiency and thoroughness. Sir Philip Knights, Chief Constable of the West Midlands Police, and Mr I. S. Manson, Chief Prosecuting Solicitor of the West Midlands, have also given invaluable assistance in the course of our enquiries. It is a pleasure to record our gratitude to our secretary, Mrs Yvonne Jacobs, for her painstaking and unstinting labours in the preparation of the manuscript. Our final thanks go to our families for their continued support and encouragement. The views expressed in this book are, of course, ours alone and should not be taken as the views of the Home Office, the Royal Commission on Criminal Procedure, respondents, or anyone else to whom we are indebted.

MICHAEL MCCONVILLE
JOHN BALDWIN

Birmingham 1980

CONTENTS

1

UNDERSTANDING THE PROSECUTION PROCESS

Understanding of the way in which the prosecution process operates in England is in its infancy. In the United States, by contrast, generations of lawyers and social scientists have been active in enquiring into, and constructing theories about, all aspects of the criminal system. This disparity cannot be explained simply by reference to the fact that less interest has been shown or less intellectual effort expended in England, though this is certainly the case. It is much more that the participants in the criminal justice system have by and large shown little enthusiasm for outside enquiry and have regarded researchers with suspicion and on occasions with fear. The danger, as they see it, is that researchers may undermine confidence in the operation of the system; they may rock the boat and challenge the *status quo*. The sort of co-operation from officials that American researchers take for granted has to be won in England through prolonged and delicate negotiation, and there is no guarantee that the enquiry will not after all be thwarted.

We do not make these observations as any *apologia* for what follows. Indeed, as far as the research reported in this book is concerned, we could scarcely have wished for more helpful respondents. Nor do we seek to air our grievances about the hostility we have encountered in the past.[1] It is rather that the climate of defensiveness, suspicion, and antagonism that English researchers have traditionally been faced with has set boundaries to the accumulation of knowledge about the criminal process, and to some extent stunted that development of explanatory models and theories which our American counterparts have so enthusiastically and successfully employed. In seeking to understand how the English prosecution system works, reliance upon the writings of academics in the United States can prove

[1] These have been discussed a good deal elsewhere: see Baldwin and McConville (1978a, 1979a) and Zander (1977, 1978 at pp. 139–41).

hazardous. For the concepts they have developed, the explanations advanced, the formal and informal working arrangements uncovered, look decidedly uncomfortable when placed alongside the English criminal system. Certain parallels, it is true, can be drawn between the two jurisdictions but they can too easily be overdrawn.

At the same time it would be misleading to suggest that little research has been carried out in England. There has in fact been a great deal, but most of it has been limited in scope, fragmentary, and essentially atheoretical. The primary motivation has been the laudable, though pragmatic, one of seeking reform of the system rather than any serious attempt to explore and understand its workings.[2] Researchers working in this tradition have confined their attention to specific steps in the system—such as pre-trial detention, police interrogation, the provision of legal advice and financial assistance, interactions within the courtroom, jury trials, and sentencing—and much has been achieved in exposing serious weaknesses at these stages of the criminal process. Worthwhile reforms have sometimes followed these endeavours and it would be wrong to dismiss the value of this work. Nevertheless, it must be recognized that producing reforms of the criminal system in a piecemeal way is unsatisfactory and can be self-defeating. It can lead to mere tinkering with one part of the system when extensive surgery is required. It may yield information about aspects of the administration of justice but may fail to increase our understanding of the working of the whole. Changing one part of the system may have unanticipated consequences elsewhere. Appreciation of the interactions of the different stages of the criminal process is crucial since, for example, decisions taken at one stage (say, when a suspect is in police custody) will as a rule have an important bearing on decisions taken by the suspect and by others at later stages. Without some consideration of underlying

[2] Campbell and Wiles (1976) see this approach to the study of legal institutions as part of a peculiarly English scientific tradition. Social science in England is, they argue,

> pragmatically conceived, utilitarian in stance, and technical in execution ... Pragmatism and an uncomplicated empiricism became, and have remained, essential features of British political and intellectual life ... The British tradition has produced an almost instinctual distrust of abstraction and theorizing. (pp. 558-9.)

Similarly incisive observations on English research have been made by Low (1978); McBarnet (1978a); Lloyd (1979) at pp. 344-74; and Campbell and Wiles (1979).

principles, without some kind of theory about how the system operates, our understanding of the system as a whole and our ability to make rational predictions about the consequences of change are unlikely to be advanced. The point is well made by Low (1978) who argues that, without any 'properly articulated theoretical underpinning',

> what are we to make of [King's] finding that a third of those who apply for bail in magistrates' courts have their applications rejected? Is this a lot or a little? Is the criminal justice system being used as an instrument for the oppression of under-privileged groups and the maintenance in power of a 'ruling class', . . . or is it on the contrary being used as an instrument for securing equality before the law? (p. 15.)

But, as many writers have found, it is very much easier to write about the desirability of explicit theoretical underpinnings than it is to construct them in the course of empirical enquiry. Even a casual reading of the literature of social science readily demonstrates that questionable interpretation often takes place in awkward or inappropriate theoretical frameworks almost as if to dress up crude attempts by researchers to superimpose their own values upon their empirical findings.

These lapses are easy enough to understand, even if they cannot be defended. Research in the social sciences cannot be the value-free activity the founding fathers envisaged, and, if some researchers have preferred to adopt a rigidly pragmatic approach to avoid the accusation that their use of theory is nothing more than the thinly disguised expression of their own prejudice, one may at least feel some sympathy for them. Most find it easier to deal with the business of collecting and analysing the findings of research than to grapple with concepts and theories that might breathe life and meaning into them. We endeavour in this chapter to set out some of the theoretical perspectives that we have found useful in making sense of the English prosecution process. We then present the results of our research in the main body of the book, and attempt in the final chapter to draw the findings together in terms of the theoretical perspectives discussed here.

THEORETICAL PERSPECTIVES

In examining the working of the criminal justice system, the natural starting-point is the perceptive analysis provided by the

American political scientist, Herbert Packer, whose work is now a classic within the broad field of socio-legal studies. Packer (1968) argued that it was useful to view any system of criminal justice according to the extent to which it corresponded to two perspectives (or models, as Packer preferred to call them) which represented poles of a single continuum. On the one hand, Packer describes a Crime Control Model which he characterizes as an administrative, rather than a judicial, approach in which the rights of individual defendants are subordinated to the bureaucratic demands of repressing and controlling criminal behaviour. Under this model, the administration of justice operates rather like a conveyor belt with decisions in the hands of officials acting for the most part outside the formal atmosphere of the courtroom. There is no basic presumption of innocence, rather the reverse, for, as Packer puts it, 'if there is confidence in the reliability of informal fact-finding activities that take place in the early stages of the criminal process, the remaining stages can be relatively perfunctory' (pp. 160–1). The underlying values of Packer's second model—the Due Process Model—are diametrically opposed to these. Here criminal procedure is viewed as an obstacle course in which checks designed to weed out potentially innocent defendants operate at every stage in the process. Formal judicial and adversarial fact-finding replaces informal, administrative fact-finding, and the acquittal of the guilty is tolerated in order to ensure that no innocent defendant is convicted.[3]

Though Packer is at pains to emphasize that these models are 'ideal types' (and, therefore, abstractions and distortions of reality) and that they are not to be viewed as normative prescriptions, there is little doubt from Packer's own work, and also from the work of others who have followed, which of the two models is viewed as the more likely to produce just and equitable results. Most writers have in fact noted an acute disjuncture between, on the one hand, a somewhat disingenuous vaunting of 'due process' values by actors within the judicial system and, on the other, the actual operation of the system itself. 'The

[3] Griffiths (1970) disputes Packer's claim to have produced two models of criminal procedure. He argues instead that Packer has provided only one—a Battle Model—in which the criminal process is portrayed as a struggle between two contending forces (the individual and the State) which exhibit 'profound and irreconcileable disharmony of interest'. (p. 367.)

criminal process', Packer writes, 'in the large majority of cases probably approximates fairly closely the dictates of the Crime Control Model'. (p. 239.) He notes, for example, in relation to the arrest of suspects, their detention and interrogation, their rights to have access to lawyers, and the protections laid down to establish a defendant's culpability in the courtroom itself, that procedures conform more closely to the Crime Control than the Due Process Model—a view that is amply confirmed by a great deal of research conducted subsequently in the United States.

Although doubts have been raised about the framework proposed by Packer,[4] and although less research on these questions has been carried out in England than in the United States, there are nevertheless certain obvious parallels that can be drawn. We shall argue in this book that, for example, the safeguards available to suspects in police custody are virtually non-existent. Yet it is at this stage that the suspect is most vulnerable and where, as Packer rightly argues, the disparity in resources between the state and the accused is greatest.[5] Furthermore, the police-suspect encounter is one of the key exchanges in the criminal process and one that may well colour what happens at later (and more public) stages. Many writers have shown that the rules regulating police interrogation in England are routinely ignored or flouted, that the suspect's right to remain silent is illusory, and that there is almost unlimited scope for an unscrupulous officer to exploit the weakness of the accused's position. The situation is indeed more favourable to the accused in the United States where the courts have striven in recent years to give meaning to his rights. In the absence of corres-

[4] McBarnet (1978b, 1979) has argued that Packer's models present a false dichotomy because, she says, there is no necessary relationship between legality and due process. She does not see deviations from standards of legality by actors within the criminal justice system in terms of accommodations or aberrations on their part. On the contrary, she argues that 'a good many of the practices in criminal justice described as informal perversions of the formal rules are in fact allowed, facilitated or upheld in the formal rules of statute and precedent'. (1978b, p. 30.)

[5] Packer summarizes the problems the accused faces in the following succinct passage:

> There is every opportunity for overreaching and abuse on the part of the police. There is no limit to the extent to which these opportunities are taken advantage of except in the police's own sense of self-restraint. Later correctives palliate but do not suffice. What actually takes place in the police station is known only to the suspect and to the police. It is not hard to predict whose word will be taken if a contradiction arises. (p. 203.)

ponding efforts on the part of English courts (which, as we shall see in later chapters of this book, have been prepared to overlook or condone even serious breaches of the rules governing the interrogation of suspects), we would argue that, in England more than in the United States, the unverifiable product of police interviews has, to use Packer's telling phrase, 'a decisively malign impact on the criminal process'. (p. 203.)

But this is merely one way in which the Crime Control Model describes well the situation in England. Further parallels can be drawn. Consider Figure 1, which shows what happened to those defendants, charged with indictable offences (i.e. those which could be tried by jury), whose cases reached the criminal courts[6] in England and Wales in 1978. Two striking features of

FIGURE 1

The disposition of defendants charged with indictable offences in England and Wales in 1978

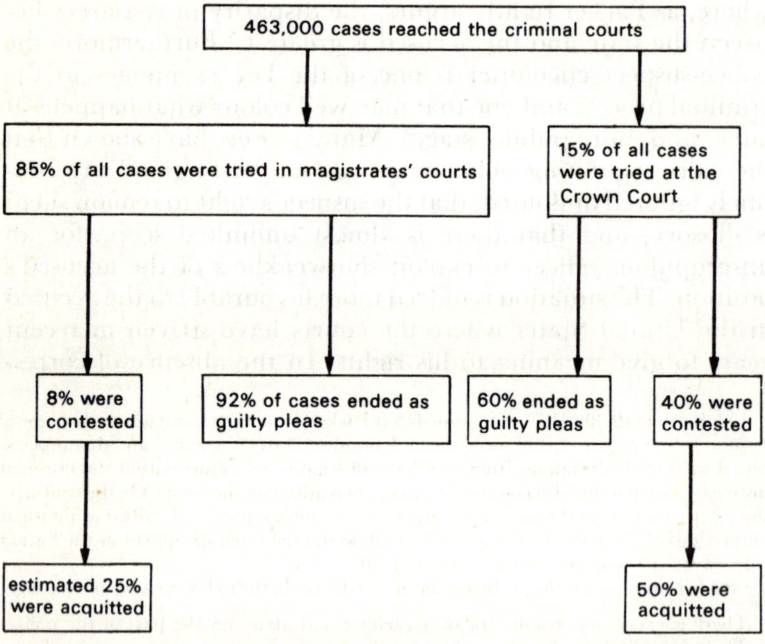

[6] No account is taken in the diagram of the 107,000 offenders (mainly children and young persons) charged with indictable offences whose cases did not reach court but who were instead dealt with by the police by means of a formal caution.

these statistics should be noted. First, the great majority of indictable criminal cases are heard in the lower criminal courts, fewer than one case in seven reaching the Crown Court.[7] Secondly, few criminal cases are contested in the courts. Indeed, the single most important feature of criminal procedure (both in England and in the United States) is its fundamental dependence upon the guilty plea. It is an extraordinary fact that almost 90 per cent of all defendants charged with serious criminal offences plead guilty,[8] and that trial by jury (the epitome of the Due Process Model) is used by only about 5 per cent of those who are eligible to be so tried. There is no clearer example of the hiatus that exists between the 'law in books' and the 'law in action' because, in the procedures which accompany a plea of guilty, the formal safeguards embodied in the rhetoric of 'due process of law' are absent; the procedural protections associated with adversarial confrontation are lacking; proof beyond reasonable doubt is not determined by an impartial jury; there is no testing of witnesses in cross-examination; inadmissible evidence (even the previous criminal convictions of the accused) may be taken into account, and the traditional remedies open to defendants on appeal are largely foreclosed. There is, in other words, an erosion of the principles of adversary justice and their replacement by essentially inquisitorial procedures. It is true that the jury is retained, but its function is on this view largely symbolic—to uphold due process values in the occasional show trial.

That the overwhelming mass of defendants plead guilty at trial has far-reaching legal and sociological implications in making sense of the criminal system. It is upon the basis of the perfunctory treatment of those who plead guilty that much of the theorizing about the criminal justice system (in the United States if not in England) has been grounded, and it is worth examining this body of writing in some detail.

It is tempting to regard the erosion of adversary trial and of

[7] In England and Wales, the magistrates' courts represent the lower criminal courts which sit without a jury. Jury trial is provided in the Crown Court (the higher criminal courts) which deal on the whole with the more serious criminal cases.

[8] Although national statistics are not as readily available in the United States as in England and Wales, the indications are that the proportion of defendants who plead guilty is even higher there: see Newman (1966); President's Commission (1967); and Blumberg (1970).

due process principles as straightforward accommodations to case-load pressures. Criminal courts have been faced by an ever-increasing number of cases, and it is often argued that, as a direct consequence of this, compromises have to be made. This explanation has been advanced by a number of American writers, among whom the most notable are Newman (1966), Alschuler (1968), and Blumberg (1970), to explain the prevalence of plea bargaining—a practice widely adopted in the United States in which more lenient sentences are offered to defendants who plead guilty. According to this view, the resources of the court system simply do not allow all defendants to be tried by jury, and deviations from due process values become an inevitable concomitant of scarce resources. This explanation has, however, been undermined in recent years by researchers such as Heumann (1975), Eisenstein and Jacob (1977), and Nardulli (1979), who have demonstrated that plea bargaining procedures are still followed when court resources are under-utilized. Others, such as Friedman (1979) and Langbein (1979), have argued that the rise of plea bargaining may have had more to do with structural changes in criminal justice (as, for example, the growing complexity of trials, and the emergence of professional police and prosecutors) than with an increasing volume of cases. Criminal courts, it seems, are not after all committed to, or even oriented to, an adversarial approach. Rather the different actors who comprise 'the court' develop working relationships which emphasize co-operation rather than antagonism and endeavour to reduce the uncertainty of trial. This has benefits for many defendants in that the sentence is predictable and may be a good deal less severe than it would have been following a trial. A co-operative stance also benefits the regular court participants by making their professional careers less insecure and disagreeable, even if this is at the expense of allegiance to legal and procedural rules.[9]

Little surprise should be caused by these observations, for generations of sociologists since Max Weber have pointed out

[9] Blumberg (1967), in a famous passage, refers to the 'short-cuts, deviations and outright rule violations' which are adopted by the court participants. He continues:

> all the significant participants in the court's social structure are bound into an organized system of complicity. This consists of a work arrangement in which the patterned, covert, informal breaches, and evasions of 'due process' are institutionalized, but are, nevertheless, denied to exist. (p. 20.)

that the formal rules of an organization will invariably be tempered or replaced by the development of an informal structure of rules which may run counter to the manifest aims of the organization.[10] This has fundamental implications for the running of all bureaucracies, strikingly illustrated in the case of the criminal courts. Here the declared goal is the rather vague one of the attainment of 'justice' according to the requirements encapsulated in the phrase 'due process of law'. This objective is refracted through a gamut of group interests, administrative pressures, individual characteristics, and the like. As Cole (1979) puts it:

> Although the traditional picture of the courtroom emphasizes adversarial attitudes, a more realistic version might stress that interactions among the major actors have many of the characteristics associated with those in a small group ... each member of the courtroom group [becomes] proficient at the work routines associated with his or her role, and it allows the group to develop stable expectations about the actions of the other members. In this way the business of the courtroom proceeds in a regularized, informal manner, with many 'understandings' among the members that are never recorded but that ease much of the work of the court. (pp. 336–7.)

The development of these relationships between court personnel—what Cole calls 'exchange relationships' to emphasize the reciprocity of their dealings[11]—can set severe limitations on the scope for reform of procedures, since the commitment of court actors to the existing routines may be sufficiently strong to counteract any modifications that may be introduced.[12]

American theorists emphasize the co-operation and cohesiveness of the various participants in the criminal system because

[10] There is a vast literature concerned with the sociology of organizations, a literature dominated by the contribution by Max Weber (see 1947 edition). See also Merton (1940); Merton *et al* (1952); Blau (1955); and Blau and Scott (1963).

[11] Several American researchers have adopted the same perspective: see particularly Blumberg (1967); Skolnick (1967); Eisenstein and Jacob (1977); Buckle and Buckle (1977); Utz (1978); Nardulli (1979); Mather (1979); and Lipetz (1980).

[12] This is well illustrated by Lipetz (1980) in her study of a Women's Court in Chicago. She writes:

> The public expects courts to dispense justice. Legislators write laws and empower courts to enforce them. Offices and organizations which employ or sponsor courtroom personnel devise policies for courtroom personnel to follow. Yet as courtroom workers begin to translate duties and regulations into everyday routines, something happens. Justice concerns are submerged as interest focuses on managing caseloads and getting work done. (p. 58.)

theirs is in large measure a plea bargaining system in which the principles of negotiation and barter over sentence and plea are widely accepted as an integral part of criminal procedure. Plea bargaining is not only recognized but regulated by appellate courts, and it seems that as many as 90 per cent of all criminal cases heard in courts throughout the United States are nowadays settled by some form of plea bargaining.[13] It is entirely understandable, and indeed appropriate, that the dominance of the practice should have generated so much theorizing about the workings of the criminal process. But it is misleading to suppose that the theoretical perspectives can be readily transposed to English courts for, although significant elements of negotiation surround guilty pleas in England[14] (which the Court of Appeal has now belatedly recognized[15]), there is no institutionalized structure within which plea bargaining takes place such as is found in most jurisdictions in the United States. In consequence, the theoretical approaches that have been developed have to be treated with caution. Nevertheless, they should not be too hastily jettisoned for, as we noted earlier, the English system is in large part a guilty plea system, and some explanation of the reasons behind the widespread waiving of the right to jury trial by defendants is required.

In the first place, it should be noted that, whatever the rhetoric of open court adjudication, in most cases all the significant encounters and exchanges which bear upon the disposition of cases take place privately outside the courtroom.[16] This can be seen clearly in the way that suspects are interviewed in police custody, a subject with which we shall deal at length in this book. It is also illustrated in relation to the question of guilty plea determination, where the advice of police officers or lawyers as a rule assumes much greater significance than any

[13] National figures are not available, but see Vetri (1964); President's Commission (1967); and McIntyre and Lippman (1970), for useful estimates of the incidence of plea bargaining.

[14] We argued in our book, *Negotiated Justice* (1977a), that plea bargaining and plea negotiation were much commoner in England than had traditionally been assumed.

[15] We have discussed the position adopted by the Court of Appeal in relation to a spate of plea bargain cases that has reached it in recent years: see Baldwin and McConville (1979b).

[16] As Jerome Skolnick (1967) has put it: 'If the adversary system is defined with only the trial in mind, we are blinding ourselves to the realities of a system that is predominantly pretrial in character.' (p. 69.)

consideration of adversary principles.[17] The most striking example of this form of private guilt determination is to be found in encounters which often occur in the Crown Court when the trial judge meets counsel before trial in his chambers to discuss a particular case—encounters which have been successfully shielded from all researchers in the field. One English judge has recently provided the following extraordinary account[18] of what can occur on these occasions:

> Bargains between judges and defendants as to sentence happen every day. It is in the interests of all concerned that they should ... The practice of Crown Court Judges varies widely. Some see counsel in their rooms whenever they are asked. Some refuse to see counsel at all. One judge ... told me that he only sees counsel he can trust ... Some judges send for counsel before the case starts and virtually give directions for 'carving it up' ... Some judges negotiate more subtly, by sending and receiving messages through their clerks or the court clerks ... Judges miss life [at the Bar] and day after day see their former colleagues only across the formal courtroom. It is good to have a chat with the lads. How tempting to sit down and sort it all out sensibly, wigs off ... The tension of open court has gone. The shorthand writer is absent. No press or public. Even the accused—around whose fate it all revolves—is not there ... In this easy atmosphere [the formal rules] can be overlooked in a genuine effort to find a sensible short-cut, off the record.[19]

Secondly, although plea bargaining and related forms of plea negotiation are practised in England, and are indeed permissible within the legal rules,[20] a much more powerful factor

[17] See on this Dell (1971); Laurie (1972); Heberling (1973); and Baldwin and McConville (1977a).

[18] The account was provided by His Honour Judge Pickles in evidence he submitted in 1979 to the Royal Commission on Criminal Procedure.

[19] For a similarly startling revelation, see His Honour Judge David (1978) who writes:

> Magistrates will be familiar with the scene. The time is 10.29. There is a knock on the retiring-room door and the clerk announces 'Counsel to see you'. Thereafter follows a swift moving scene, more reminiscent of a cattle auction than a court of law, and the business of the day is all but disposed of. (p. 74.)

[20] The key case here is *Turner* [1970] 50 Cr.App.R. 352 which gives the accepted legal position on plea bargaining. The Court of Appeal stated:

> There must be freedom of access between counsel and judge. Any discussion, however, which takes place must be between the judge and both counsel for the defence and counsel for the prosecution. This freedom of access is important because there may be matters calling for communication or discussion, which are of such a nature that counsel cannot in the interests of his client mention them in open court ... Again,

operates to induce defendants to plead guilty. This is the so-called discount principle, a sentencing practice under which those who plead guilty are customarily given a lighter sentence than they would have received had they been convicted after a full trial. This policy raises serious questions about the voluntariness of guilty pleas tendered as a result but, as we shall argue in the final chapter, the legal rules encourage the practice.[21] Several American writers have referred to this sentencing policy as evidence of the existence of 'implicit' plea bargaining,[22] and there can be little doubt about the potent influence it has in discouraging contested trials. The research that we have ourselves conducted on this question (Baldwin and McConville (1978b)) showed clearly that enormous reductions in both the length and form of sentences were awarded to those who pleaded guilty.[23] This factor alone goes a long way towards explaining why so few defendants eligible to be tried by jury opt to do so. Most prefer to be dealt with in the lower courts where the sentencing powers of the magistrates are much more circumscribed than are those of judges in the Crown Court. Indeed, contrary to popular view and despite the concern voiced in official circles about the number of defendants who nowadays choose to be tried by jury rather than before magistrates,[24] it appears from the research that we conducted in the Birmingham Crown Court in 1975 and 1976 that relatively few defendants whose cases reach the Crown Court are themselves responsible for the decision. We found that in only one case in

---

counsel on both sides may wish to discuss with the judge whether it would be proper, in a particular case, for the prosecution to accept a plea to a lesser offence. It is of course imperative that so far as possible justice must be administered in open court. Counsel should, therefore, only ask to see the judge when it is felt to be really necessary.

[21] The Court of Appeal has made it plain on several occasions that defendants pleading guilty can anticipate sizeable reductions in sentence: see Thomas (1979) at pp. 50 2.

[22] See particularly Newman (1966); Newman and NeMoyer (1970); Heberling (1973); Heumann (1978) at p. 158; and Friedman (1979).

[23] We calculated the extent of the sentence discount by comparing the sentences given to two samples of defendants who pleaded guilty in the Birmingham Crown Court with a control group of defendants who had been convicted after contesting the case in court. 57 per cent of one of the groups of those who pleaded guilty, and 50 per cent of the other, were given non-custodial sentences whereas only 31 per cent of the matched group of those convicted after trial received such sentences. We discuss this research in greater detail at pp. 197–8.

[24] See particularly the report of the James Committee (1975).

ten tried in the Crown Court did the defendant himself determine the venue of trial.[25] There is, then, no great enthusiasm evident among defendants to have cases tried in the Crown Court, still less to contest them; and it is pressures within the criminal system itself which induce a high level of compliance with bureaucratic objectives.

Numerous researchers in England and in the United States who have examined why defendants plead guilty have been struck by the peripheral role that most defendants seem to play in reaching that decision. For, though in one sense the defendant is the key actor in the whole scenario, it is clear nonetheless that he rapidly becomes relegated to an inferior role in the court. In an organizational sense, it is perhaps inevitable that his legal advisers and the others who comprise the courtroom workgroup should occupy a pre-eminent role. They are after all much more familiar with court routines than is the defendant, and they can offer advice on the basis of knowledge of how the system works in practice. The defendant, who is likely to be confused and unfamiliar with the intricacies and routines of the court, is in a weak position to question or reject the advice that is offered.[26] Indeed, he will in most cases be foolish to do so. Most defendants, it seems, are relieved and happy to entrust the case to their legal advisers and to follow whatever advice they are given. It was clear from the research that we carried out in Birmingham, one aspect of which involved interviewing defendants tried in the Crown Court, that many felt an acute sense of powerlessness in this situation. One defendant summed up the sentiments of many others when he observed that defending and prosecuting lawyers are 'the cast of the play, you're just the casual one-day actor'.[27]

[25] From information kindly supplied to us by the West Midlands Prosecuting Solicitor's Department on 2,406 cases tried in the Birmingham Crown Court in 1975 and 1976, we discovered that 49 per cent of cases were of such a serious nature that they were triable only in the Crown Court, and that 40 per cent of cases were tried in the Crown Court on the prosecutor's application. It is important to note, however, that, in those cases that were contested, slightly more than a quarter reached the Crown Court on the defendants' election.

[26] See the excellent discussion of the defendant's position in Bottoms and McClean (1976) at pp. 55–8.

[27] The same point was made, if more bluntly, by another defendant who stated that:

> from the accused's point of view, it's like a guy on a desert island, with all the little sharks coming in for a little nibble ... Everything's stacked against the accused ... [My barrister] refused to ask lots of questions owing to the fact that he's one of the

Given this emphasis upon the superficiality of treatment of defendants in the criminal process, it is perhaps surprising that a thoroughgoing 'conflict' perspective has not been more widely used by writers describing the workings of the criminal justice system. Important contributions have been made by several theorists (most notably Chambliss and Seidman (1971)) who have viewed the enactment and enforcement of law as reflections of the ability of particular groups to shape the legal system to protect their own class interests. This perspective could be applied to the way that courts themselves operate, and Chambliss (1969) has argued strongly that:

> The activities and policies of law-enforcement agencies, which sometimes appear irrational or whimsical to outside observers, are in fact quite rational (albeit not necessarily desirable) activities which are designed to have the consequences of maximizing organizational rewards and minimizing organizational strain. This general principle is reflected in the fact that in the administration of the criminal law those persons are arrested, tried, and sentenced who can offer the fewest rewards for nonenforcement of the laws and who can be processed without creating any undue strain for the organizations which comprise the legal system. (pp. 84–5.)

Numerous writers, such as Hall (1952), Chambliss (1964), Hills (1971), and Thompson (1975), have argued that this approach has considerable relevance to the *enactment* of laws such as those relating to theft, vagrancy, and drugs, but greater difficulties have been encountered when researchers have turned their attention to the *enforcement* of legislation. There have been, it is true, a number of convincing demonstrations of the way that selective enforcement activities on the part of police officers can be squared with a conflict perspective,[28] but, when attention is focused on what happens inside the courtroom (in isolation from other stages in the criminal process), the perspective is only weakly supported. Although it is not difficult to find empirical evidence showing discriminatory practices by some

---

flag wavers. I don't know whether he wants to be a Q.C. or what. I was just dissatisfied with them all in general—putting it bluntly, they all basically piss in the same pot.

See further Baldwin and McConville (1977a) at pp. 84–94.

[28] An excellent analysis of these studies in relation to the 'social construction of official statistics' is provided by Box (1971) at pp. 166–217; see also Chambliss and Seidman (1971) at pp. 271–394.

courts, there is little of substance which demonstrates disparities of treatment along class lines.[29] It seems that, if a conflict framework is to contribute to an understanding of the judicial as opposed to the criminal process, it has to be grafted on to a view of the courtroom which recognizes the institutional demands of the courtroom bureaucracy and the narrow sectional interests of the individuals who comprise it. Chambliss and Siedman (1971) in effect do precisely this in their discussion of the American guilty plea system when they argue that specifically bureaucratic pressures operate to create the system but that 'how favourable a bargain one can strike with the prosecutor in the pretrial confrontations is a direct function of how politically and economically powerful the defendant is' (p. 412)—a proposition that is in fact scarcely supported by the available empirical evidence.[30]

These considerations bring us to a more general observation—that the administration of justice is an inherently political process for, as Cole (1979) puts it, 'it is engaged in the formulation and administration of public policies where choices must be made among such competing values as the rights of defendants, protection of persons and property, justice and freedom. That various groups in society interpret these values differently is obvious.' (p. 32.) If this be so, we may conclude that, when one considers the factors that explain the Anglo-American guilty plea systems, reference to the role played by police officers, lawyers, or other members of the court, although a necessary part of any explanatory framework, is not of itself a sufficient explanation. The broader socio-economic system within which the criminal courts operate cannot be left out of account.[31]

[29] Several researchers have purported to demonstrate 'class justice' but, when account has been taken of the numerous interacting variables, most of these claims have turned out to be exaggerated, if not entirely misplaced. On this, see the critique prepared by Hagan (1974) in relation to disparities in sentencing.

[30] It is fairly easy to supply anecdotal demonstrations, such as the plea bargain struck by Vice-President Spiro Agnew (on which see Kress (1974)), but more systematically collected evidence is difficult to find. Perhaps the strongest empirical evidence in favour of the proposition comes from those studies which show that having the financial means to retain a private lawyer (as opposed to a public defender) has some influence on the severity of the sentence imposed: see, for example, Newman (1956); Oaks and Lehman (1970); and Casper (1972).

[31] The most strident development of this thesis is given by Bankowski and Mungham (1976).

A related point concerns the legal framework within which the guilty plea system develops and flourishes. We would contend that it is not satisfactory to argue, as several American writers come dangerously close to arguing, that the reliance upon guilty pleas arises because the legal rules which predicate adversary trial are twisted or disregarded in the interests of courtroom personnel. It is in our view going too far to say, as for example does Blumberg (1967), that deviations from the rules merely reflect the limited resources available to deal with intolerably high case-loads. Some account must be taken of the legal rules themselves. What is the content of these rules and what sanctions can be brought to bear where there are breaches? Consideration of the rules reveals that they frequently embody ambiguous standards of legality and that, far from upholding the rights of individuals, they permit, legitimate, or even encourage violations of those rights. In an important series of articles, McBarnet (1976, 1978a, 1978b, 1979) has argued that, while many writers have assumed that the formal legal rules constitute the essence of legality, analysis of the exact specification of the rules often contradicts this assumption. In her examination of the laws relating to arrest, for instance, McBarnet (1979) contends that it is a mistake to regard the discretionary or discriminatory activities of police officers as mere accommodations to the rules or as breaches of them. One must rather look at the content of the rules and at what the courts are prepared to treat as acceptable police behaviour. 'Analysis of the "law in the books" on police behaviour', she writes, 'does not tell us what the police do but a good deal about what the police are legally allowed and legally expected to do.' (p. 28.) When interest is shifted to the 'law in the books' in the way that she advocates, it becomes apparent that the rights of suspects are scarcely enshrined in the law at all for, as McBarnet herself puts it, the law does not incorporate its own rhetoric. Thus the justification for the departures from legality is to be found not in the behaviour of individuals but in the law itself and in the way it is interpreted by the courts. In a telling passage, McBarnet (1979) observes that:

> Legality requires equality; the law discriminates against the homeless and jobless. Legality requires that officials be governed by law; the law is based on post hoc decisions. Legality requires each case be judged on its own facts; the law makes previous convictions grounds

for defining behaviour as an offence. Legality requires incriminating evidence as the basis for arrest and search; the law allows arrest and search in order to establish it. Legality embodies individual civil rights against public or state interests; the law makes state and the public interest a justification for ignoring civil rights. (p. 39.)

This perspective offers a valuable corrective not only to Packer's description of the two polarities of criminal justice (which are seen in McBarnet's terms as a false dichotomy[32]) but also to the fashionable preoccupation of researchers with the 'law in action'. This suggested reversion to the more traditional study of law provides a new perspective which we shall examine critically in the course of this book.

It is misleading to suggest that the sort of injustices that arise within the English system can be attributed to, say, a handful of corrupt police officers, or to incompetent lawyers, or even to lazy or foolish judges. No doubt such individuals exist and may in isolation cause appalling injustice. But most miscarriages of justice which occur within our system cannot be explained in these terms. What we see as of greater importance is the formal structure of legal rules and procedures which allow and even facilitate the erosion or violation of the rights of defendants. In other words, accepted legal procedures require examination as well as violations, real or apparent. In this context, it is worth employing the distinction that has been made by Kipnis (1978), building on Rawls (1971), between 'aberrational' injustice and 'systemic' injustice. Aberrational injustices arise as a result of mistakes or errors of judgment; they are incorrect outcomes of a sound system, a system which is framed to avoid such results. Systemic injustice, on the other hand, results not from human error but from fundamental structural weaknesses within the system itself.[33]

[32] McBarnet (1978a) argues as follows: 'the operation of the law is not a subversion of the substance of the law but exactly what one would expect it to produce; the law in action is only too close a parallel to the law in books; due process is for crime control' (p. 31).

[33] Kipnis (1978) neatly illustrates this distinction by reference to a quality control analogy. He writes:

> Two vials of antibiotic may be equally contaminated. But depending upon the process used to produce each, the contamination may be aberrational or systemic. The first sample may come from a factory where every conceivable step is taken to ensure that such contamination will not take place. The second vial may come from a company which uses a cheap manufacturing process offering no protection against

We shall, therefore, concentrate upon what we see as 'systemic' weaknesses in the English prosecution system, and explore the nature of the relationship between the legal structure and the ability of individuals to enforce rights assumed to be built into that structure. We shall argue that the rights of individuals are at many points uncertain and ambiguous, that responsibilities of those in the prosecution process are ill-defined, and that the adversary model produces numerous conflicts and contradictions. Anyone trying to make sense of the way that the English prosecution system works must recognize that the role of the police is absolutely central. But it is a paradoxical role, for they are required under the adversarial approach to pursue partisan and fearless prosecution, yet at the same time to make dispassionate decisions about whether a prosecution is justified. We shall contend, however, that, in explaining how mistakes, faulty judgment, or injustices occur, it is misleading to isolate police officers or other individuals for criticism. Attention must be paid instead to the structure of the system itself.

---

contamination. There is an element of tragedy if death results when all possible precautions have been taken: there just are limits to human capability at our present level of understanding. But where vital precautions are dropped in the name of expediency, the contamination that results is much more serious if only because we knew it would take place and we knew what could be done to prevent it. (pp. 314–15.)

2

THE BACKGROUND TO THE RESEARCH AND ITS OBJECTIVES

BACKGROUND TO THE RESEARCH

The history of research into the English criminal justice system is very short. Only within the last twenty years have social scientists singled out the activities of police officers, judges, lawyers, and other court personnel as subjects worthy of attention. This development has no doubt been linked to the emergence of criminal law as an academic subject in its own right, the expansion of higher education, and the increased interest in the social sciences, particularly sociology. There was in the 1960s a burgeoning of interest by lawyers and others in the operation of the criminal courts, reflected in a spate of empirical enquiries into various aspects of the system. There have been few genuinely collaborative ventures by lawyers and social scientists working together on an equal footing on interdisciplinary research of this nature. The traditions of the two disciplines are so different that the perspectives adopted by researchers from each, and the way that research has been conceived, have raised many fundamental questions about the nature of the research enterprise itself. As Willock (1974) drily observes, sometimes 'legal Chippendale and sociological G-plan can clash disastrously' (p. 12). This clash of perspectives has tended to lead to piecemeal research, limited 'fact' gathering exercises, and an overwhelmingly atheoretical approach. Narrow topics (such as bail, legal advice and representation, remuneration of lawyers) have been subjected to scrutiny, sometimes in fine detail. As we noted in chapter 1, much of this research has been reformist in character and a great deal of it oriented towards the solution of specific problems. Are too many people being held in custody who could safely be released on bail? Is legal advice available where it is most needed? Is the rate of acquittal too high? Are professional crooks exploiting the rules of evidence and subverting the aims of the criminal system? Though we do not wish to suggest that such research is not worthwhile, it is nevertheless important to recognize that research which sets out to provide answers to such specific problems gets off on the wrong footing because the very definition of a problem is itself problematic. Such an approach, apart from running the obvious risk of taking for granted the very thing that needs to be tested, can lead the researcher to ignore competing perspectives and explanations. The reason is that social problems are often defined by dominant groups in society—they are situations which threaten some vested interest and require a solution that will re-establish social equilibrium. But social problems may also be defined by those at the receiving end, and for them the problem is not the breakdown of social control: it may well be the dominant interest itself.[1]

This question of the definition of problems has fundamental implications for the conduct of research in the social sciences. It raises acute difficulties when, as in our case, the body funding the research is a government department or some other official organization. The fact that our research was funded by the Home Office (and later by the Royal Commission on Criminal Procedure) immediately raises questions about the extent to which we were able to develop our own research proposals and to operate as independent researchers. It is to be expected that government departments and other official bodies should want answers to problems they have defined as existing rather than to those that they do not recognize, and a great deal of research in the past has been funded on this basis. The danger with policy research of this kind is not simply that the scope of the study is narrowly circumscribed but that the remit of the funding body or its stated expectations may distort the interpretation of the results and the presentation of findings. This danger can be seen in the following passage taken from an article by Clarke (1977), a member of the Home Office Research Unit:

Anyone designing policy-oriented studies must pay heed not only to

[1] That most research conducted by social scientists is concerned with disadvantaged groups, such as deviants, ethnic minorities, the old, or the poor, raises serious ethical questions. Because such groups are relatively powerless, they are much less likely to refuse to participate in social scientific enquiries than are other groups in society. Kelman (1972), in an excellent analysis of the ethical dilemmas that face social researchers, rightly argues that there is a danger that research may merely serve to strengthen established interests at the expense of disadvantaged groups. Important discussions of this danger are found in Douglas (1971); Becker and Horowitz (1972); Galliher and McCartney (1973); Sagarin (1973); and Barnes (1979).

the usual scientific standards of argument and proof, but must also be acutely aware of the constraints operating in the real world ... In so far as he makes use of theory, he should strive to frame explanations in terms of variables over which the administrator has a degree of control. (p. 125.)

That administrative concerns should seek to direct research is understandable enough; that they should artificially force explanations into manageable categories is thoroughly unscientific.[2] It must be said, however, that, though we were aware of the dangers, neither the Home Office nor the Royal Commission on Criminal Procedure sought to place serious restrictions on the way we wished to carry out our research. No attempts were made at any stage of our enquiry to divert us from our stated aims, and no pressures were brought to bear to persuade us to pursue avenues we felt unproductive or uncongenial. So, despite some initial fears that our academic interest in the criminal process and our independence as researchers might be compromised by the pragmatic or administrative preoccupations of the Home Office or the Royal Commission, we found that no real constraints were placed in our way in formulating the proposals or in conducting the research itself.[3] Indeed, from the outset, the Home Office made clear that, while their primary interest in the enquiry related to current debates on acquittal rates in the Crown Court,[4] they wanted us to cast our net wide and to examine all aspects of criminal procedure that might have a bearing upon the final disposition of cases at trial.

In the previous chapter we discussed some of the theoretical perspectives that have proved useful in helping us understand the way in which the prosecution process in England works. In this chapter, we set out the details of the research that we have undertaken. We discuss the objectives that we have sought to pursue and provide information on the samples and the methods we have adopted. Before we do this, however, it is necessary to say a little about the background to the project and to indicate

[2] On this and related questions, see the perceptive analyses of Morris (1975) and Wiles (1976).

[3] We did encounter, however, difficulties when the Home Office raised doubts about the wisdom of our publishing certain findings: see Baldwin and McConville (1979a).

[4] This debate had been sparked off by the comments of the then Metropolitan Police Commissioner, Sir Robert Mark, who observed in 1973 that rates of acquittal in the Crown Court were 'too high to be acceptable'.

how the research reported in this book relates to the findings that we have already published.

In our previous two books, *Negotiated Justice* (1977) and *Jury Trials* (1979), we dealt with separate aspects of English criminal procedure. In *Negotiated Justice*, a book which to our regret is more often remembered because of the hostility it provoked from senior ranks of the legal profession than because of its substance,[5] we argued that aspects of English criminal procedure—specifically the lack of effective monitoring of police interrogation and the practice that has developed of awarding a sizeable reduction in sentence to those who plead guilty—produce a situation in which the great majority of defendants can be expected to plead guilty. In Figure 1, presented on p. 6 above, the proportions of defendants who plead guilty in English courts were shown, and it is clear from this Figure that even in the Crown Court a majority of all defendants pleaded guilty at trial in 1978. This reliance upon the guilty plea, we argued, is the central feature of the English criminal system. Yet one of the most interesting facts to emerge from the Crown Court statistics (as given in the *Judicial Statistics* published annually by the Lord Chancellor's Department) is the extraordinary variation of guilty plea rates between different Crown Court centres throughout the country. These statistics have shown that certain Courts have a consistently higher guilty plea rate than do other Courts. For instance, the lowest proportion of defendants pleading guilty is to be found in London (about 40 per cent) and the highest in the North Eastern Circuit (about 70 per cent), and these proportions have been maintaind over the years ever since the statistics were first collated. Unfortunately, the *Judicial Statistics* nowadays present the rates only according to Court Circuits (of which there are seven in England and Wales), and there is no doubt that these large units disguise the extent of variation in plea rates between separate Courts within each Circuit. In the course of our research, we visited six Crown Courts in large cities, and examined the court files for the years 1973 and 1974,[6] and we found variations in guilty plea rates from 51 per cent in Liverpool to 77 per cent in Newcastle upon

[5] The furore to which the book gave rise is discussed in Zander (1977) and Baldwin and McConville (1978a, 1979a).

[6] We are indebted to Kathlyn Bristow and Ann Keith, who were formerly employed as Research Fellows on the project, for carrying out this examination.

Tyne and 79 per cent in Birmingham.[7] Few questions have ever been asked by legal commentators about these kinds of variation, and there is no reason to suppose that they can be explained in terms of the types of defendant or criminal offences in the different areas, and the precise nature of the factors that might explain the overall patterns remains elusive. No doubt some attention needs to be paid to the activities and structure of courtroom workgroups—such as has been done so successfully in the United States by Eisenstein and Jacob (1977) and by Mather (1979), amongst others[8]—but research of this nature has scarcely begun in England. In the present context, one important point to make about the statistics relating to guilty plea rates is that the two Crown Court centres in which we have conducted most of our research, Birmingham and London, have respectively the highest and the lowest plea rates of any Crown Courts in the country.

We carried out the fieldwork for this project in the Birmingham Crown Court over a twenty-month period in 1975 and 1976, during which time 2,406 defendants were tried, 79 per cent of whom pleaded guilty. No more than 370 defendants—15 per cent of the sample as a whole—were actually tried by jury, and the outcomes of their cases were dealt with at length in our book, *Jury Trials* (1979). A further 116 defendants pleaded not guilty and were acquitted at the Crown Court without their cases reaching the jury. These were cases in which the trial judge, for a variety of reasons, decided that the matter should not be determined by a jury, and he himself took the decision by directing the jury to acquit or else by ordering that a verdict of not guilty be recorded before the case had got off the ground in court. These are an important group because some 40 per cent of all acquittals at the Crown Court arise in this way. Indeed, within our sample of Birmingham cases, it is remarkable to note that more defendants gained such acquittals than obtained acquittals by jury. The fact that so many cases collapse at court deserves close investigation because it raises fundamental issues about the formulation and control of the case for the prosecution. If, for example, defendants against whom there

[7] The other rates were 60 per cent in Cardiff, 67 per cent in Manchester, and 74 per cent in Leeds. Further details of this exercise are given in Baldwin and McConville (1979c) at p. 42.

[8] See our discussion chapter 1 at pp. 8–10.

is insufficient evidence are being placed on trial, it is necessary to examine the judgment and motivation of those who institute charges, and to discover why weak cases of this type are allowed to proceed so far. If, on the other hand, individuals against whom there is abundant evidence are being acquitted, it is important to know whether this is because of prosecutorial inefficiency or because of matters over which the prosecution has no control. In short, whether there is a problem with such cases and what the problem may be is the central issue, and, since so many misconceptions surround prosecution practice in such cases, we devote chapter 3 of this book to a detailed analysis of ordered and directed acquittals and chapters 4 and 5 to a discussion of the problems that arise when the prosecution evidence is palpably weak.

This leads naturally to a consideration of a second concern of this book: to gain an understanding of the case for the prosecution (chapters 6–9).[9] As we have already mentioned, the criminal process in England is under-researched, and there has been no systematic attempt to examine the way in which cases are constructed against defendants. In order to achieve this, some basic questions need to be answered, and a major part of this book (chapters 3–5) is concerned with a descriptive analysis of pre-trial criminal proceedings. The sorts of question with which we deal relate to such matters as the role of the police in gathering evidence; the extent to which the prosecution relies upon civilian witnesses and upon forensic evidence; the circumstances surrounding police interrogation of suspects; the frequency and nature of oral and written statements of defendants; the relationship between confession evidence and offence type, plea and outcome; and the significance of confession evidence to the prosecution case as a whole (chapters 6–7). Questions of this kind require investigation because virtually nothing in England (and little elsewhere) is known that bears upon

[9] This part of our research was separately funded in 1979 by the Royal Commission on Criminal Procedure. After we had completed the fieldwork on contested cases in the Crown Court—research which had been entirely funded by the Home Office—we were approached by the Secretary of the Royal Commission on Criminal Procedure about the possibility of examining the role of confession evidence in a series of Crown Court trials. This was a subject which had been close to our hearts for some time as it is central to questions such as the determination of guilty pleas. After a period of solid but exceedingly amicable discussion about how the research would proceed, we were awarded a grant from the Royal Commission to conduct this work.

them. The answers that we provide are subject to certain limitations. We did not, for example, study cases that are disposed of in the lower courts; we failed to persuade barristers to co-operate in any aspect of our enquiry;[10] and we were unable to gain access to certain key exchanges in the process, such as interrogations.[11] These matters either proved beyond our resources or resulted from our failure to overcome professional and institutional resistance. Particular limitations are discussed in detail at various points in each chapter and, as can be seen, we were able to use other sources to supplement our research when certain information was missing.

SAMPLES AND METHODS ADOPTED

Our main concern was, then, to produce a picture of the composition of prosecution cases, the manner in which they are assembled, and the effectiveness of the controls to which the prosecution is subject. In attempting to do this, we were extremely fortunate to obtain the full co-operation of the police and prosecuting solicitor's department in Birmingham, who greatly facilitated our enquiry. In describing how critical decisions were taken by the prosecution, we devised questionnaires, which were completed prior to the trial by police officers and by prosecuting solicitors on all 2,406 defendants who fell within the sample. The questionnaire administered to police officers covered the following main items:

—method of committal (paper, oral, part oral)
—length of time between first court appearance and committal
—reasons for undue delay
—whether the defendant was remanded in custody or on bail
—the factors taken into account in deciding to charge the accused (including statements of admission made by accused; seriousness of alleged offence; value of property involved; attitude of complainant; strength of evidence)
—existence of unusual features which influenced the final choice of charge(s).

[10] Details of the difficulties we encountered in our efforts to persuade the Bar to participate in our research are summarized in Baldwin and McConville (1979c) at pp. 23–4.

[11] Our request to the Royal Commission on Criminal Procedure that we be allowed to observe a small number of police interviews with criminal suspects was turned down.

The questionnaire which was administered to prosecuting solicitors immediately following committal of the case to the Crown Court dealt with different aspects of prosecutorial decision-making, specifically:

—who saw the case papers before the committal proceedings (senior police officer, Director of Public Prosecutions, Police Prosecuting Solicitor, independent solicitor engaged by police, counsel)
—whether anyone suggested or requested that anything further be done in the preparation of the evidence
—if so, the nature of the comments made
—whether these comments were acted upon and, if they were not, why not
—the nature of the most serious offence in respect of which the defendant had been committed for trial
—whether the case was one which could be tried only at the Crown Court; whether the defendant chose to be tried in the Crown Court; whether application for trial in the Crown Court was made by the prosecution
—where the application for trial was made by prosecution, the reasons for this decision (e.g. seriousness of offence; prior criminal record of defendant; jointly tried with another who faced serious charge; value of property involved).

In a separate questionnaire, the police supplied details of each defendant's criminal record and penal history, together with their suspicions of involvement in uncharged criminal activity, particularly of a serious, persistent, or organized nature.[12] The response rates that were achieved for these three questionnaires in Birmingham were as follows:

Police pre-committal questionnaire:
2,397 returned out of 2,406 = 99.6% response
Prosecuting solicitor's pre-trial questionnaire:
2,288 returned out of 2,406 = 95.1% response
Police criminal background questionnaire:
2,352 returned out of 2,406 = 97.8% response

It is important to note that these questionnaires were not designed to elicit attitudes or opinions about the prosecution process. They were concerned primarily with why decisions were made, the factors that were taken into account, and the preparation of the case as a whole. Collection of this sort of

[12] Further details of the questionnaire that was used are given in Baldwin and McConville (1979c) at pp. 110–16.

information, which is more factual than attitudinal, was seen as of greater relevance in understanding decisions that were taken in the 2,406 cases than the gathering of the opinions of police officers, prosecutors or others about the prosecution process.

But we also explored the underlying reasons behind prosecutions and the explanations that different parties offered when cases failed to get off the ground in court. For this purpose we interviewed police officers and administered questionnaires to prosecuting solicitors, defence solicitors, and trial judges and, to obtain some appreciation of the consequences of being prosecuted in such circumstances, we interviewed the defendants in question.

Although we have said that most of our research was conducted in the Birmingham Crown Court, we have always recognized the dangers in concentrating upon a single Court, and we attempted, therefore, to replicate our findings whenever possible. This replication was carried out in London where we conducted interviews with police officers and made use of a great deal of material kindly made available to us by the Metropolitan Police. In 1975, the then Metropolitan Police Commissioner, Sir Robert Mark, allowed us to interview some four hundred police officers about the outcome of cases that had been tried by London juries[13] and supplied us with Committal Papers relating to these cases. As we describe in chapter 4, we attempted to assess, on the basis of these papers, the strength of the evidence against each defendant to determine whether the prosecution was itself justified. In addition, the Metropolitan Police completed, for all defendants tried in the seven Crown Court centres in London in a three-month period in 1975, the same standardized questionnaire that had been completed by officers of the West Midlands Police for the Birmingham sample concerned with each defendant's criminal record, suspicions of serious uncharged criminal activity and the like. Altogether 2,292 defendants were tried in the Crown Courts in London in the three-month study period, and questionnaires were completed for us in 2,253 cases (98.3 per cent).[14]

[13] The results of this exercise, together with details of the procedures adopted, the samples used, and the response rates achieved, are given in Baldwin and McConville (1979c).

[14] The achievement of these extraordinarily high response rates is due almost entirely to the efforts expended on our behalf by Inspector Stuart Harris of the West Midlands

As we describe in chapters 6–7, the research that was separately funded by the Royal Commission on Criminal Procedure involved in essence teasing out the degree of importance played by confessions in Crown Court trials.[15] The samples we used for this purpose were: (i) the 500 contested trials heard in the Birmingham Crown Court in 1975 and 1976; (ii) 500 Birmingham cases in which there had been a guilty plea in the same period; and (iii) a sample of 476 cases tried in London in 1979, 205 of which had ended in guilty pleas, 271 of which were contested.

CONCLUDING COMMENTS

We attempted to examine the English prosecution system against the background of knowledge that is currently available and in the context of the conclusions we have drawn from our wider research. When we began our research in 1974, our intention was to examine the outcome of contested trials in the Crown Court, and it soon became obvious that decisions taken at an early stage of the process often had a great influence over decisions that fell to be taken later. What was not clear, however, was the critical importance of pre-trial procedures and practices on the ultimate disposition of cases. We quickly realized that the adversarial model of justice was not much in evidence, and that the main purpose of open-court adjudication related not to questions of guilt or innocence but to sentencing those who had already pleaded guilty. And it also became apparent that many guilty pleas, far from representing a recognition of culpability on the part of defendants, were a direct product of inherent pressures within the system which militate against contested trials. What we saw as the context of our research became, therefore, a major focus of interest in its own right.

In a real sense, the determination of guilt antedates the trial, and, in seeking to explain this, it is necessary to examine the overall structure of the criminal process, its design, and thrust,

---

Police, Chief Inspector Malcolm Dines of the Metropolitan Police, Mr I. S. Manson, the Chief Prosecuting Solicitor of the West Midlands and his Chief Administrative Officers, Mr N. Brown and Mr L. Kenny. It is appropriate that we should express our great indebtedness for the work carried out by all these.

[15] A preliminary analysis of the results that we presented to the Royal Commission is given in Baldwin and McConville (1980).

and to analyse the nature of the formal rules and the relationship between rules and practices. Many of those who have attempted such an appreciation have adopted a normative stance but this approach has difficulties, principally the choice of standard against which evaluation is made. Feeley (1976) has expressed the weakness of such evaluations in the following passage:

> Typically legal goals tend to be viewed as self-evident or easily identified and are posited without much ado. Frequently they are not even restated by the researchers with much precision or explicitness. Thus the basis of comparison—the standard against which reality is measured—is rarely clearly identified and operationalized ... One indication of their vagueness is that these posited ideals can often be countered with distinctly different views that others have derived from the same body of laws. (p. 499.)

It cannot be assumed, simply because there is a gulf between the formal rules on the one hand and the activities of legal actors on the other, that the system is working badly or that it is in need of reform.[16] The more important question is why there is a gap: whether, for example, it is an aberrational and unintended by-product of rules and procedures or whether it is the result of deliberate actions on the part of individuals or groups. And in this analysis, the rules themselves cannot be assumed to have an explicit and unambiguous meaning. They are just as deserving of scrutiny as the practices themselves. These and other questions are the subject of the final chapter, but we wish to re-emphasize here that the appreciation we provide is intended to be explanatory, not prescriptive.

[16] In relation to evaluating plea bargaining practices, we have attempted to set out some of the criteria against which negotiated settlements might be assessed: Baldwin and McConville (1979b).

3

ACQUITTALS WITHOUT A JURY

INTRODUCTION

Considerable controversy has been generated in recent years over the subject of rates of acquittal in English criminal cases, especially those tried at the Crown Court. The origins of the debate can be traced to the mid-1960s, when details of numbers of defendants acquitted in trials in higher courts became available for the first time. The Association of Chief Police Officers (1966) undertook the collation of rates for different areas of the country and produced what seemed at the time a startling picture: almost 40 per cent of those who pleaded not guilty in the higher courts were acquitted. The acquittal rate is nowadays even higher, almost as high as 50 per cent. Though some legal eyebrows were raised when acquittal rates were first made public, it was not until the issue was tackled head on by Sir Robert Mark that the whole subject became a matter of heated political debate. More than any other contributor, Mark (1973) set the tone of the debate throughout the 1970s when he argued forcefully that 'the proportion of those acquittals relating to those whom experienced police officers believe to be guilty is too high to be acceptable' (p. 10), and he contended that certain defendants (particularly professional criminals) and their legal advisers were able to exploit defects in the legal system to their own advantage.[1] Not surprisingly, Mark's views provoked a good deal of huffing and puffing from the higher echelons of the legal profession, though this dwelt more upon his criticisms of certain members of the profession (especially his reference to a minority of criminal lawyers 'more harmful to society than the

[1] Mark re-iterated here a point that had been made with some force by the Criminal Law Revision Committee (1972) in their highly controversial report on the rules of evidence. The Committee stated that:

> there is now a large and increasing class of sophisticated professional criminals who are not only highly skilful in organizing their crimes and in the steps they take to avoid detection but are well aware of their legal rights and use every possible means to avoid conviction if caught. (para. 21.)

clients they represent'[2]) than to his references to rates of acquittal *per se*. Of greater importance, however, than the often intemperate response of the profession was the stimulus given to research by these observations. Three studies in particular—those of Zander (1974a), Mack (1976), and Baldwin and McConville (1979c)—would probably not have taken the form they did had it not been for the peculiarly acrimonious context in which they were conceived.

The main area of controversy has been concerned with rates of acquittal before juries, although Mark himself had surprisingly little to say about juries. What has been all but overlooked throughout the debate is the truly staggering proportion of acquittals brought about not by jury trial but by the failure of the prosecution to provide enough evidence even to reach the level at which the trial judge can safely leave the determination of the defendant's fate to the jury. It is quite remarkable that one of the most important statistics to emerge from recent issues of the *Judicial Statistics*, published by the Lord Chancellor's Department—that slightly more than four in ten acquittals involve cases in which the judge rather than the jury assumes responsibility for the acquittal—has been consistently ignored by protagonists in the debate on rates of acquittal in the Crown Court. These cases fall into two categories of roughly equal size—those in which the prosecution offers no evidence against the defendant ('ordered' acquittals) and those in which the trial judge, having heard part of the case and being of the view that there is insufficient evidence to leave the case to the jury, directs the jury to acquit ('directed' acquittals).

It is worth pausing at this point to examine in greater detail the available statistics on ordered and directed acquittals. The figures given in the *Judicial Statistics* for 1979 (Cmnd. 7977) show that there was an overall acquittal rate of 48 per cent in those cases in which defendants pleaded not guilty in the Crown Court. In only 57 per cent of these acquittals was a jury actually responsible for the verdict; in 24 per cent of acquittals the trial judge had directed the jury to acquit, and the remaining 19 per cent were ordered acquittals. Very similar proportions obtained in earlier years in each of these categories. There are also certain

[2] The Chairman of the British Legal Association, for example, was reported to have described this comment as a 'monstrous slur' and one that was 'getting close to seditious or criminal libel' (*New Law Journal* vol. 123 (1973) at p. 1029).

interesting regional variations in the figures, with the proportion of non-jury acquittals in 1979 varying from 35 per cent (in the Western Circuit) to 54 per cent (in the North Eastern Circuit). Further examination of the *Judicial Statistics* reveals that this regional pattern has held for a number of years, with some areas consistently producing the highest proportions of non-jury acquittals, other areas the lowest. Such patterns are striking, and it is tempting to speculate about why they have occurred, but, since almost nothing is known about the nature and seriousness of the cases involved, let alone the factors that produce them, explanations can only be speculative.

Earlier research in this country (of which there has been very little) has reached somewhat divergent conclusions about how such acquittals should be viewed. Zander (1974a), for example, argued that 'there is bound to be a feeling that in too many cases the prosecution presses for trial when the evidence never warranted such a decision' (p. 47).[3] McCabe and Purves (1972a), who carried out the only other English study of non-jury acquittals, reached a less disquieting conclusion. Although they identified certain cases in which the evidence was too weak to justify prosecution (and in which 'a conviction would be a welcome, if surprising, bonus'), they saw the prosecution in the great majority of cases as justified in terms of wider social and peace-keeping policies that the police were pursuing.[4] Since McCabe and Purves viewed such policies as 'marked by moderation and balance', they argued that the police approach was defensible.

OUR RESEARCH IN BIRMINGHAM AND LONDON

It was against this background that our own research, which was as we have said primarily concerned with the outcome of cases tried by jury, was conducted. In the course of this research, we encountered 88 cases involving 116 defendants, tried at the

[3] Zander cites one senior barrister as stating that:

> A large number of cases are committed for trial which should never have been committed at all because the evidence is insufficient ... The more experienced judges and Recorders stop these cases at the close of the case for the Crown, but there are of course a large number of inexperienced Recorders who are not sufficiently certain of themselves to do this. (pp. 47–8.)

[4] As, for example, in an affray when the ringleaders and peripheral figures were prosecuted so that a jury could more fully understand the seriousness of the incident.

Birmingham Crown Court in 1975 and 1976, in which 64 defendants were acquitted by order of the trial judge and 52 on his direction. This number of ordered and directed acquittals was in fact slightly higher than the number of jury acquittals (114) in the same period. One aspect of the research involved eliciting from the prosecution—the police and the prosecuting solicitor or, where relevant, the Director of Public Prosecutions (D.P.P.)[5]—the reasons why the prosecution had collapsed and whether or not weaknesses in the case had been foreseen. We also sought the views of the trial judge on what had happened in court and interviewed the defendants in question to gain some idea of the consequences to them of being put on trial. The response rates of the four groups we contacted in Birmingham about the cases of the 116 defendants were as follows:

Police officers	98.3%
Prosecuting solicitor (or D.P.P.)	91.4%
Trial judges	83.6%
Defendants	62.1%

All of these groups were approached after the trial had been concluded. In the case of judges and prosecuting solicitors, standardized questionnaires were used which included, *inter alia*, questions about why acquittals had been ordered or directed. The questions asked were simple and direct. For example, where an acquittal was directed, the trial judge was asked whether this was because:

—the charge was ill-founded in law
—the prosecution offered no evidence
—the prosecution in the course of the trial invited the jury to acquit
—a special plea of autrefois convict or acquit was made out
—there was no evidence upon which a jury properly directed could convict
—there was insufficient evidence upon which to leave the case to the jury
—of some other reason.

We were permitted to conduct lengthy tape-recorded interviews with the police officers responsible for the handling of each case and with the defendants. This enabled us to evaluate

[5] We had hoped to involve the Bar in our inquiry, but the Senate of the Inns of Court and the Bar refused to allow any barrister to participate. This is further discussed in Baldwin and McConville (1979c) at pp. 23–4.

how defendants had been affected by their experiences and their reactions to being put on trial and, in the case of the police, to find out why the acquittal had occurred and if it had been foreseen. The specific questions put to police officers included the following:

—please would you give the reasons for the acquittal in this case?
—if no evidence was offered by the prosecution, please would you state why not?
—did you expect an ordered/directed acquittal at any stage?
—if so, would you say at what stage?

In addition to any other questions put to them, all respondents were given the opportunity to comment upon the outcome and the factors that produced it.

We also carried out a partial replication of this study in London in which we interviewed police officers (along identical lines as the interviews in Birmingham) from the Metropolitan Police District in order to obtain their views about the outcomes of over 400 contested trials heard in 1975 in the seven Crown Court centres in London.[6] As in Birmingham, our main objective in this exercise was to ascertain opinions about cases tried by jury, but we also encountered 65 non-jury acquittals, of which 14 were ordered and 51 directed by the judge. These cases made up 14.8 per cent of the sample of contested trials, a somewhat lower proportion than was found in Birmingham.[7] We obtained officers' views on 61 of these 65 acquittals (93.8 per cent), and we shall use this material in the course of the present chapter for comparison with views expressed about cases in Birmingham.

The response rates we achieved in Birmingham and London were encouragingly high[8] and we were able to form a clear idea

[6] As explained in chapter 2, the exercise conducted in London was of a limited nature. Since it was not possible to monitor on a daily basis the progress of cases in London, we were advised that it would not be worthwhile contacting trial judges for their views as they would not be able to recall details of cases after even a short lapse of time.

[7] See Baldwin and McConville (1979c) at p. 40.

[8] The only exception was the rate for defendants, which was in fact lower than response rates we had achieved for defendants tried by jury (72 per cent) and for those who had pleaded guilty (81 per cent). The explanation for the lower response rate in non-jury acquittals lies in the fact that the present sample, unlike the other two samples, includes no one sentenced to a term of imprisonment. Response rates for those in prison were as a rule exceptionally high (see Baldwin and McConville (1977a) at p. 4), whereas many defendants involved in cases in the present sample proved elusive and many others were successfully interviewed only after repeated visits to the defendant's home.

of the reasons the cases had failed. Before dealing with the views that were expressed, it is important to establish at the outset that the cases which form the subject matter of the present chapter warrant serious consideration. Few could be treated as trivial cases, the charges representing a rough cross-section of the Crown Court work-load with violent and property cases predominating. Table 1 shows the type of offence with which the 116 defendants in Birmingham, and the 65 in London, were charged, compared with other defendants who were tried by jury in the two cities in the same period. The results given in the table indicate that the types of offence which made up the samples of ordered and directed acquittals were serious in nature and represented a fairly typical cross-section of the case-loads of the courts in question. Similarly, in terms of age and sex, those involved in ordered and directed acquittals were roughly comparable to the sample of Crown Court defendants as a whole, though they were, as a group, somewhat less likely to have been previously convicted of a criminal offence. Indeed, 45 per cent of them had never previously appeared in court on a criminal charge, and very few in either city were regarded by the police as serious or professional criminals. It was clear to us from the interviews we conducted with defendants and from the information supplied by the police that the great majority of defendants were bewildered individuals who lacked experience of the criminal justice system and who found themselves caught up in complex legal proceedings. For some of those involved, it was a drama for which they were ill-equipped and, even though they managed to secure acquittals, the fact of being forced to stand trial frequently had, as we shall see later, serious effects on their lives.

Given the seriousness of the charges and the potentially severe consequences to defendants of being prosecuted, it is important to examine why these cases ended as they did. For Birmingham cases (for which we had fuller details), the most important sources of information were the questionnaires completed by judges immediately after trial and the tape-recorded interviews that we conducted with police officers. The trial judge is, after all, responsible for making the formal decision to terminate a trial and can therefore accurately supply his reasons for making that decision, whereas the police officer, having handled the case from the outset, is in a much better position to provide full

TABLE 1

Type of offence involved in ordered and directed acquittals in Birmingham and London compared to the type of offence tried by jury

(*a*) *Birmingham cases*

	Ordered or directed acquittals	(%)	*All jury cases*	(%)
Violent offences (including robbery)	43	37.1	143	38.7
Sexual offences	6	5.2	16	4.3
Burglary, theft, and handling offences	46	39.6	151	40.8
Other property offences	10	8.6	23	6.2
Motoring offences	2	1.7	13	3.5
Other offences	9	7.8	24	6.5
	116	100.0	370	100.0

(*b*) *London cases*

	Ordered or directed acquittals	(%)	*All jury cases*	(%)
Violent offences (including robbery)	9	13.9	77	21.5
Sexual offences	3	4.6	10	2.8
Burglary, theft, and handling offences	29	44.6	150	41.9
Other property offences	14	21.5	37	10.3
Motoring offences	5	7.7	57	15.9
Other offences	5	7.7	27	7.6
	65	100.0	358	100.0

background details than the judge. Using these two sources of information, combined with relevant details supplied by the prosecuting solicitor or D.P.P., we were able to ascertain why most of these cases had been terminated.

Before examining these factors, two important points should be noted. In the first place, only exceptionally was any disagreement voiced by any of the respondents about the trial judge's decision to stop a case. In only seven of the directed acquittals in Birmingham (13.5 per cent) and seven in London (13.7 per cent) could a police officer have been described as disgruntled with a particular decision. For ordered acquittals, it is the prosecution itself which, by offering no evidence, in effect makes the decision to terminate a case. So there was even less quibbling with the outcome on the part of the responsible police officer. Indeed, it became clear that, in the great majority of cases which ended in ordered or directed acquittals, the result had been at least half-expected by the investigating police officer, if not at the very outset of the prosecution, then at least by the time the case reached court. The second point is that the prosecution commonly contended that there was little that could have been done to strengthen the evidence. It would be quite wrong to assume, as some writers have done, that all these cases were the result of sloppy or inadequate investigation and preparation by the police.[9] This may well have been so on occasions, but there were many cases in which the prosecution produced a strong case at the outset only to find that events beyond their control brought about its downfall in court.

Since respondents generally had no difficulty in identifying what went wrong in these cases, it was not surprising to find that there was a high level of agreement between them as to the factors responsible. Though respondents often identified a number of factors, we attempted to discern the most important for the purposes of our analysis. We therefore collated the information received from respondents and we then devised various categories summarizing the basic reasons which brought about the early termination of cases.[10] The broad outline of these categories is shown in Table 2. In the rest of the chapter, we examine these categories in some detail, citing the comments made about particular cases by the respondents we contacted. In this analysis, we have amalgamated the categories under four main headings: (i) domestic disputes (17 defendants in Birmingham and London); (ii) failures of key prosecution witnesses (59 defendants); (iii) cases in which the defendant was regarded as peripheral or involved in separate offences for which he or others had already been convicted (41 defendants); (iv) cases with insufficient evidence (39 defendants). These four categories are not mutually exclusive (several in groups (i), (ii) and (iii), for example, include cases in which the evidence is weak). Taken together, they cover about 90 per cent of cases for which we had information.

[9] See, for instance, the reviews by J. A. G. Griffith in *New Society* vol. 50 (1979) p. 751, and by P. Hillyard in *Journal of Social Welfare Law* (1980) p. 187.

[10] For the sake of simplicity, we have combined ordered and directed acquittals. There are certain differences in the factors that produced each type of acquittal, but on the whole these differences are less important than the similarities.

TABLE 2

The factors that explain ordered and directed acquittals

	Birmingham defendants	(%)	London defendants	(%)
Domestic disputes—no useful purpose served by pursuing the matter further	15	13.3	2	3.3
Failure of key prosecution witnesses to appear at trial	12	10.6	4	6.5
Failure of key prosecution witnesses to come up to proof in court	29	25.7	14	23.0
Cases in which the role of the defendant was marginal and the ringleaders had already been convicted	21	18.6	14	23.0
Cases in which the defendant had earlier pleaded guilty to a separate offence, and it was not thought worthwhile pursuing this matter	6	5.3	0	0.0
Cases with insufficient evidence to proceed to the jury	23	20.3	16	26.2
Some other reason	7	6.2	11	18.0
Inadequate information available	3	–	4	–
	116	100.0	65	100.0

THE FINDINGS

(i) *Domestic disputes*

These cases, which were more common in Birmingham than in London, are particularly interesting in that they are indicative of the ways in which the courts are sometimes prepared to circumvent the formality of trial in order to reach pragmatic and expeditious solutions to delicate domestic problems. Although serious injuries had been inflicted in some of these cases and there was an overwhelming body of evidence to implicate the defendant, it was nonetheless thought that no useful purpose would be served by employing the full machinery of justice to establish this. The procedure adopted in all of these cases was for the judge to bind over the defendants and many of their victims 'to be of good behaviour and keep the peace'. What this means is that defendants (or victims) promise to avoid further trouble, and agree to forfeit a stated sum of money if they fail to keep the promise.[11] A good deal of informal discussion and negotiation took place out of court between the various parties involved in each of the cases, and the matter was as a rule finally settled in a discussion between counsel and the judge in the judge's chambers. There are many obvious parallels between these informal discussions and those that sometimes occur in settlements of plea in the Crown Court,[12] though there seemed on the whole to be greater satisfaction with the outcome of cases within the present sample. By adopting this solution, the necessity of an expensive trial is avoided, as is the stigma of conviction, while at the same time a check can be maintained on a difficult or potentially dangerous situation. We cite below a few examples of the comments we received from different respondents in Birmingham[13] about the outcome of these cases:

Cases 14–15 [An assault involving two men arising out of a landlord-tenant dispute]

Judge: The prosecution had charged both men and they were committed separately for trial. The only evidence was what each man had said about the other while claiming that he himself was acting in self-defence. The prosecution clearly could not ask the jury to believe one man on the trial of the other and then ask the jury to disbelieve that man in his own trial.

Prosecuting solicitor: It was in the best interests of the case.

Police officer: It came as a complete surprise. Had the injuries to [defendant 14]—the fractured skull—deteriorated, then he would have died and the other man would have been charged with murder. It is completely wrong to bind over in such a case. The defence and prosecuting solicitors had words together, and it was generally agreed that the charge would be reduced from section 18 wounding to section 20 and that they would plead guilty to that. But then they elected to go for trial in the Crown Court.

Defendant 15: It was bad because I've not had a chance to prove my innocence. Being bound over is like being found guilty. I was not satisfied with my barrister because he persuaded me to forego a jury trial against my wishes.

Case 179 [A landlord-tenant dispute in which the victim's conduct was very provocative]

[11] Further details of the courts' powers to bind over defendants are given in McClean and Wood (1969) pp. 150–2; and Hampton (1977) pp. 327–8.

[12] See the discussion above at pp. 9–11.

[13] In all cases quoted in this book, details which might identify any individual concerned have been disguised.

Judge: Injuries were negligible and doubtless there was some aggravation on each side. Usually the best way of dealing with this kind of case is to bind over *both* parties to keep the peace (which can of course be done without any conviction) and this is what I did in this case. Normally a case like this would have been dealt with in the Magistrates Court.

Prosecuting solicitor: It was the right course, having regard to the circumstances of the case.

Police officer: Under the circumstances, it was the best way to end the case. It was stressed to [the victim] that the case against the defendant was not very strong and that if [the victim] pursued it, his bad character would be brought out in court and the defendant would probably be acquitted anyway. There was no point proceeding further ... The police are very reluctant to get involved in such cases—we usually try to get both parties to make up and to keep the peace. We were obliged to take action because an allegation had been made and [the victim] wouldn't agree to any other course at that stage.

Defendant: It was fair. We were both bound over so I am satisfied now.

Case 278 [A domestic dispute in which the evidence was very confused and unsatisfactory]

Judge: The prosecution took the view that the defendant and the prosecution witnesses were probably equally to blame for the disturbance and both sides agreed that the case should be dropped and all parties bound over to keep the peace.

Police officer: I didn't think much of [the victim] as a witness and, if it had gone to the jury, I don't think we would have got a conviction. In getting him bound over, we achieved our purpose in preventing a recurrence of the incident, without having a trial.

Defendant: I hit him quite badly because he was really bad—in hospital. But he asked for it. He hit me first, then I hit him back. My barrister said it was his own fault. I was thinking they'll probably say I was guilty and I'd get a fine. I didn't think they'd dismiss the case. I think the bind over was fair all round.

These cases can be seen as illustrations of the way that courts on occasion adopt pragmatic solutions to what are often confused and complex social situations. Few of the defendants interviewed took great exception to the course taken, and some were relieved that prosecution witnesses had also been bound over. In short, it appeared to several defendants that the bringing of charges had helped defuse a volatile domestic situation, and the police were by and large satisfied that a bind over provided some protection against any recurrence.

(ii) *Failures of key prosecution witnesses*

The commonest factor that explains ordered and directed cases in the Crown Court is, according to our analysis, that key witnesses for the prosecution either fail to appear at court or, if they do appear, give their evidence in an unsatisfactory manner. Sometimes a case is destroyed because the witnesses have disappeared, but more frequently cases collapse because a key witness gives his evidence in an unconvincing or unreliable way. Where the poor performance of a witness is unexpected, there is little the prosecution can do. But it is worth noting that often no surprise was occasioned by what had happened: indeed, in as many as four out of ten cases in this category, the police feared from the outset that prosecution witnesses would present difficulties. In such cases, the prosecution is more open to criticism since it can be argued that a prosecutor should take into account the credibility of witnesses in deciding whether or not to institute charges. If a prosecution hinges upon the word of an untrustworthy or unreliable witness, there are strong reasons for not proceeding. The variety of problems that the prosecution faces is illustrated in the following quotes:

Case 63 (*London*) [A key witness was a man serving a lengthy prison sentence]

Police officer: There were no witnesses other than [the man in prison] and only formal police evidence. I expected an acquittal from the beginning as he was not reliable at all. I wasn't surprised at all but we had to charge [the defendant]. But it would have been unsafe to let the case go on.

Case 122 (*London*) [A cashier at a supermarket disappeared after a fellow employee had been charged with theft]

Police officer: We couldn't produce the girl as a witness. She had left home and disappeared. We had been to the Crown Court on three previous occasions and the judge eventually gave us no more time to find her.

Cases 36–7 (*Birmingham*) [A case of car theft]

Judge: The prosecution was not in a position to go on, because an essential witness was not there. The matter had been adjourned before. I did not feel that any more public money should be wasted so I refused the prosecution's application for an adjournment.

Police officer: The prosecution witnesses did not turn up. I know that [the defendant] had done it, but we couldn't do anything without the witnesses. On the day, and even before, I wouldn't have been surprised if they had been acquitted since the evidence wasn't particularly strong against them, particularly the fact that I had three witnesses with more previous convictions than the two chaps we were trying.

Case 44 (*Birmingham*) [A case of violence]

Judge: The prosecution case rested entirely on the evidence of one witness, the complainant. His evidence before the jury was inconsistent in material respects from the statement he made to the police.

Prosecuting solicitor: The complainant was unable to give the same evidence in cross-examination as examination-in-chief. He had deviated enormously from his statement.

Police officer: The person who let us down at the Crown Court was the complainant. When he was in court, he stated that he couldn't remember who had hit him and he mentioned something about there being two men. He was a man of very low intelligence. He was very nervous and he probably didn't really know what happened on the day of the incident. The result was right. At first we thought we had got a fair case because he made a good statement but, when it came to the crunch, he said he wasn't sure.

Defendant: The other bloke started coming with insults, provoking me, so I said 'Shut your mouth' and he made a swing at me. He's an old man and I don't think he's all that sane, but I sidestepped and hit him. I'm sorry I did it now, him being old and that, but other people have since told me he had it coming to him. The judge in the case was very, very straightforward. He saw the truth wasn't being told by him, so he stopped the case after the police evidence. He was telling so many versions, it was obvious he was lying. I expect he was frightened of losing his job.

Case 273 (*Birmingham*) [A case of theft]

Judge: The evidence given by witnesses for the Crown was unreliable. It would have been unsafe to convict upon it.

Prosecuting solicitor: The evidence was 'tainted' and the case was unsafe to leave to the jury. Two of the main prosecution witnesses had long criminal records and it was clear that lies were being told.

Police officer: I think we expected an acquittal really. We had difficulty in establishing the truth. It was difficult to know whom to believe. It came as no great surprise to us when the judge directed an acquittal.

Cases 495–6(*Birmingham*) [A case in which a police officer was viciously assaulted in a fracas at a dance hall]

Prosecuting solicitor: The only prosecution witness—a police officer—giving evidence of the defendants' alleged assault upon him, gave his evidence in such an unsatisfactory way that it would not have been safe to leave the case to the jury. There was a suspicion that the witness was not telling the truth.

Police officer: The judge wasn't happy about the evidence of the officer. I put it down to inexperience on the part of the officer. The judge, who was perfectly fair, said that it was blatantly obvious that the officer had to defend himself, but the officer either forgot that he had used force or else was scared about saying that he had used force. It was blatantly obvious but he denied it throughout. There was no need for him to deny it as he was quite entitled to use all reasonable force. They tore him to shreds on it—he couldn't cope because he wasn't experienced—he'd never been in the Crown Court before. The poor chap was scared anyway. It was a very strong police case, otherwise I would never have charged them. But in court it crumbled.

These cases exemplify an important point: a proportion of Crown Court cases will always fall down for reasons largely beyond the prosecution's control. The non-appearance of witnesses or their failure to come up to proof are inevitable hazards that any prosecutor must face and ones that even the best organized system must tolerate. It follows that it would be both unfair and incorrect to lay blame at the prosecution's door in many of these cases. Equally, however, it is clear that some cases would not even have got off the ground had a more discriminating prosecution policy operated, particularly in those cases which rested upon the evidence of witnesses whose unreliability was known to the police from the outset.

(iii) *Cases in which the defendant was regarded as peripheral or involved in separate offences for which he or others had already been convicted*

We have noted earlier how the outcome in many ordered or directed acquittals represents a pragmatic compromise. We have seen how, for example, in relation to certain domestic disputes, the prosecution may decide, for policy reasons, to abandon a case even though they might reasonably anticipate that it will end in conviction. This policy element assumes somewhat greater significance in the 41 cases within the present subgroup. Most of the defendants in question were involved with others, and the prosecution decided that, having secured convictions of the ringleaders, it was not worth pursuing the matter further. A question raised by cases within this category is why the defendants concerned were prosecuted in the first place. One answer is that given by McCabe and Purves (1972b), who suggest that the prosecution of 'peripheral' defendants frequently 'serves to introduce before the jury evidence about the circumstances and extent of the crime which might go a long way towards convincing the jury of the guilt of those who were its prime movers' (p. 39). In other cases, the evidence against peripheral defendants is considerably weakened if co-defendants plead guilty and cannot, or will not, be used as prosecution witnesses. To give one extreme example we encountered within the present sample, two youths charged with possessing keys used for stealing cars told us in interviews how they had tossed a coin to determine who should plead guilty to the offence and thereby avoid implicating the other. As before, we cite a few of the comments made by the respondents we contacted about the outcome of cases within this broad category:

Case 36 (*London*) [A woman charged with receiving stolen shoes which represented a very small part of a large haul]

Police officer: She was one of the loose leaves on the tree. She'd only had three pairs—quite rightly the judge thought this was peripheral.

Case 143 (*Birmingham*) [A youth, involved with two others, charged with taking a car without consent]

Judge: The prosecution offered no evidence against this defendant as the others jointly charged pleaded guilty. An identifying witness said that she did not get a good look at the face of the third man in the car, and the admissions of the other two accused were not admissible against him.

Police officer: Once the other two pleaded guilty, the evidence wasn't all that strong. If all three had carried on pleading not guilty, I have no doubt that [this defendant] would have been convicted.

Case 229 (*Birmingham*) [A man charged with handling stolen goods, the proceeds of a burglary which had been committed by three other men who pleaded guilty]

Prosecuting solicitor: Three other defendants pleaded guilty and it left very little or no evidence against this defendant.

Police officer: I think that this defendant's involvement was slight inasmuch as the property was passing through his premises rather than him having a great deal to do with it. If the case had run its full course, I would have been surprised if he had been acquitted. But if there had been a trial for all four, an acquittal in his case wouldn't have surprised me as much as in the others because he was a minor cog.

Defendant: As far as justice goes, it was pretty fair. But, looking at it, it was stupid and a waste of money. The way the case went on, the police knew themselves I wasn't guilty.

Case 334 (*Birmingham*) [A case of handling a stolen television set]

Judge: Having had a plea of guilty from the burglar, the prosecution was content to offer no evidence against his girlfriend who was found with some of the proceeds.

Prosecuting solicitor: The defendant was charged with handling some of the goods stolen by the man with whom she was co-habiting. In view of the fact that he pleaded guilty and she was a woman of no previous convictions, the prosecution took the same view that they take with wives of men from whom stolen goods are recovered, i.e. not bother to charge them. No evidence was therefore offered.

Police officer: Her counsel suggested to the prosecuting counsel that there was very little evidence that she had received the stolen television set knowing it to be stolen. She was going to plead not guilty and I think a sort of compromise was reached between defence and prosecuting counsel. Prosecuting counsel suggested to the judge that, even after a trial, there would be a lot of doubt as to whether a conviction would ensue and the chances are that, even if she had been found guilty, she would have got a conditional discharge or something like that. So I think you can say that justice was seen to be done—it was an easy way round. I wouldn't disapprove of this kind of compromise because it would have been a very costly business for little end result.

No doubt in some cases within this category there was an element of overkill and the prosecution's net had been cast too wide. In other cases, the police had reasonable grounds on which to proceed against the defendant and, once the main goal of the prosecution had been achieved, they took the view that there was no point in continuing further. Considerations of time, money, and effort sometimes dictate a strategic withdrawal.

(iv) *Cases with insufficient evidence*

A final group of cases we examined comprises those which fail in court simply because the prosecution does not produce enough evidence even to get the case off the ground. It will be clear that our classification of ordered and directed acquittals does not relate to distinct categories, and it would be wrong to suggest that only cases within the present category are ones in which the evidence is weak. There was insufficient evidence in some of the other cases classified under different headings, but, because there was some other readily identifiable factor which was seen by respondents as directly producing the acquittal, we have chosen not to include them within this category. The cases dealt with here are, therefore, those that collapsed purely because the evidence produced by the prosecution was deemed insufficient to allow the case to proceed to the jury. It is noteworthy that few of these acquittals came as a surprise, and in most cases, as the following quotes suggest, the outcome was at least half-expected.

Case 226 (*London*) [A simple shoplifting case]

Police officer: A doctor gave evidence that she was on drugs which made her forgetful and depressed. Her story was always that she had forgotten the handbag she had taken was on her arm. I realized that she had made a mistake really and that it was right to acquit her. Her story was consistent throughout.

Case 85 (*Birmingham*) [A case of a defendant charged with burglary]

Police officer: We ourselves thought the evidence was quite thin. The stolen property was found in his bedroom but he had been out at work and had no lock on his door and it was feasible that the others might have put the property into his room. None of the others implicated him and we had no real evidence against him. We had just enough evidence to charge him. It wasn't a question of being oppressive to him, but now I think we shouldn't have proceeded against him. I was uncertain about whether he would be convicted from the outset but we thought it wise to leave it to the jury to decide.

Case 174 (*Birmingham*) [A case in which a second-hand dealer was charged with handling a stolen television set]

Police officer: I don't think we expected a conviction from the start. I suppose, when we looked at the evidence we'd got, we thought we'd lose it unless he pleaded guilty. Actually we thought the defence would make a submission of no case to answer at the committal stage, but they just let it go through. So the acquittal came as no surprise to us at all. On the evidence we'd got, it was a thin case—we expected an acquittal, to be honest.

Case 357 (*Birmingham*) [A case of stealing a car]

Police officer: Since the ownership of the car was in doubt, it was unsafe to let the case go to the jury. It was always a case which could go either way. It depended on whether the defendant actually went into the box to give evidence. If we could have got that far, the case might have gone the other way. But the evidence was pretty thin so I wasn't surprised by the verdict. It was quite fair on the evidence, though there were a lot of suspicious circumstances about the case.

Defendant: It was a waste of time and public money, I think. The police persisted in keeping the case going on no evidence. They, better than anyone else, must have known there was no evidence. I think they were only frightened of me complaining if they got it chucked out at an earlier stage. They jumped to conclusions—it was too late to go back once the charge was in. Instead of cutting their losses, packing up there and then, and admitting they'd made a mistake, they kept it on in the hope of it going the wrong way. Everybody I spoke to about it thought it was ridiculous that I'd even been charged on this evidence. I'd read the depositions and I knew there was no evidence at all.

Case 448 (*Birmingham*) [A charge of being carried in a car taken without the owner's consent]

Judge: This was a case where, apart from alleged oral admissions, there was just sufficient evidence to leave the case to the jury. The police officers' evidence as to the alleged oral admissions was seriously in conflict with each other and their own previous statements.

Police officer: The evidence was a little bit thin from the outset but as you will appreciate it is not for us to judge the matter. It's our job to present the evidence to the court which they rejected as being insufficient in the end. This kind of charge is always a difficult one. It relies very much on verbal admissions or a written statement. Because there is an element of doubt over verbal statements, it is crucial to have the evidence spot on, which it wasn't in this case.

Doubts must be raised about whether such cases ought ever to have been brought and, as the quotes indicate, second thoughts on this were sometimes expressed by the prosecution. Often the police officer interviewed felt that, because someone had been arrested as a result of a specific allegation, the prosecution was obliged to have the matter settled by a court, even though the evidence might be only flimsy or circumstantial in nature.

CONCLUSION

Our analysis of ordered and directed acquittals demonstrates that a high proportion were not cases in which the prosecution evidence was weak. In many of them, the prosecution was confident that a conviction would be secured. Often they were cases which collapsed because of unforeseen, and unforeseeable, contingencies, or else they were ones in which the prosecution was abandoned for reasons of policy or expediency (as, for example, to avoid re-awakening hostilities or to save time and expense). But there were other prosecutions which are less easily defended either because of known doubts about key witnesses or because of inherent weaknesses in the evidence. For the reasons given on p. 46, the figures given in Table 2 underestimate the proportion of cases in which the prosecution evidence was thin. Taking all ordered and directed acquittals together, about half were cases in which the evidence, judged by the comments made by our respondents, was incipiently weak and in which doubts must be raised about the wisdom and fairness of proceeding in the first place. Nor should one underestimate the suffering to individuals that prosecution in such cases occasioned. It was clear from the interviews that we conducted with defendants shortly after their cases had been concluded that many had suffered appalling consequences as a result of their experiences, consequences which were only partly alleviated by their eventual acquittal. As we have already noted, it is a mistake to assume that all the defendants were legally or factually innocent of the charges they faced. Nevertheless, many of them were involved in cases in which the prosecution evidence was, to say the least, flimsy—often insufficient to make guilt or innocence even on paper other than an open question. The following examples, which we cite *verbatim* from the tape-recorded interviews we conducted with defendants, give some idea of the sorts of comment we encountered:

Case 5 [A directed acquittal in which a girl was charged with criminal damage]
I was terrified. I couldn't sleep at nights wondering what would happen to the baby if I went to prison.

Case 21 [A directed acquittal involving a young mother]
It just scared me to death. I think it was terrible. It's just about ruined my life. I have lost the custody of my baby and fighting the custody will be very expensive.

Case 54 [A directed acquittal on an assault charge]
It has upset everything. It made me very ill—I was off work for six

weeks. I couldn't sleep with the nightmares it gave me. My wife was worried too. She lost many nights' sleep.

Case 56 [A directed acquittal in a case involving a sexual assault]
I find it hard to forget—I try to work hard at other things but it's difficult to put something like this behind you. In my own mind, I feel embarrassed when I see people, wondering whatever they must think.

Case 190 [A directed acquittal in a case involving a sexual assault]
I'm very bitter. They should never have brought the case. The girl was telling different stories and I had never been in trouble before. She treated it all as a big joke. But it was awful for me and a terrible strain for my wife. I couldn't think of anything else I was so worried about the case, in case it got into the papers. Even being acquitted, we've had to move house because the neighbours, I'm sure, wouldn't have let their daughters play with ours.

Case 203 [A business man acquitted on the judge's direction on charges of false accounting]
I have lost my business and all my prospects. I have lost at least £6,000—probably more. All my business friends seem to have deserted me. One of the reasons why I couldn't set up business again is that nobody would allow me credit. My wife hasn't been the same woman since then—can you imagine a burden like this hanging over you for more than a year?

Case 245 [An ordered acquittal in a case involving an assault]
People still look at me—they know you've been to court for assault. It makes me feel terrible. It makes me feel like a murderer. I don't like people to know—I wish I could scrub it out. After twelve months, I suppose I'll be in the clear, but I suppose I've got a black spot to my name.

Case 256 [A directed acquittal on two theft charges]
I lost my job and it's a job I'll never have again. The heartache it has caused was terrible. Now I'm on social security and I'm expecting the electricity to be cut off. I don't see anybody now—people feel wary, they don't want to know you because they know you've had dealings with the police. I used to have faith in British justice but this has knocked a big chunk out of it. The police tried to force me to make a statement. I couldn't make a statement because I had none to make. The police were convinced of getting a verdict of guilty. They may think it's a minor case but it's a man's reputation that's at stake. We had no worries before, but now I'm behind with H.P. payments and all these debts are accumulating

because I'm out of work. I've never been in trouble before and I didn't know the procedure.

Case 381 [A research technician whose acquittal in a fraud case was ordered when the prosecution offered no evidence]
I lost my job—that was gone, and I've had quite a bit of difficulty in getting another job. When I told them about the case, they terminated the contract instantly. It was quite obvious why—I could see their point of view. Obviously there's this whole thing about no smoke without fire. It's been a major embarrassment—my worst six months ever.

Given the suffering caused to some defendants, it is appropriate to examine the possibility of identifying such cases in advance of trial. Early identification of weak cases would not only avoid the suffering and hardship occasioned to the defendants in question but would also produce considerable savings in terms of the scarce resources of the court. However, in attempting to identify weak cases, it must be borne in mind that some cases, which do not end in acquittals, may also be incipiently weak. It is therefore necessary to examine the question of weak cases in much broader terms, and it is with these broader issues that the next chapter is concerned.

4
PRE-TRIAL IDENTIFICATION OF WEAK CASES

INTRODUCTION

As was noted in the previous chapter, some commentators view an acquittal rate of some 50 per cent in contested trials as attributable to the rules of evidence and procedure, the quirks of jury trial, or the practices of defence lawyers that enable the guilty to go free; others would have it that the prosecution is at fault in pursuing some cases without any real hope of success and with insufficient evidence to justify putting the accused on trial. It would of course be wrong to regard every acquittal as a failure of the system.[1] As we have seen in the previous chapter, many cases collapse in court because of the unavoidable hazards that even the best organized system has to confront. Moreover, a system which has built into it a succession of separate and independent checks may be expected to throw out at some later points in the process a proportion of cases which have successfully passed earlier checks. A recognition of this feature of the prosecution system has led one solicitor to make the following observation:[2]

> It cannot be stressed too strongly that there is no evidence to suppose that there is a plague of prosecutions as a result of the lack of curbs on police prosecution powers. There is evidence to suppose that cases are brought to trial where, once it comes to the crunch as it were, the prosecution offers no evidence against the defendant, as there is in law no case for him to answer.

Although there is some truth in this statement, it is nonetheless doubtful whether it represents a correct assessment of the problem. Indeed, the important exploratory research conducted by McCabe and Purves (1972a) had earlier suggested that certain

[1] See, for example, Lord Devlin (1960) who writes: 'If the success of a system of criminal prosecution is to be measured by the proportion of criminals whom it convicts and punishes, the English system must be regarded as a failure. Far too many people who have in fact committed crimes escape punishment.' (p. 113.)

[2] A Midlands solicitor 'A Question of Public Prosecutions' *Law Society's Gazette* vol. 74 (1977) pp. 208–9.

cases were being pursued in the Crown Court which ought not to have reached court at all. As was noted in the previous chapter, when McCabe and Purves examined acquittals which the trial judge himself had directed, they found that a majority had been brought about either because the defendant had been able to advance a credible explanation about his activity or because the prosecution case had been fatally weakened by witnesses failing to come up to proof. There was another group of cases, involving seven defendants, which appeared to the researchers to have been weak from the outset of the prosecution. These cases were weak, according to McCabe and Purves, 'in the special sense that . . . the weakness of the prosecution case was apparent before the defendant was committed for trial, and it might be presumed that the prosecution was pressed for reasons other than the expectation of a conviction' (p. 36). Though they identified few cases within their sample as inherently weak (and the authors themselves stress that the significance of such cases ought not to be exaggerated), the study nonetheless suggested that certain cases were being pursued which would not survive a rigorous screening system. Often it is difficult to differentiate those cases which are weak *ab initio* (and therefore possibly identifiable) from those in which collapse at trial is retrospectively attributed by the various parties to an inherent and ineradicable flaw in the evidence.[3]

In devising our own research, we set out to discover whether any cases were being pursued in the Crown Court in which the evidence was insufficient to justify charging the suspect and, if there were such cases, whether it was possible to identify them in advance of trial. In other words, we sought to distinguish between incipiently weak cases and those cases in which the prosecution was justified in evidentiary terms in initiating the charges even though the case became flawed at some later point in the proceedings.

THE METHODS ADOPTED IN IDENTIFYING WEAK CASES

In attempting to determine the extent to which it was possible to identify weak cases in advance of trial, we relied mainly upon the same two samples of Crown Court cases described in the

[3] In a separate study, McCabe and Purves (1972b) considered that many of the cases which had ended with the judge directing the jury to acquit had been prosecuted when the chances of conviction were slight. See also Zander (1974a).

previous chapter. As noted in Table 1 on p. 36, the first sample consisted of the 486 contested cases tried in the Birmingham Crown Court in 1975 and 1976, the second of the 423 defendants whose cases were heard in the seven Crown Court centres in London in 1975.[4] Although we sought information from a variety of sources in identifying weak cases, the principal method that we adopted was to subject the prosecution case to independent scrutiny. The Lord Chancellor's Department in Birmingham and the Metropolitan Police in London kindly supplied us with copies of all the committal papers (statements and depositions) relating to cases within the samples, and these were examined by two highly experienced individuals—one a retired Chief Constable, the other a retired Justices' Clerk.[5] The two assessors were asked, amongst other things, to determine whether, on the basis of the evidence adduced in the committal papers, the prosecution was justified in charging the accused. In none of the cases was this assessment made with any knowledge of the result of the trial, and as far as possible the committal papers were sent to the assessors for scrutiny immediately following committal proceedings.[6] The two assessors were in addition making their evaluations wholly independently of each other. As far as we are aware, this is the first time that researchers in England have carried out this kind of detailed and independent examination of the strength of the prosecution evidence in a series of criminal trials.[7]

The exercise was one in which the assessors were asked to act, as it were, as examining magistrates: to decide whether the evidence disclosed a case for the defendant to answer. Before turning to the results, it is necessary to discuss the precise purposes of the exercise and its limitations.

In the first place, it is conceivable that a judgment that a particular prosecution was not justified may be no criticism of

[4] A small number of cases were excluded from the original sample of contested trials because defendants had changed their pleas to guilty in the course of the trial.

[5] The two assessors were Mr A. F. Wilcox, CBE, QPM (formerly Chief Constable of Hertfordshire) and Dr J. P. Wilson, OBE (formerly Clerk to the Sunderland Justices and an editor of Stone's Justices' Manual between 1952 and 1968).

[6] About two-thirds of all the assessments in Birmingham were in fact made before the trial was concluded. It was not, however, possible to send committal papers for the London sample to the assessors in advance of trial because that sample had been selected from cases already disposed of by the courts.

[7] A small number of researchers in the United States have made use of panels of expert assessors: see particularly the study of Rosenthal (1974) of personal injury settlements.

the prosecution. This follows from the fact that the prosecution may have information which is not contained in the committal papers and which would not be available to the assessors. The police might have, for example, detailed information on the background of the defendant or on the witnesses that would not be contained in the committal papers. Again, in an exceptional case, the prosecution might have evidence that they do not propose to introduce at the trial. In a burglary case, for instance, the police may be led to the defendant by finding his fingerprints at the scene but decide for tactical reasons not to use this material at trial if there is other evidence (such as a written confession) which provides an apparently strong case against the defendant.[8] Although committal papers usually disclose the whole of the prosecution case, on some occasions they do not. More frequently, they do not fully describe the reasons the prosecution wishes to proceed.

A second difficulty associated with paper assessments of this kind relates to the question whether the prosecution has adduced sufficient evidence to justify charging the accused. What the prosecution is required to do is, to use the traditional legal terminology, to make out a *prima facie* case. This means that, before an issue can be submitted to the jury, the judge must be satisfied that there is evidence which, if uncontradicted, could lead a reasonable jury to convict the defendant. If the judge is not satisfied of this, he will direct the jury to acquit. This is one of the formal protective rules of the English criminal system, but, though it is simply stated, it is far from scientific. For the amount and quality of evidence necessary to satisfy the test cannot be measured objectively. Whether there is sufficient evidence is essentially a matter of judgment, and for some cases individuals may reasonably differ on the same evidence. In the light of this, it must be emphasized that, while we believe that the opinions of the assessors provide a good indication of the strength of each case, their judgments cannot be regarded as scientifically exact.

The final and most important limitation relates to the weight that can be given to what are, after all, subjective evaluations. If it is thought desirable to spot in advance of trial the weak or

[8] The police in one case, for example, declined to use fingerprint evidence against one suspect so that he would not be persuaded to wear gloves if he were to commit a similar crime in the future.

the hopeless case, reliance on a subjective evaluation is a price that must be paid. But this does not by any means invalidate the present exercise. The methods we adopted allowed us to test the assessors' opinions by comparing them with the subsequent history of each case at trial. We were also able to set the prospective views of the assessors against information collected from the police on standardized questionnaires immediately following each committal and against information gathered after trial from interviews with the police officer responsible for the handling of the case in court. Comparisons of this kind enabled us to measure the accuracy of the assessments and, as will be apparent later, they served to reinforce our confidence in the value of the exercise.

THE FINDINGS

(i) *The views of the assessors*

For various reasons, it proved impossible to obtain committal papers for all the cases included in the Birmingham and London samples. Sometimes this was because the papers could not be released to us pending an appeal or because a case was *sub judice* for other reasons. In London, it was simply not possible to locate a full set of committal papers in all cases because they were not in the hands of the Metropolitan Police from whom we obtained the papers.[9] In the event, we managed to supply the two assessors with full sets of committal papers for 471 of the cases in the Birmingham sample (96.9 per cent) and 336 in London (79.4 per cent) and the analysis which follows is primarily based upon the assessors' views of these 807 cases. For comparative purposes, we conducted a similar exercise on a sample of 500 guilty plea cases heard in the Birmingham Crown Court in 1975 and 1976. These cases formed a one in four sample of all guilty pleas heard in this period, and reference will be made to them at appropriate points in the ensuing discussion.

The first finding to emerge from this exercise was that, in the overwhelming majority of cases, the assessors were satisfied on the evidence disclosed in the committal papers that the prosecution was justified in charging the accused. Whatever

[9] A small number of the London papers were lodged at the office of the Director of Public Prosecutions, and we are indebted to the Director for supplying copies for our use.

misgivings they may have had about the desirability of prosecuting particular individuals or about the appropriateness of some cases being sent for trial to the Crown Court,[10] the assessors were agreed that the vast majority of defendants had at least a case to answer. There were, however, a number of cases in each city in which the assessors were convinced that the prosecution case was so weak that there was no case for the defendant to meet. In Birmingham, 39 cases (8.3 per cent of all cases for which information was available) and in London 21 cases (6.2 per cent) did not, in the opinion of the assessors, rest on a standard of evidence sufficient to reach the minimum required in law. Of these 60 cases identified as hopelessly weak, 8 are excluded from the following discussion, either because important additional evidence, not available to the assessors and admitted at trial, was adduced by the prosecution after the committal papers had been served[11] or because the charges against the defendant at trial were very different from those he faced at committal. In such circumstances, there is little value in discussing assessments based upon wholly different considerations from those that eventually obtained at trial.

When the remaining cases were examined, it became quite clear that the assessors formed strong views about the strength of the prosecution and even the propriety of pursuing the matter in court. The following comments made by the two assessors illustrate the remarkable degree of agreement between them. It is also particularly important to note that all the following extracts were made in cases that ended in acquittal:

Case 43 [Two men, one being the defendant, were lawfully present in the house of the complainant. Out of the presence of the defendant, the other man took the complainant's handbag and made off. Both were charged with robbery]

Assessor A: There is no evidence that the defendant took the bag. The

[10] In a number of cases, the assessors drew attention to charges which they believed were too trivial for a Crown Court hearing and which ought to have been tried summarily. For a discussion of this question, see Pendragon in *Law Society Gazette* vol. 72 (1975) pp. 348–49.

[11] We ascertained details of additional evidence from the police officers whom we interviewed after the conclusion of each trial. In most cases in which additional evidence was adduced after committal, its importance was slight and had no real bearing on the outcome of the case in court. In such cases, we did not consider that the assessments had been unduly affected by the absence of the new evidence so they were not excluded from the analysis.

complainant says it was the other man. There is no suggestion that the robbery was planned or that the proceeds were shared. The allegation is that the other man took it.

Assessor B: There is no evidence that this defendant was implicated in the alleged offence.

Case 49 [A case of unlawful wounding in which two men attacked the victim and a third man—the defendant—gave the victim comfort and assistance after the assault]

Assessor A: The jury may accept the defendant's story in the absence of evidence of his participation.

Assessor B: There is no evidence that the defendant attacked the injured party. None of the witnesses implicates the defendant and the injured party thinks that he was the furthest away when the attack occurred. This prosecution may have been misconceived.

Case 91 [The defendant, a passenger in a car, was charged with possession of drugs found in the driver's car door compartment]

Assessor A: The defence that the accused did not know the drugs were in the car will probably be accepted. There is nothing to connect the accused to the drugs.

Assessor B: I do not think there will be a conviction of this defendant on the facts. There is no evidence against him.

Case 100 [The defendant was charged with going equipped for theft. He was walking in a street with another man when they were stopped by the police. On being searched, the other man was found to have four car keys in his pocket]

Assessor A: There is little to support the charge. There is no evidence that the accused possessed the keys and the defence that the keys had nothing to do with the accused is likely to be accepted.

Assessor B: There is little evidence of possession and none of intent. I do not consider that there was any case against this defendant.

Cases 134–7 [A shopkeeper alleged that a packet of chewing-gum was taken from his shop by one of the four defendants. He did not see the incident and was unable to say which of the four was responsible for the theft]

Assessor A: There is no evidence to identify which of the accused took the gum and there is little evidence of common design. This is an outstanding example of the abuse of a Crown Court being required to deal with a case which ought not to have got beyond the magistrates.

Assessor B: I do not consider that there is adequate evidence against any of the accused. All the accused denied the offence. At the end of the day (apart from acting on a hunch) there was no effective evidence against any of them.

Case 308 [An allegation of theft between friends]

Assessor A: The circumstances of this case are likely to strike the jury as fishy. The credibility of the prosecution witnesses appears doubtful.

Assessor B: There are at least six discrepancies between the evidence of the several witnesses, some on vital issues. There are too many holes in the evidence.

Case 381 [The defendant was charged with theft of a credit card]

Assessor A: The papers disclose no evidence that the accused stole the card. Apparently it was issued to him in the normal way.

Assessor B: A strange case where I doubt whether the charge preferred will stand up. I cannot understand why this defendant was charged with theft of the card. The prosecution sounds like an afterthought.

Cases 392–4 [This case arose out of a fight between four men known to each other. One of the injured parties alleged that a small sum of money was taken from his jacket in the course of the fight. The three others involved were charged with robbery]

Assessor A: There is a lack of corroboration and a jury will find it difficult to believe any of the parties. The case is confused and the witnesses unreliable. It would be unsafe to convict.

Assessor B: This case is so confused and confusing that I do not consider that a conviction can be obtained against any of the accused. I cannot see this prosecution succeeding.

All the above comments relate to cases that were tried in the Birmingham Crown Court. Similarly forceful observations were made by the assessors about cases within the London sample:

Case 28 [An allegation of assault occasioning actual bodily harm arising out of a domestic dispute that took place some considerable time before a complaint was made to the police]

Assessor A: There is no medical evidence of the injuries alleged to constitute actual bodily harm. It might have been preferable to let the victim prefer the charge himself.

Assessor B: This is a poor case. The injuries were first recorded four to five months later and no medical evidence has been called. I consider that the parties could well have been left to pursue their own remedies.

Case 86 [The defendant was charged with handling a television set. It could not be established whether the set had been stolen, although the police received information that it was]

Assessor A: There is no evidence that the set was stolen and no proof that the defendant knew it was stolen.

Assessor B: I do not consider that there is sufficient evidence of receiving or of dishonesty by this accused.

Case 123 [The accused was on his own in a street with a stone in his hand. He was charged with possessing an article with intent to damage property]

Assessor A: The evidence of intent to damage is dubious. It seems to me that there was little to justify arrest.

Assessor B: This is a charge which should never have reached the Crown Court and which is unlikely to succeed.

Case 282 [A case involving a man charged with dishonestly handling a sports jacket found at his flat]

Assessor A: There is no evidence that the jacket had been stolen. The evidence is lacking.

Assessor B: There is no evidence that the goods had been stolen and I doubt whether this case can be established.

Case 383 [A charge of driving whilst unfit by reason of drink]

Assessor A: The doctor called to examine the accused said that he was not unfit and the specimen of blood contained alcohol below the accepted level. The police made the arrest because they thought that the defendant was unfit; it would have been preferable to await confirmation from the doctor.

Assessor B: The low alcohol content, as determined by analysis, coupled with the doctor's evidence should result in an acquittal.

These comments give some idea of the views expressed by the assessors about the small, but important, group of cases which were, in their opinion, so weak that the prosecution was not justified in terms of the amount and quality of the evidence adduced. That all the defendants were acquitted lends considerable weight to their assessments. In many of these cases no doubt the defendant had, in the eyes of the police, something to explain. He may, for example, have been present at the scene of a crime and been seen to act in a furtive or suspicious manner. Alternatively, he may have been evasive and uncooperative when questioned. Nevertheless, when the evidence which the police had been able to gather was dispassionately considered by individuals not personally committed to the prosecution, it appeared that there was little to substantiate the charges. In terms of the evidence presented, the prosecution in these cases seemed to have been misconceived.

Whilst the views of the assessors are quite unambiguous in this respect, the critical question is the extent to which it is safe to rely upon their judgments. In other words, it might be objected that the methods adopted amount to no more than the replacement of one set of subjective opinions (those of the prosecution) with another set of opinions which are equally impressionistic. For several reasons, however, we think that the views of the assessors have to be accorded greater respect than this objection might suggest. It was possible to compare all assessments with the actual result of the case in court, and also to evaluate their views in relation to the opinions of police officers (and others) contacted after the trial had been concluded and in relation to information we collected from the prosecution immediately following committal proceedings. When these comparisons were made, our confidence in the judgment of the two assessors was considerably reinforced.

(ii) *The outcome of cases identified as weak*

One major advantage of our method of prospective identification of weak cases is that it allowed the assessments to be set against the outcome of the cases at trial. If the cases picked out by the assessors were in fact so weak that the prosecution was not justified, one would anticipate that most if not all would collapse in court. One would not expect that all such cases would necessarily result in acquittal because cases may become stronger in court than they appear on paper, as, for example, where defendants make unexpected admissions in the witness box or a co-defendant supplies damning evidence. In such borderline cases, the outcome may be thoroughly unpredictable if the prosecution is allowed to proceed.[12] There will be scope for reasonable differences of view in many cases as to whether the evidence has reached the minimum required in law before the case can proceed to the jury. This consideration is not, however, of major importance and the value of the opinions of the assessors rests primarily upon the prosecution failing in those cases identified as weak. Examination of the fate of defendants involved in those cases identified as weak showed that, in both Birmingham and in London, the overwhelming majority resulted in the acquittal of the defendant. Table 3 sets out the results on this.

[12] It is settled that the Court of Appeal can dismiss an appeal against conviction even in cases where they are of the view that the trial judge ought to have ruled that there was no case for the defendant to answer at the close of the prosecution's evidence if the accused gives evidence and incriminates himself: *R.* v *Power*, [1919] 1 K.B. 572.

TABLE 3

The outcome of cases for which one or both assessors expressed the view that the prosecution was not justified

	Birmingham	(%)		London	(%)	
Case ended in an ordered acquittal	16	48.5	84.8	0	0.0	84.2
Case ended in a directed acquittal	4	12.1		3	15.8	
Case ended in a jury acquittal	8	24.2		13	68.4	
Case ended in a conviction	5	15.2		3	15.8	
Case excluded because of new charges or important additional prosecution evidence	6	–		2	–	
	39	100.0		21	100.0	

As the table demonstrates, the assessors were remarkably successful in identifying cases that were incipiently weak; indeed, over five prosecutions in six of those seen as not justified ended in acquittal.[13] This in itself strongly suggests that it is possible to identify in advance of trial many cases which ultimately end as acquittals.[14] Moreover, the bald figures presented in the table underestimate the extent to which the assessors were successful. For instance, *case 206* in Birmingham is classified in the table as ending in a conviction yet the detailed comments of the assessors and the facts of the case show that our classification obscures the accuracy of the assessment that was made. In this case, the defendant was initially charged only with unlawful wounding, having restrained a plain clothes police officer who was trying to arrest another man. At trial, the defendant was acquitted of this charge but convicted of common assault, a much less serious charge. As the following extracts show, the assessors accurately forecast the outcome, even though this could not be reflected in Table 3:

[13] As we have noted in the previous chapter, fewer cases were withdrawn from the jury in London than was the case in Birmingham. The reasons for this must remain speculative but see the views in Zander (1974a) cited above at p. 32.

[14] It may seem surprising that twenty-nine cases in which the evidence was weak were allowed to go before the jury. The explanation is that, as other research (McCabe and Purves (1972a); Zander (1974a)) has suggested, some judges are reluctant to assume the responsibility for terminating cases once a jury has been empanelled.

Assessor A: There seems little justification for the charge. Assault or obstructing a police officer would have been more appropriate and would probably have led to a plea before the magistrates.

Assessor B: This is a trivial matter where a charge of obstructing the police would have sufficed. I consider that the assault and injury were too trivial to support a charge of an indictable offence.

Two other cases (one in each city) involved multiple charges in which the defendant was acquitted of the main offences and convicted only of a minor count; in one further case, the police officer interviewed said he was 'surprised' that the defendant was convicted; and in two others the officer stated that the prosecution case was not very strong. But even if such qualifications are ignored, we can claim that the assessors were remarkably accurate in identifying the weak or hopeless cases in both the Birmingham and London samples.

(iii) *The opinions of others involved in the trial of those cases identified as weak*

As we discussed in the previous chapter, we conducted interviews after the conclusion of each contested trial with the police officers in Birmingham and London who had been responsible for handling the case. In addition to these interviews, we sent questionnaires to the trial judge and to the prosecuting solicitor for every contested trial in Birmingham. The information that we collected from these sources enabled us to test how far the opinions of the assessors were shared by others closely involved in the trial. It might be thought that there are dangers in putting too much emphasis upon this exercise because in a very weak case the police or prosecuting solicitor might seek to rationalize their decision to proceed by claiming that the original decision to prosecute was well justified and that the case was wrecked only because a flaw had subsequently developed. It quickly became apparent, however, that all those approached gave their views extremely frankly, with a full recognition of the evidentiary weaknesses.[15] In most cases, the respondents' views were entirely consistent with the opinions of our assessors that the prosecution was doomed from the start. The following quotations are illustrative of this:

[15] We have commented elsewhere on the abilities of many of those contacted in the course of our research to rise above general prejudices they may have held when discussing the outcome of a particular case: see Baldwin and McConville (1979c) pp. 34–5.

Case 86 (*London*) [A case involving handling a television set believed to be stolen]

Police officer: It was a very weak case and I wasn't surprised by the acquittal.

Case 315 (*London*) [A case arising out of allegations that a small child had been sexually assaulted]

Police officer: We knew from the beginning that it was a pretty weak case. I don't think that any of the police officers involved were surprised at the outcome at all.

Case 366 (*London*) [A case of car theft in which the defendant claimed that he believed the car to have been abandoned]

Police officer: To be quite honest, I expected a not guilty verdict from the outset.

Case 43 (*Birmingham*) [A case of robbery]

Police officer: There was no evidence actually available to prove that the defendant was present when the offence took place and he was not identified by the prosecution witness who knew him.

Case 49 (*Birmingham*) [A defendant charged in connection with a fight which took place outside a public house]

Police officer: It was pretty obvious to me all along that there was insufficient evidence for him to be convicted. It was only right that the defendant was acquitted: any other verdict would have been wrong.

Case 134–7 (*Birmingham*) [A case involving four youths said to have stolen a packet of chewing-gum from a shop]

Police officer: There was definitely insufficient evidence to convict any of these defendants. I strongly agreed with the judge's decision to order an acquittal. The officer who took the decision to charge was quite within his rights, but I certainly wouldn't have done it.

Judge: My view was that there was insufficient evidence to convict any of these defendants . . . In my opinion, this case never ought to have been committed for trial at all—if the committal proceedings had been done properly either by the prosecution or by those who represented any of these defendants it would not have been committed.

Prosecuting solicitor: There was little or no evidence to sustain a successful prosecution.

Case 174 (*Birmingham*) [A case involving a second-hand dealer charged with receiving a stolen television set]

Police officer: On the evidence we'd got, it was a thin case—we knew that from the start. We expected an acquittal, to be honest. Actually, we thought the defence would make a submission of 'no case to answer' at the Committal stage, but they just let it go through.

Case 381 (*Birmingham*) [A case involving the use of a credit card in alleged offences of deception]

Prosecuting solicitor: The prosecution offered no evidence in view of the fact that there was insufficient evidence available to justify a conviction. It had been hoped that additional evidence would have been available but it was not.

As these comments demonstrate, there can be little doubt that those involved in these trials had grave misgivings about the prospects of conviction. In a few of the cases no doubt the decision to proceed (or the decision to allow the case to go to the jury) was finely balanced,[16] but for most cases respondents took the view that there was little point in pursuing the matter in the expectation of a conviction.

(iv) *Views expressed by police officers at committal*

A final source of information relevant to the assessors' views was derived from the police after the committal proceedings were completed. In cases falling within the Birmingham sample,[17] a questionnaire was administered to the police in every case immediately following the defendant's committal to the Crown Court. As explained in chapter 2, this questionnaire, which was completed for every case passing through the Crown Court, was concerned with certain factual matters such as whether the defendant was on bail or in custody, and the number of weeks between committal and his first appearance in court. But the primary purpose of the questionnaire was to ascertain at that early stage the reasons for instituting proceedings against the accused. To that end, the police were asked to indicate which, if any, of a list of factors they had taken into account in deciding to charge the accused. The list presented to the police included factors such as the defendant admitting the offence in a signed statement or orally, the seriousness of the alleged offence, or the attitude of the complainant in the case. One particularly important factor was that 'the evidence was not very strong but it was deemed proper for the court to decide'. In almost a half of

[16] Sometimes this was apparent in the comments we received from respondents. In *case 328* in Birmingham, for example, the trial judge said: 'This was a very weak case but just sufficient to go to the jury. The accused did not give evidence, but the jury had no hesitation in acquitting.'

[17] It was not possible to collect comparable information in London, given the retrospective nature of the sampling procedures we were forced to adopt.

all the cases that the assessors had identified as weak, police officers had themselves ticked this last category. Indeed, asking the question in this form produced a rather curious result, for we found in most cases when this category was viewed by the police as relevant that they had actually amended the questionnaire by striking out the word 'very' from the category 'evidence not very strong . . .'. This provides a clear indication that, in such cases, police officers were fully aware of the limitations of the prosecution evidence at the committal stage and long before the date set down for trial in the Crown Court.

As we have already seen, the assessors were of the view that, in 60 of the 807 cases they examined, the prosecution had not brought forward enough evidence to warrant placing the accused on trial. In other words, more than one case in every fourteen failed to reach even a *prima facie* level. This finding relates only to cases in which the prosecution was wholly unjustified, and it is important to note that the assessors identified other cases in which they thought that, though the prosecution was justified in charging the accused, there was no justification in respect of some of the counts in the indictment. In the Birmingham contested sample, the assessors said that there were a further twenty cases in which one or more counts were unjustified, and, in the London sample, nine such cases. Examination of these cases revealed that in all save two the accused was acquitted on the counts regarded as unjustified. Combining these results, therefore, it appears that 7.4 per cent of all contested cases were brought without sufficient evidence and a further 3.6 per cent contained one or more counts which were not justified by the available evidence.

WEAK CASES AMONG THOSE IN WHICH THE DEFENDANT PLEADED GUILTY

The assessments discussed so far were based upon contested trials only, and it would be wrong to infer that the same pattern applies to all cases committed for trial. In order to ascertain the extent to which this picture was relevant to other cases heard in the Crown Court, we asked the assessors to scrutinize a further 500 cases heard in Birmingham in which the defendant had pleaded guilty.[18] No assessment could be made in two of

[18] The sample of guilty plea cases was drawn over the same time period as the main sample so that the assessors would have no idea which cases were contested and which were not.

these cases and, of the remainder, the assessors concluded that the prosecution was not justified in charging the accused in eleven cases (2.2 per cent).[19] Bearing in mind that there were four times as many guilty pleas as there were contested trials in Birmingham in the sample period, it would appear, therefore, that overall about 3.5 per cent of all cases committed for trial were not justified in terms of the evidence adduced by the prosecution.

A plea of guilty in circumstances in which there is in truth no case for the defendant to answer brings two different interests into conflict. On the one hand, it might be said that it is in the public interest that those who are indeed guilty should admit their guilt. This permits society to punish those who have transgressed the law, saves the cost, time, and trouble of proving culpability, assists the morale of the police, and reinforces public confidence which might be weakened if wrongdoers escape their deserts. On the other hand, the Anglo-American criminal justice system is intended to ensure the punishment only of the guilty and, if defendants plead guilty where the prosecution has failed to establish a *prima facie* case on paper, they are bypassing all the safeguards provided by the system against unjust punishment. It must be emphasized that we are not presently concerned with whether innocent people are pleading guilty. The views of defendants, police officers, and others in these cases raise the possibility that some who pleaded guilty were innocent, whereas, for other cases, it is clear that the defendant was factually guilty or at the least involved in some way in the commission of a crime. The more important question in the present context is why people against whom the evidence is slight or non-existent nevertheless plead guilty. This is a complex question that we have considered at length elsewhere (Baldwin and McConville 1977a, pp. 59–82) and to which we shall return in the final chapter. It is sufficient to note here that some defendants pleaded guilty because they were guilty in fact, that some simply wanted to get the case over as quickly as possible, and that others were badly advised or put under pressure to enter a guilty plea. In our interviews with defendants involved in contested cases identified as weak by the assessors,

[19] In a further twelve cases, some charges in multiple-count indictments were said to be completely unsupported by evidence. It is noteworthy that the defendant's guilty plea to other counts was generally accepted in these cases.

there was, for example, plenty of evidence to suggest that the defendants in question had been offered inducements to plead guilty. We quote below from interviews we conducted with two defendants in Birmingham, both of whom were acquitted at trial, which indicate the sort of temptations that are dangled before defendants.[20]

Case 210 [A case which arose out of an incident in which a police officer was assaulted]
My barrister came downstairs to see me at the trial and said that if I pleaded guilty to [the least serious charge], I'd be guaranteed a £10 fine and the other charges would be dropped. When I refused, he said he was pleased. He said 'You'll walk out of this. You'll definitely get an acquittal.'

Case 310 [A domestic dispute]
When we were waiting to go into the court, the policeman spoke to the prosecuting barrister and said, 'We've got a very thin case.' The prosecution offered a deal to my barrister and my barrister told me that it was a good offer. I said, 'No—I'm going in on the original charge and pleading not guilty.' He didn't advise me to accept the offer: it had been offered to him, he offered it to me. He didn't press me—it was only a ten minute chat.

It hardly needs stressing that, faced with inducements of this sort, the weak, naive, or less resilient might well be tempted to forego their right to trial and instead plead guilty.

THE NATURE OF CASES IDENTIFIED AS WEAK

It seems clear that, if an effective screening mechanism had been introduced at an early stage in the prosecution process designed to sift out those cases in which there was insufficient evidence against the accused,[21] most if not all of the cases picked out by the assessors as inherently weak would not have been pursued, and it is important to find out what types of case and what sorts of defendant would have been affected. Examination of the samples in Birmingham and London revealed that the cases identified as weak were a very mixed bag, embracing offences such as robbery, wounding, taking and driving, and theft. Slightly more than one third were offences of theft,

[20] For further examples of advice to plead guilty being given to defendants who were eventually acquitted, see Baldwin and McConville (1977a) at pp. 78–9.

[21] As we shall see in the next chapter, there may be non-evidentiary reasons for pursuing a prosecution in certain cases.

handling, and burglary and about the same proportion involved offences of wounding or assault. None of the cases appeared to be of a particularly serious nature. They involved for the most part small amounts of property, technical assaults, or minor woundings. In the Birmingham group, for example, there were ten cases of burglary, all of which involved small amounts of property, the value of which was less than £1 in seven cases. Similarly, of the four robbery cases, one concerned a handbag snatching incident and three were cases in which small amounts of property were alleged to have been taken during fights. All four incidents occurred between acquaintances or persons well known to each other. The overall picture was reinforced when the backgrounds of the defendants involved were taken into account. Of those involved in weak cases in both cities, over 40 per cent had no criminal record, almost exactly 80 per cent had never been sentenced to terms of imprisonment, and none was regarded by the police as a serious, professional criminal. Although there may be differences of view about whether the offences in question were serious or not, it can at least be confidently stated that none of the offences represented threats to public safety.

CONCLUDING COMMENTS

Two general implications may be drawn from all this. First, an effective screening mechanism based upon evidentiary considerations would primarily affect cases that are contested and that at present lead to the acquittal of the accused. It would also affect, though less markedly, some cases that presently end in conviction. These cases are either those in which the defendant pleads guilty (whatever the evidence) or those in which the question whether the prosecution had made out a *prima facie* case is borderline. Secondly, it would bear almost entirely upon comparatively minor infractions, involving defendants regarded by the police as thoroughly unprofessional.

The assessors were able to identify with great accuracy cases which were incipiently weak and, for the most part, weak beyond redemption. Put another way, the results strongly suggest that a small proportion of Crown Court cases could safely be discontinued early in the process without serious loss, and perhaps with considerable gain in terms of saving the scarce resources of the system and, more importantly, by sparing defendants the anxiety and turmoil of prosecution. For not only did the great majority of cases viewed as weak by the assessors actually end in the acquittal of the defendants in question, but it was clear that others closely involved with the trial readily acknowledged the crippling limitations of the prosecution evidence and, so far as the police themselves were concerned, these limitations were often recognized at the very outset of the prosecution. Taken together, these different considerations provide convincing evidence of the accuracy of the judgment of the assessors and of the possibility of identifying weak cases in advance of trial. But one consideration must be borne in mind: for, had all the cases judged to be weak by the assessors been screened out at an early stage, some defendants who were factually guilty would have escaped conviction and sentence. No doubt there are some observers who would argue that this makes the case for early termination unacceptable. It must be pointed out, however, that every decision not to prosecute, whether made by the police, the Director of Public Prosecutions, or anyone else, involves the risk of setting free defendants against whom a prosecution might have succeeded. Any attempt to predict the likely outcome of a case involves a subjective evaluation of such risks, and it is a question of whether the risk is within tolerable limits. Examination of cases identified as weak by the assessors suggests that there are good arguments for early intervention and that, even if the non-prosecution of a minority who would have been ultimately convicted is regarded as a loss to society, the competing advantages are of much greater significance. The number of unnecessary trials could be reduced[22] with the consequent saving in terms of cost, delay, and court time. More important, many defendants (some of whom may be quite innocent of the charges brought against them) would be relieved of much unnecessary distress.

We cited in the previous chapter the interviews we conducted with defendants who had been involved in ordered and directed acquittals, and we noted the serious consequences several had suffered as a result of being put on trial. It is worth re-emphasizing the same point in relation to those defendants who had

[22] In a few cases, as was discussed in the last chapter, the removal of a weak case could prejudice other cases. This would occur where the prosecution of the weak case (without any hope or expectation of a conviction) might assist in the conviction of other defendants. We pursue this point further in the following chapter.

been involved in weak cases. It is true that a few defendants experienced a sense of elation simply because they had been acquitted, but this feeling was as a rule tempered by other considerations. They complained, for instance, about the treatment they received at or following arrest; being detained in custody overnight or over the weekend; their families not being informed of where they were being held; not being made aware of their rights; being threatened or bullied during interrogation; and of having inconvenient or oppressive conditions imposed on bail. But on the whole they found the consequences of prosecution itself harder to bear. These consequences were particularly severe for those who had never been in trouble before—the press publicity, the adverse effects upon their reputation and social standing, and the disruption to their domestic life. Some were left feeling jaundiced or embittered because they had been needlessly put through an ordeal, which had been financially punitive as well as costly in terms of the emotional stress on themselves and their families. Perhaps the most striking thing to emerge was the sharp distinction they drew between the actual court proceedings and the need for them. Defendants had little but praise for the way in which the judge and their legal advisers had handled the case but were often scathingly critical of the prosecution's decision to proceed in the first place. The following extracts from interviews that we carried out with defendants in Birmingham (all of whom were eventually acquitted) illustrate these points:

Case 100 [A case in which the police alleged that the defendant had stolen car keys in his possession]

Well, it was fair, but I should never have been in court in the first place. I had to have time off work to go to court. I didn't get paid and I can't claim. It was a waste of the taxpayer's money and everything.

Case 244 [A case involving a licensee involved in a pub brawl]

It was a bit of a mess-up by the police, I think. I always thought the police were doing a good job under hard conditions, which I still appreciate. I wouldn't like to have to do some of the things they do. But where an ounce of common sense could have made a difference between right and wrong, they weren't interested. I can't say much about justice as I wasn't put in a position where I had to be judged. The only thing I would really criticize was the action of the police.

Case 310 [A domestic dispute]
If you were found not guilty, you'd be over the moon. Justice in the Crown Court is excellent but the police side of it is deplorable. They were justified in investigating but no more than that. Being completely detached, it was chaotic. I wasn't asked to help with inquiries, I was arrested on the word of one person. They made up their minds when I was charged that I was guilty, and nothing after that would change their opinion. Immediately after I was charged, the company I was working for received an anonymous telephone call and I was dismissed. For six months I was on unemployment benefit. As it is, I've just found myself a better job.

Case 328 [A case surrounding alleged illegal application for a passport]
So far as the Crown Court is concerned, I've got nothing to grumble about, nothing whatsoever. I was not treated unfairly there, I will never say that I was. What I wonder is why I was accused, why the charge was brought against me. The press gave it such publicity that it harmed my reputation and my business suffered to a considerable extent.

What emerged from our interviews was that eventual acquittal was small comfort when adverse consequences flowed from the mere fact of being put on trial. The criminal system cannot, of course, guard against the effects of being put on trial because these result from matters over which the court has no control. If it is thought desirable to prevent such consequences, attention should be directed towards examining whether such cases should be tried at all. It would be wrong to conclude from the results presented in this chapter that no attention is given to this question in England or that no protective procedures have been set up to deal with it.[23] The available evidence strongly suggests, however, that these procedures are operating imperfectly. In the next chapter, we examine the mechanisms that currently exist in England, and attempt to discover why weak cases and, more generally, those cases that ended in ordered and directed acquittals were allowed to pass through some, if not all, of the checks that might have been expected to terminate them.

[23] Such procedures are, however, much more highly developed in the United States where the proportion of cases 'diverted' from the courts is very much higher than in England. On this, see particularly Vera Institute (1977) and Eisenstein and Jacob (1977).

5

THE PROTECTIVE MECHANISMS OF THE PROSECUTION SYSTEM

INTRODUCTION

English legal and administrative procedures are specifically designed to guard against two broad errors: the conviction of any who are possibly innocent, and the placing on trial of those against whom there is no real evidence. Among the rules designed to prevent the conviction of the innocent is the requirement that it is for the prosecution to prove beyond reasonable doubt that the defendant is guilty. In discharging this burden, the prosecution is confined to admissible evidence, and if it fails to bring forward sufficient evidence upon which a reasonable jury could properly convict, the defendant must be acquitted. It is not for the defendant to prove his innocence: all he need show is that there is a reasonable doubt as to his guilt.[1] Rules of this kind are formal rules and they constitute an integral part of open court adjudication in the adversary system.

Additional considerations apply to the second issue—ensuring that only those against whom there is sufficient evidence are charged and sent for trial. Here, many of the protective rules are less open to scrutiny; they are less formal and less well-defined. However, they do exist. Before charging a suspect, the police must be satisfied that there is sufficient evidence against him, though they have considerable latitude in the interpretation of this requirement. Usually the prosecution evidence will be scrutinized internally or by a prosecuting solicitor before or after charges are laid, and the defence has a similar opportunity to test the evidence after charges have been laid. In cases destined to be tried in the Crown Court there is a further check—at committal proceedings the defence may submit that there is no case for the defendant to answer on the evidence adduced by the prosecution and request the magistrates to make a decision. Finally, before a case comes on for trial at the Crown Court, prosecuting counsel may himself determine that there is

[1] Strictly speaking the defendant does not have to show even this. It is sufficient that there is a reasonable doubt, and this may be apparent in the prosecution evidence itself.

insufficient evidence upon which to proceed and take steps to terminate the prosecution. If for any reason these mechanisms function imperfectly (or fail to operate at all), there is a risk that a defendant may be sent for trial upon insufficient evidence. If this happens, an innocent person may needlessly be put to the trouble, expense, and anxiety of a court appearance the outcome of which should never have been in doubt.

In the two preceding chapters, we examined cases which, in the vast majority of instances, ended abruptly at trial in the acquittal of the defendant. This in itself suggests that the criminal justice system is able to provide real protection for those accused who are possibly innocent. The protective mechanisms operated successfully in the sense that in these cases they did prevent the conviction of defendants against whom there was insufficient evidence. In evidentiary terms, the right result was eventually reached. But it is less certain that existing safeguards are adequate in stifling prosecutions based on insufficient evidence. The criminal justice system provides a number of checks to prevent such occurrences and, in some respects at least, the system corresponds to Herbert Packer's Due Process Model. As we saw in chapter 1, Packer (1968) represents this model of the criminal system as an obstacle course in which 'each of its successive stages is designed to present formidable impediments to carrying the accused any further along the process' (p. 163). In a celebrated passage, Packer compares this model with what he terms the Crime Control Model, which emphasizes speed and efficiency in case disposal—resembling an assembly line more than an obstacle course.[2] Pursuing this analogy, one might argue that, within the English system, the need to satisfy the police, prosecuting and defence solicitors, counsel, and magistrates that the case is fit to proceed represents a series of hurdles that must be overcome if a case is to reach trial. However, it will be apparent from much of the discussion in the two previous chapters that it is difficult to reconcile this model with the finding that weak cases were allowed to proceed a considerable way through the process. This was not true of all cases. The cases discussed covered, on paper at least, the whole spectrum of evidence-sufficiency from the inherently weak to the manifestly strong, their only shared characteristic being that, when

[2] See Packer (1968) pp. 149–73. The models are critically evaluated by Griffiths (1970); Bottoms and McClean (1976) pp. 226–39, and McBarnet (1978a).

the crunch came, there was not enough evidence available or it was unreliable or of poor quality. As we have seen in the previous chapters, fatal weaknesses may develop at any number of points prior to trial. Our present interest is not, however, in the whole range of cases examined, but with those cases which were incipiently weak either because there was never any *prima facie* case at all or because there was no reasonable prospect of a conviction. The screening system was not effective and the important question is why the various checks failed to work. It is useful to examine this by looking at the separate protective mechanisms of the system, and a good starting-point is the stage at which most cases failed—at the Crown Court itself.

CHECKS PROVIDED AT THE CROWN COURT

As we have seen, an important group of cases are terminated by the trial judge ordering an acquittal to be recorded without the case even reaching the jury. This generally arises, not from any independent action on the part of the trial judge, but at the instigation of prosecuting counsel. Upon receiving a brief to appear for the Crown in a criminal case, it is the duty of counsel to examine the prosecution evidence, to request if need be that additional inquiries be made before proceeding further, and to decide whether a case for the defendant to answer has been made out. The source of these duties is well put by Brown (1975) in the following passage:

> [It] is counsel's responsibility to undertake the presentation of the case in court. It is he who has to stand up before the court to put the prosecution case, to meet questions put to him by the judge, to meet legal arguments put by the defence and to see that the prosecution case is fairly presented and that all weaknesses in the defence case are identified and fairly exposed to the court. If, in the event, criticisms of the way in which the prosecution is conducted are raised, it is counsel for the Crown who bears the responsibility. (p. 3.)

The proper discharge of these duties was evident in a number of cases within our samples. We did not have the benefit of speaking to counsel directly[3] but it was clear from information provided by other respondents (particularly the police) that often the immediate cause of the abandonment of the prosecu-

[3] As noted earlier, it was a matter of regret to us that the Senate of the Inns of Court and the Bar had ruled that no barrister co-operate in any aspect of our inquiry.

tion was the advice of counsel. In some cases, counsel's scrutiny of the paper evidence was enough to convince him that the matter should not be allowed to proceed. In others, being uncertain of the strength of the case on paper, counsel requested that particular witnesses be re-interviewed, and decided to abandon the case only when he had assessed this new information. We cite below some examples in which counsel's active role was decisive in bringing cases abruptly to an end:

Case 43 (*Birmingham*) [A case of robbery]
Police officer: Our view was that this defendant might have been an accomplice, although not necessarily responsible for the robbery. But subsequently prosecuting counsel advised us to interview the complainant again to see whether she would be willing to identify this defendant in court as one of the assailants. When interviewed again she said that he was not present and our barrister then said that there was insufficient evidence to put the defendant on trial.

Case 308 (*Birmingham*) [A charge of theft]
Police officer: On the morning of the court hearing, prosecution counsel said in strong terms to offer no evidence. I took his advice and we offered no evidence.

Case 330 (*London*) [A charge of indecent assault]
Police officer: The complainant woman positively identified the defendant as the person who entered her flat and indecently assaulted her. When she came to court, she told me before the trial started that the accused was not the man. I brought this, as I was duty bound to, to the notice of our counsel. He told me to speak to the complainant again. I did so and she was adamant he was not the man. Counsel then discussed this with the judge and decided to offer no evidence.

Case 425 (*London*) [A case of shoplifting]
Police officer: This was an allegation of shoplifting of property valued at less than £1 in which the defendant claimed absentmindedness. Counsel spoke with the judge before the case about the amount of property involved, the fact that the defendant had suffered terribly in the war, and his general state of health. Counsel took a very sympathetic view of the defendant, decided that he couldn't stand up to a trial and in view of this offered no evidence against him.

These examples illustrate the sort of influence that counsel may exercise over the fate of particular cases. Counsel can terminate a prosecution or ensure that any doubts he entertains are satisfactorily resolved before agreeing to proceed. The experience and conscientiousness of counsel is thus itself an important check on the bringing of misconceived or oppressive prosecutions.

It does not follow that the possible intervention of counsel is an infallible safeguard or even an effective fetter on the prosecution. That hopelessly weak cases were allowed to reach trial is some indication of this. As we have seen, several cases collapsed at trial simply because there was little or no evidence against the defendant. Even trial judges are on occasions critical of the prosecution. In one case in Birmingham, for instance, in which the judge had directed the jury to acquit, the judge expressed himself 'horrified that the charge was brought and that it got through the prosecuting solicitor's department'. This strongly suggests that some cases, passing through the hands of prosecution counsel, ought to have been terminated by him and not allowed to limp through to trial. One can only speculate about why such cases reach trial. In some cases, there is room for differences in point of view. Prosecution counsel may decide, after a careful assessment of the brief, that there is sufficient evidence to get the case off the ground in court, but this opinion may not be shared by defence counsel or by the trial judge. In finely balanced cases, such evaluations are difficult, and counsel should not be criticized merely because his opinion does not win the day. In clear-cut cases counsel is more open to censure. If there is no real evidence against the defendant, counsel is at fault if he continues to press the prosecution. This is likely to happen, for example, where counsel is inexperienced in criminal matters. Barristers with little or no experience are sometimes instructed to appear at the Crown Court, and in such circumstances their opinion on the merits of the prosecution case may be less than helpful.[4] Another difficulty is that some barristers are not sufficiently familiar with the brief properly to assess the prosecution evidence. This may arise from pressure of work or because the brief is delivered to them so late that there is insufficient time for proper consideration. We have discussed elsewhere the adverse consequences this may create on the defence side,[5] but the problem has wider implications, as the

[4] We have noted elsewhere the limited experience of certain barristers in fighting cases in the Crown Court: see Baldwin and McConville (1977b).

[5] Baldwin and McConville (1977a) pp. 110-11. See also McCabe and Purves (1972a) pp. 44-5, and Bottoms and McClean (1976) pp. 158-9.

following comment by Danks (1975), a chief prosecuting solicitor, shows:

> The problem of the returned brief is not only a difficulty for barristers but also for solicitors. One day I had 25 briefs returned, one afternoon, seven of them fights, and all of them for the next day. That is no way to run a business and it ought not to be beyond the wit of the legal profession to design a system which avoids such difficulties, or at least alleviates the position. (pp. 70–1.)

The dangers of this practice hardly require elaboration, and situations must arise in which counsel, whatever his level of experience, is not well placed to make a careful assessment of the strength and propriety of particular prosecutions. He may in consequence embark upon a course that he would not have taken under more favourable conditions.

Whilst independent scrutiny by counsel is one check upon the prosecution, it is not always sufficient. Moreover, it is a check which comes, if at all, at a late stage in the proceedings, as a rule immediately before the case is due to be tried. This inevitably causes distress to the defendants involved and has adverse consequences for the efficiency and cost of the administration of the Crown Court. It is often not appreciated that the late collapse of cases can disrupt other court business, delay the trials of other defendants, waste the time of police officers, court staff, and judges, and involve considerable costs in terms of the fees paid to solicitor and counsel and the expenses of witnesses and potential jurors.[6] For all these reasons, it is desirable in the interests of everyone that weak or hopeless cases be spotted as early as possible in advance of trial.

CHECKS PROVIDED AT COMMITTAL PROCEEDINGS CONDUCTED IN THE MAGISTRATES' COURTS

One obvious point of intervention is at the magistrates' court. All cases that are to be tried in the Crown Court must first be committed for trial by magistrates at what are known as committal proceedings.[7] Under this procedure, the function of the

[6] On the waste of resources caused by the collapse of cases in the Crown Court, see further McCabe and Purves (1972a) pp. 31–2.

[7] There are limited exceptions, as where the Court of Appeal orders a new trial or where a voluntary bill of indictment is preferred, but these are of little numerical importance.

magistrates' court is not to determine whether the accused is guilty of the offence charged but to ensure that there is sufficient evidence to justify sending the defendant for trial at the Crown Court. The point was well put by Lord Widgery, CJ, in 1973 in the following passage:[8]

What is the function of the committal proceedings for this purpose? Is it, as the prosecution might contend, simply a safeguard for the citizen to ensure that he cannot be made to stand his trial without a *prima facie* case being shown; or is it, as [counsel for the applicant] would contend, a rehearsal proceeding so that the defence may try out their cross-examination on the prosecution witnesses with a view to using the results to advantage in the Crown Court at a later stage? . . . For my part I think that it is clear that the function of committal proceedings is to ensure that no one shall stand his trial unless a *prima facie* case has been made out. (p. 435.)

It might be expected, in view of these comments, that committal proceedings would provide an effective screening mechanism that would at least prevent the Crown Court from being clogged up by hopelessly weak cases. It is now clear, however, that adequate review of the prosecution evidence at committal proceedings is, save in a small minority of cases, little more than legal fiction. To understand why this is so, it is necessary to examine the different forms of committal that may be employed and their use in practice.

By section 7 of the Magistrates' Courts Act, 1952, a magistrates' court inquiring into an offence as examining magistrates shall commit the accused for trial if it 'is of opinion, on consideration of the evidence and of any statement of the accused, that there is sufficient evidence to put the accused upon trial by jury for any indictable offence'. The type of committal proceedings to which this section relates is commonly known as 'full committal proceedings' or 'old style committal'. Committals of this kind generally begin with a short opening address by the prosecutor outlining the substance of the case against the defendant. Witnesses are then called by the prosecutor, examined orally by him, and cross-examined by the defence. The

[8] *R.* v. *Epping and Harlow Justices, ex parte Massaro* [1973] 1 Q.B. 433. This was a case in which the prosecution refused to call the victim of an alleged assault to give evidence at committal proceedings, even though the defendant wished to cross-examine her. The defendant was committed on the basis of other supporting evidence and his application for an order of *certiorari* to quash the committal order was refused. See further Hopkins (1976).

evidence of the witnesses is recorded in the form of depositions. At the conclusion of the prosecution evidence, the defence can submit that the evidence produced is not sufficient to warrant committing the defendant for trial, and the magistrates must then decide whether or not to uphold the submission. If the submission is upheld, the defendant is immediately discharged. This procedure, which was the only form of committal until 1968, had been heavily criticized over the years. Lord Devlin (1966) described it as 'the biggest waste of all', and Williams (1959) said that it 'could be abolished for all the good it normally does in saving innocent persons from vexatious prosecutions'. The principal criticism was that it was a cumbersome and time-consuming procedure, wasteful of resources, and needlessly prodigal of magistrates' time.[9] Full committal proceedings were not without their defenders,[10] but eventually legislation was introduced to provide for an alternative form of committal.

The new procedure, introduced by the Criminal Justice Act, 1967, has, if nothing else, the merit of simplicity. Section 2 of the Act enables a court to receive a written statement taken from a witness at an early stage to save his attendance at the committal.[11] If the magistrates are satisfied that all the evidence before the court is in the form of written statements of this kind, section 1 of the Act provides that the magistrates may commit the defendant for trial for the offence without consideration of the contents of those statements unless either the defendant (or one of them, if there are several) is not legally represented or the defence requests the court to consider a submission of no case to answer. Under this procedure, which has come to be known as

[9] Allen (1958) put the case against in these terms:

Taking depositions, word by word and sentence by sentence (sometimes through an interpreter), is a lengthy process even in the most straightforward cases; magistrates, at least in populous centres, are quite sufficiently occupied nowadays with their summary jurisdiction, and it seems to be high time that the whole system was overhauled and justices and their clerks relieved of a tedious and superfluous duty. (p. 653.)

[10] The arguments for and against are canvassed in Napley (1966), and Gardner and Carlisle (1966).

[11] A written statement is admissible as evidence to the same extent as oral evidence, provided that the conditions laid down in section 2(2) are satisfied. These conditions are, in general terms, that the statement purports to be signed by the person who made it; that it contains a declaration by that person that it is true; that, before the statement is tendered in evidence, a copy is given to the defence; and that there is no objection by any of the other parties to the statement being so tendered.

a 'paper committal' or 'section 1 committal', a defendant may be committed for trial without the magistrates hearing or reading the evidence in the prosecution's case. Unlike full committals, the section 1 procedure can be completed in minutes.

In purely administrative terms, the section 1 committal procedure has certain major advantages over old-style committals. Its cheapness and speed could not possibly be matched by full oral proceedings even in the simplest case. But this is not the only yardstick, and the section 1 procedure is by no means always superior. Under the section 1 procedure, the evidence consists of statements elicited from witnesses by the police. This evidence can present certain difficulties, as pointed out by Napley (1966) in the following passage:

> statements prepared with a view to prosecution are taken by police officers and not lawyers; as a result they frequently contain inadmissible and imprecise material. This, however, is by no means the major objection to such statements. There is a certain technique involved in the preparing of proofs of evidence ... This technique of statement taking, which is also found at the heart of successful cross-examination, is the ability by suggestion to implant into the mind of a witness or potential witness some belief, as to facts, which he henceforward adopts as his own recollection. (pp. 491–2.)

Statements taken by the police may appear firmer and more reliable than is warranted, and it may well be in everyone's interests to have the evidence tested in the absence of the jury. But there is a second, and more important, advantage to full oral proceedings. Where magistrates are required to hear and consider the evidence, there is at least the possibility that weak cases may be thrown out at that stage. How frequently magistrates intervened in this way was a matter of considerable interest in the debates leading up to the introduction of section 1 committals although no reliable figures were available. The Tucker Committee (1958) had stated, however, that between 3 and 4 per cent of charges were discharged by examining magistrates,[12] but some commentators thought the true figure may have been even lower.[13]

[12] Tucker Committee (1958) para. 7. The Committtee gave no information at all on how they had reached this figure.

[13] See, for example, Allen (1958) at p. 653, and Harrison (1955) who wrote: 'Magistrates rarely decide that there is not sufficient evidence to commit the accused, especially if he is well known or if the allegations are serious.' (p. 157.)

This difficulty notwithstanding, it can still be claimed for full oral proceedings (unlike those under section 1) that they provide in theory at least a good opportunity to test the strength of the prosecution and a forum in which the weak and misconceived may be taken out of the system. In theory also, the two procedures are alternatives, paper committals not being designed to replace entirely old-style committals.[14] In practice, however, section 1 committals have almost entirely displaced old-style committals, and, though there are murmurings that the old procedure is nowadays being used somewhat more frequently, information that we have collected indicates that it is still highly exceptional for even a few of the witnesses in a case to be called upon to give evidence at the committal stage. Even in the 116 cases in our sample which had ended as ordered or directed acquittals, none had involved full oral proceedings and in only four was some evidence given in oral form. Indeed, out of the 2,406 cases sent for trial in the Crown Court at Birmingham in the period of our research, no more than four had taken the form of full oral committals, and there were only eighteen others in which some of the evidence had been given orally. The remaining 99 per cent of committals had followed the section 1 procedure. The upshot of this was that, in the overwhelming majority of cases, there was no effective scrutiny of the prosecution's case by the magistrates. The chaff proceeded on its way with the wheat.

It is of some importance to establish how this situation has come about. Why is it that almost all cases go through committal proceedings, as it were, by default? The reasons are not yet altogether clear, but some factors can be readily identified. In the first place, there is little doubt that many defence lawyers lack the necessary skill and experience to mount a proper

[14] As Gardner and Carlisle (1966), the leading proponents of section 1 committals, note:

> We are anxious to see that any reform should satisfy all the purposes of the present systems, namely to inform the accused of the case he has to meet; to see whether there is a *prima facie* case for trial by jury; to commit the accused for trial to a particular court ... on bail or in custody. Our proposals, we believe, satisfy all these requirements. An accused who is uncertain of the prosecution's case after reading the written statements or who wishes to challenge or test the strength of the case against him can elect committal under the [full oral] procedure. So, too, where the accused after considering the written statements of the witnesses decides to submit that there is no case to answer, he can elect the [full oral] procedure. (p. 501.)

challenge of the prosecution's case at committal—an observation acknowledged even by leading defence advocates themselves.[15] For many busy practitioners, paper committals offer a possible escape route. But this situation is not helped by the fact that defence solicitors very commonly receive the committal papers for the first time on the day of the hearing,[16] and the possibility of the defence making any thorough assessment of the evidence is virtually non-existent.[17] It is true that defence solicitors could seek an adjournment where this happens, but many are reluctant to postpone the trial, particularly if the defendant is in custody. Finally, one must draw attention to the part played by magistrates at the committal hearing. A number of commentators have alleged that the advantages of full committals are frustrated by the timidity of magistrates who see their function merely as rubber-stamps for the prosecution and who, in any event, lack real confidence in their own ability to decide upon cases of importance. One solicitor, writing about old-style committals, put the point forcefully in the following passage:[18]

> The real demerit of the present system would seem to lie only in the reluctance of magistrates to acquit at committal proceedings. In many cases, the accused has in fact to establish that he was innocent of the

[15] Thus Napley (1966) writes: 'The strongest argument which can be used against the continuation of the [old-style] preliminary inquiry is that the average practitioner does not employ it to the best advantage; others, although present at the inquiry, appear barely to employ it at all.' (p. 491.)

[16] As part of the pilot work for the present research, we sent questionnaires to twenty-five defence solicitors handling cases for trial at the Crown Court in Coventry. It was apparent from the completed questionnaires that most of the defendants concerned had been committed for trial without the prosecution's case being scrutinized by the defence. Indeed, it was hardly possible in most cases for any such examination to take place, because the defence solicitors had been given the committal papers only on the day of the committal itself. We were very sorry to learn, shortly after this finding had been disclosed to members of the Law Society (which had given its approval to the pilot study in the first place), that the Law Society could not after all allow solicitors in Birmingham to answer the questions we wished to put to them about such matters: see, further, Baldwin and McConville (1979c) p. 25.

[17] The introduction of paper committals was based upon a number of important assumptions, in particular that written statements would be served upon the defence well before the hearing, that the defence would be prepared at an early stage, and, in consequence, be in a position to assess the prosecution evidence and to elect full committal in a weak case. See, for instance, Gardner and Carlisle (1966); Carlisle (1967); and Samuels (1968).

[18] E. Goldrein (1959); see also Napley (1966), and Morris (1976). The Association of Chief Police Officers (1978) noted that, in sixteen of the 102 cases of the ordered or directed acquittals that they examined, there had been an unsuccessful submission of no case to answer at the committal proceedings: see para. 20.22.

crime charged before the Bench will find that there is no case to answer. If there be any suspicion that he might be guilty of the charge, the easy way out for the court is to shelve the burden of responsibility by committing the accused for trial. Time and time again, there is a serious and argued plea by the defence that no jury would possibly convict on the evidence before the court, the accused is committed for trial, and subsequently acquitted. (p. 274.)

There may be other reasons for the great popularity of section 1 proceedings,[19] but it is abundantly clear that full committals are nowadays rarely used. There is in consequence no consideration of the evidence by the magistrates (unless the defence raises objections), and indeed this is the object of the provisions. The responsibility for ensuring that there is a case to go for trial has as a result been shifted away from the magistrates. Although defence solicitors may be criticized for not exercising their right to require the court to consider whether the evidence is sufficient, the primary responsibility for identifying weak cases falls on the prosecution, whose duty it is to proceed only where the evidence justifies that course. In order to understand how weak cases get into the system, it is not sufficient to look to the section 1 procedure as the source of the problem; instead it is necessary to examine the activities of the prosecution.

CHECKS PROVIDED BEFORE COMMITTAL BY THE PROSECUTION

Unlike almost all other common law jurisdictions, there is no system of public prosecution in England. There is instead a variety of systems which have grown up over the years without any organizing principle. The overwhelming majority of prosecutions are handled by the police, but in discharging their responsibilities they are not in principle distinct from other citizens.[20] Before deciding whether to proceed against an indi-

[19] Some have alleged that defence solicitors protract proceedings in order to extract a financial advantage: see the letter from R. Watts in the *Solicitor's Journal* volume 118 (1974) at pp. 778–9, and Sir Robert Mark's article in *The Observer* 6 April 1975. The matter was also ventilated by the James Committee at para. 233.

[20] The Royal Commission on the Police (1962) put the position thus:

> The police of this country have never been recognised, either in law or by tradition, as a force distinct from the general body of citizens. Despite the imposition of many extraneous duties on the police by legislation or administrative action the principle remains that a policeman, in the view of the common law, is only 'a person paid to perform, as a matter of duty, acts which if he were so minded he might have done voluntarily'. (para. 30.)

vidual, the police may seek legal advice.[21] In some parts of the country, the police rely upon solicitors in private practice for advice, but most regions now have prosecuting solicitors' departments. Where the police have recourse to such advice, there is obviously considerable scope for lawyers to influence the decision whether or not to prosecute. The principles on which such advice is based are not widely known and, given the wide variations in structure, can scarcely be uniform. Such information as is available, however, suggests that many of the principles in question are directed to ensuring that only those cases with sufficient evidence should be allowed to proceed. These principles require some elaboration.

The decision whether or not to prosecute is, perhaps, the most important and most difficult decision to be made by those responsible for the conduct of criminal cases. A wrong decision either way can have serious consequences for the suspect or for the wider community. Not unexpectedly, therefore, this question has often been at the forefront of public debates and from time to time officials have disclosed the sorts of consideration that they take into account. Barnes (1975), an Assistant Director of Public Prosecutions, sets out the way in which the Director's office deals with this question:[22]

> First of all we ensure that there are no insuperable and fatal defects to the case ... Next, if we are satisfied that there is no fatal flaw in the case, we go on to consider, not so much whether there is a *prima facie* case, but whether or not there appears to be a reasonable prospect of a conviction ... We [then] have to consider whether, in its widest sense, it is in the public interest to institute proceedings. (pp. 26–7.)

Others have defined the criteria more narrowly, requiring only that there be sufficient evidence to justify putting the individual

[21] In certain circumstances, this is obligatory. There are some forty statutes listing offences for the prosecution of which the fiat of the Attorney-General is needed, and over sixty which require action by the Director of Public Prosecutions or his consent. In addition, the Prosecution of Offences Regulations (1978) lays down in section 6 that the chief officer of police of every police area shall give the Director information with respect to a range of offences where it appears that there is a *prima facie* case for proceedings.

[22] This view echoes that put forward by Sir Norman Skelhorn, a former Director of Public Prosecutions, set out in Wilcox (1974), and accords with that of the current Director in his evidence to the Royal Commission on Criminal Procedure: see Director of Public Prosecutions (1978) para. 92.

on trial,[23] not that there should be a reasonable prospect of conviction, but all are agreed that the evidence must at least establish a *prima facie* case.[24]

If the police accepted legal advice in all cases and if that advice was based upon the considerations set out above, it might reasonably be expected that few weak cases would ever reach the Crown Court. That this is manifestly not so requires some explanation. The first factor to be taken into account is that the prosecuting principles are not as hard and fast as they might at first seem, and may easily become weakened when individual cases have to be considered. In the following passage, Danks (1975) speaks of a dilemma sometimes faced by prosecuting solicitors: 'It sometimes happens that there are thin cases. These are the ones where someone finds it hard to decide whether or not a prosecution should take place. Or, perhaps more accurately, where they cannot make up their minds not to proceed.' (pp. 71–2.) One way out of this dilemma, he suggested, was to have a full committal and to invite the justices to commit only if they are satisfied that there is a proper case for trial. Some would argue that there ought not to be a prosecution in such cases because of the risk that the justices may commit the defendant for trial out of an undue sense of caution.[25] It follows that some cases are proceeded with which ought to be discontinued, even where legal advice has been sought and accepted by the police. But there are other important reasons why this potential safeguard works imperfectly.

Prosecutions may be commenced in one of two ways: by information and summons, or by arrest and charge. Under the first method, the evidence is reviewed at different levels within the police hierarchy, and the decision to proceed is made usually at chief inspector level or above. The defendant retains his liberty, and the police have ample time in which to decide whether to proceed, and to take legal advice if this is considered

[23] A former Attorney-General said that, in the ordinary case, he had to consider 'whether the evidence goes beyond mere suspicion and is sufficient to justify a man being put on trial for a specific criminal offence': *H.C. Debates* vol. 483 (1951) at col. 682.

[24] See further Prosecuting Solicitors' Society (1979). Other considerations may mean in practice that no prosecution is instituted even where there is a *prima facie* case: see, for example, Barnes (1975).

[25] The view put forward by Danks was in fact attacked by Samuels (1975) as 'wrong' and 'oppressive'.

necessary or appropriate. Where the police are satisfied that it is proper to proceed, an 'information' is laid before a magistrate who may issue a summons to bring the alleged offender before the court. For most serious offences, however, the police have power to proceed by way of arrest or summons. Where a suspect is arrested, he is taken to a police station. The arresting officer gives an outline of the facts to another officer (normally the charge sergeant) and, if the other officer is satisfied of the substance of the case, the suspect will generally be charged and remanded on bail or in custody. The major problem with the arrest and charge procedure is summarized by the Prosecuting Solicitors' Society (1979) in the following passage:

> Under the arrest and charge procedure the obligation of the charging officer to lay his case before the charge sergeant is little or no safeguard to the arrested individual ... It would be exceptional for the charging officer to have had time, by that stage of his investigation, to take formal written statements from the witnesses. The view of the charge sergeant or other officer accepting the charge must therefore be gained from what he is told by the investigating officer. As an independent check this must be almost without value. (para. 3.3.)

Although there are serious shortcomings in the information and summons procedure,[26] it allows the opportunity of seeking legal advice before proceedings are instituted. In practice, at least in serious cases, the police generally decide to proceed by way of arrest.[27] Indeed, of the 500 contested cases dealt with by the Birmingham Crown Court in 1975 and 1976, only about 5 per cent were cases in which the summons procedure had been used, and a comparable picture appears to obtain in London.[28] It follows that, in the overwhelming majority of cases, the only checks upon the prosecution are those provided by the police themselves, and lawyers are not able to scrutinize the evidence until after the prosecution has been instituted. For practical purposes, then, the prosecuting solicitor is rarely in a position to give his opinion on the advisability of a particular prosecution

[26] For example, summonses are often issued by an assistant to the Justices' Clerk, and magistrates themselves need have no formal legal training nor is there any obligation on them to seek advice from their Clerk.

[27] Even in the magistrates courts in England and Wales, at least 76 per cent of those proceeded against for indictable offences in 1978 had been arrested: Home Office, *Criminal Statistics (1978)* Cmnd. 7670, Table 8.1, p. 156.

[28] See further Leigh (1975) at pp. 21–2.

before charges are laid, and a potential safeguard against the bringing of a weak case is lost.[29]

Even where the prosecuting solicitor is approached by the police before the decision to charge is taken, there may be difficulties. For there is no obligation upon the police to seek legal advice in most cases and, if they do, they are not obliged to accept the advice given. The police are the clients of the prosecuting solicitor, and the prosecuting solicitor cannot compel them to undertake a particular course of action.[30] Where the prosecuting solicitor becomes involved in a case, tensions may remain, as in the following case:

Case 206 (*Birmingham*) [A case of an assault on a police officer]
Police officer: Initially, the prosecuting solicitors said they were going to offer no evidence in relation to assault and just do the defendant for obstruction and deal with her at the magistrates' court. But I insisted that an assault charge went on and the defendant then promptly elected trial by jury. There was an assault so it was not vindictive in that sense, but it was vindictive in that I know the woman she is and her involvement in crime ... In a dispute like this, you can get aggravation from the prosecuting solicitor through the gaffers but once the person is charged it leaves the prosecuting solicitor no way out; they've got to fall in line with what I want to do.

The lack of independence in the relationship between the police and the prosecuting solicitor may mean, therefore, that legal advice is overridden and that the final course of action remains firmly in police hands.

Various consequences follow from these procedures and the relationships that exist between prosecuting solicitors and the police. In the first place, prosecuting solicitors are on occasion forced to conduct a prosecution that they would much rather have terminated.[31] In the second place, there are few cases

[29] The same can, it seems, apply to the Director of Public Prosecutions. Barnes (1975), for example, indicated, in relation to the task of editing committal papers, that 'not infrequently a file will only reach our office eight, ten or twelve weeks after a man has been committed in custody' (p. 33).

[30] See, for example, Danks (1975) at p. 65.

[31] See, for example, the Prosecuting Solicitors' Society (1979) who argue:

> Almost all members have experience of being instructed to proceed with cases where although there was slender *prima facie* evidence clearly and inevitably the case would fail in the court of trial. This is a significant problem particularly if the significance or otherwise is measured in terms of impact upon the life of an individual and of his family of a misconceived criminal prosecution. (para. 3.6.)

A similar point is made by the Director of Public Prosecutions (1978) at para. 91.

indeed in which intended prosecutions are abandoned before committal as a result of advice received from the prosecuting solicitor. This is difficult to quantify but our conversations with police officers in Birmingham and London suggested that the number of such cases was minimal. This was confirmed in a formal interview that we conducted with the Chief Prosecuting Solicitor of the West Midlands as part of our own research.[32] When asked how often he advised the police not to proceed with a case that was due for hearing at the Crown Court, he replied:

> In a very small number of cases. It is to be borne in mind of course that before the police recommend proceedings the file has been through a number of hands and they are very conscious of the fact that cases indeed ought not to be run unless there is a good case. I am perfectly happy that they go along with the view that I hold: that not only should there be a *prima facie* case but a reasonable likelihood of obtaining a conviction.

However, the result is that, whether by default or otherwise, available legal expertise is not effectively brought to bear in the overwhelming majority of Crown Court cases until after the committal for trial has taken place, and another potential check upon weak or misconceived prosecutions is foregone.

Nothing of substance is known about the nature of the advice that is offered to the police by prosecuting solicitors or of the frequency with which advice is offered. We were able to examine this question using information extracted from the questionnaires completed by the prosecuting solicitors on the 2,406 cases disposed of in the Birmingham Crown Court in the study period. It was apparent from this analysis that formal legal advice was rarely given to the police, apart from the editing of witness statements to get rid of inadmissible evidence. Formal advice as such was given in only 81 cases (3.4 per cent), 54 of which were prosecutions handled by the Director of Public Prosecutions. In 41 of these cases, the advice related primarily to the preferment of charges, and in 35 there was a recommendation that the police attempt to obtain further evidence. There were no signs whatever that the prosecution was prepared to use committal proceedings to expose weaknesses in its case and

[32] The interview, which was conducted in 1976, was tape-recorded. A typed transcript of the interview was agreed with the Chief Prosecuting Solicitor.

thus secure an early disposal.[33] Of all the cases in the Birmingham sample, there were only four full committals and eighteen in which some evidence was given in oral form. On the few occasions on which the paper committal procedure was not used, it was almost without exception at the instigation of the defence not the prosecution. In practice, it seems, the critical decisions are made by the police, and they cannot fairly claim that the fault lies with a lawyer if a weak case reaches the Crown Court. Once a charge is laid, an understandable inclination to protect the police from a civil action for wrongful arrest makes it unlikely that a lawyer would advise that charges be withdrawn.[34] Lawyers are scarcely involved in the early pre-trial review of the case.[35] If we are to understand how cases of little substance reach the Crown Court, it is to the activities of the police that we must turn.

Many legal commentators have wrongly assumed that the police will proceed only where the evidence establishes at least a *prima facie* case.[36] It is clear, however, from previous research (as well as from the two preceding chapters) that this assumption cannot be sustained, and that there are occasions on which the police, as they themselves acknowledge, press charges in the absence of supporting evidence and, more frequently, when

[33] Cf. the evidence of the then Director of Public Prosecutions in the Confait inquiry conducted by Sir Henry Fisher (1977). The Director said that his Department 'sometimes takes the initiative' to have full committal proceedings 'in cases where we consider that the circumstances are such that it is desirable to see precisely what a particular witness will or will not say in relation to the matter' (para. 27.5).

[34] See the observations to this effect of Sir Robert Mark *The Observer* 23 March 1975, to which a spokesman for the Law Society replied:

> The real trouble is that once a police officer had made an arrest it is difficult to get him off the hook; the charge is often allowed to go its full course rather than abandon the prosecution with the risk of civil proceedings (*Law Society's Gazette* 26 March 1975 at p. 339).

[35] In evidence to the Royal Commission on Criminal Procedure, the Association of Chief Police Officers (1979) presented figures on a survey of 6,137 acquittals at the Crown Court in 1977. The figures, they claimed, showed that 'the police do seek legal advice in the vast majority of cases which subsequently result in acquittals at Crown Court' (para. 20.20). The figures do not, however, show the stage at which legal advice was sought. In the absence of this information, it is wrong to draw the inference that advice was generally taken before charges were laid. The information we have presented from our research shows that advice is rarely taken at this critical early stage and that the value of legal advice given after charge is considerably reduced.

[36] See, for example, Williams (1959) who writes 'prosecutions are generally brought by the police, who rarely make a charge unless they have a *prima facie* case' (p. 84). See also Allen (1958) at p. 653.

there is no reasonable likelihood of a conviction. In their study of jury acquittals, McCabe and Purves (1972b) identified a group of cases which they termed 'policy prosecutions', where charges were pursued with ends in view other than the prospect of conviction. In one police area, for example, theft of bicycles was so common that anyone found in possession of machines reported stolen, without a totally credible explanation, was prosecuted, and, in another area, all those involved in pub brawls were charged. Our interviews with police officers responsible for handling cases within our samples enabled us to explore this question in some detail.

It must immediately be stated that it is far from clear what is meant by 'policy' in this context. No doubt the police do operate general guidelines in considering whether to prosecute, but it was only rarely that such policy guidelines came to the surface in our interviews. More often we noted how an individual officer's response had been conditioned by the particular circumstances of an offence rather than by any policy directive. Moreover, it is sometimes possible to defend (if not to justify) the decision to prosecute in a weak case on tactical grounds.[37] An example of this was provided by *case 91* in Birmingham, in which a car, occupied by two men, was stopped by the police. A search revealed a quantity of illegal drugs, and the police, though readily acknowledging throughout that they took the view that the drugs belonged to the driver of the car, nevertheless decided to proceed against both men. They did so for purely tactical reasons to prevent the driver throwing the blame on to an absent and uncharged passenger. They also believed the strength of the case would be improved if the passenger, under cross-examination, could be induced further to implicate the owner of the drugs. In the event, the latter pleaded guilty and the prosecution chose not to offer evidence against the other man. Another example is provided by the following case taken from the London sample:

Case 111 (*London*) [A fight developed in a street over non-payment of a debt between the defendant and the victim, as a result of which the victim died. At one stage of the fight, the defendant's brother intervened, although he did not actually strike the victim. Both men were charged with manslaughter and at the trial the defendant was convicted and his brother acquitted]

[37] The position is analysed by Heydon (1971).

Police officer: I was satisfied with this result. The main reason for charging the brother was to ensure that his family, who all witnessed the fight, would give evidence in court. It was thought prudent to bring out all the evidence in court and then leave it to the jury to decide. Justice was done in the end.

In a few cases, it appeared that the police had proceeded reluctantly, under pressure from the complainant, as in allegations of shoplifting from big stores or where the complainant was a particularly troublesome character. One example will suffice to illustrate the point:

Cases 314–7 (*Birmingham*) [Four youths charged with burglary]
Police officer: The officer who took the decision to charge was quite within his rights ... He got a little bit tired of the youths being cheeky to him and it might have been that he wanted to teach them a lesson. And the complainant is the sort of person who can stir up trouble for the police if we don't follow the book in dealing with his complaint. Once they had been charged, the officer had no alternative, but no jury could possibly have convicted any of them on this evidence.

But there were not many cases in which such distinct policy issues were apparent and, when they arose, they no doubt raised acute moral dilemmas for the prosecution. Whether one is troubled by such prosecutions or indifferent to them depends largely upon one's own definition of justice and the sort of balance that one chooses to strike between the rights of innocent citizens as against the proper punishment of the guilty. We return to this question in chapter 10, but we can say here that we came across only one case in which, in our opinion, the policy behind the prosecution was truly perverse. This was a case of unlawful sexual intercourse involving a young West Indian and a girl with whom he was living. The boy was unaware of the girl's true age and her parents were happy with the relationship. The hostel at which the boy was living had, however, upset the police on previous occasions by giving legal advice to residents in trouble. The police officer in charge of the case explained the background to the prosecution in these terms:

Case 51 (*Birmingham*)
We don't normally take USI's to court. We normally caution, but we didn't in this case because it was part of police policy at that time. It was a decision made by the Superintendent that this one

should go to court. The decision was taken to show this hostel that they have to be careful in giving advice by their social workers to these West Indians, but it backfired this time. He was acquitted, as he should have been, and it should not have been taken to the court in the first place.

We stress that no such 'policy' elements were present in the overwhelming majority of cases, or at least none that we were able to discern. It seems clear that, if we are to understand how weak cases limp through to the Crown Court, the main reason lies in the assessment of the amount and quality of the evidence by police officers. This raises the question whether the police are as a body competent to decide whether there is enough evidence to give any chance of successful prosecution. There can be little doubt that, in a proportion of cases, the police genuinely believed that there was a case to answer in circumstances in which no competent lawyer would have reached such a decision. For many cases, however, the police were fully aware of the limitations of the case from the outset. Sometimes they hoped that the defendant would plead guilty or would put up a poor show before a jury, or else that the matter would be disposed of in the lower courts. It is noteworthy that many more defendants exercised their right to be tried by jury in the cases identified by the assessors as weak than in the sample as a whole.[38] But the prosecution more commonly proceeded because it was believed that, no matter how slender the evidence, the final decision must be that of the court not the police. Time and again in the course of interviews with us, the police justified their action by saying that 'it was best to let the court decide'. Such an approach is not defensible in legal theory for, although there is no requirement that prosecutions be undertaken only where there is a reasonable likelihood of conviction,[39] it is well

[38] In Birmingham, the overall proportion of defendants who themselves elected trial was almost exactly 10 per cent, whereas in weak cases it was 54 per cent. Since in summary trials there is no advance disclosure of the prosecution evidence to the defence, it is advantageous to elect trial in the Crown Court where the case is weak to obtain this. See, on this point, the recommendations of the James Committee (1975) paras. 212–30.

[39] The Director of Public Prosecutions has recently stated that it would be wrong to prosecute just to give the matter a public airing, and that the principle is that he has to be satisfied 'that there is more than a 50 per cent chance of conviction before I will prosecute' (*The Observer* 27 January 1980). This may well be the principle on which the Director operates but it is not universally followed by the police nor is it enshrined in the law.

settled that there must at least be a case for the defendant to answer. Nor is it defensible in practice, for the consequences may be serious in terms of court time, public expense, and social upheaval for the defendant involved, costs which, apart from the occasional judicial rebuke, are not borne by the police.

CONCLUSION

We conclude that the main problem is not that the weak case will never be identified, the hopeless hived-off, the ill-conceived weeded out. The problem is that identification and final disposition are unnecessarily delayed, that thin cases are needlessly protracted. Cases perish by slow torture when what is required is a swift and early application of the executioner's axe. Counsel may be open to criticism on some occasions for allowing a weak case to go before the court, and judges may sometimes be at fault for failing to call a halt to a purposeless trial. But weak cases ought not to be committed for trial in the first place. They get through because committal proceedings do not provide anything approaching an effective screening procedure. It is well to repeat the comments of Sir Henry Fisher (1977) who saw the problem thus:

> There is obviously scope for using committal proceedings to a greater extent to test the prosecution's case. But this will not happen unless there is either a defence submission or the person appearing for the prosecution himself draws the attention of the magistrates to a point of difficulty in the prosecution's case. And this will not happen unless there is a careful and dispassionate survey and review of the evidence by the counsel, solicitor or police officer responsible for presenting the case on committal, a survey devoted not only to seeing whether there is evidence to support the charge but whether there are any weaknesses in the prosecution's case which should be brought out before the magistrate. (para. 27.6.)

As the system is presently organized, committal proceedings are not used to test the prosecution's case, and all the indications are that neither prosecution nor defence scrutinizes cases with sufficient care before requesting or giving consent to the paper procedure. The ultimate *de facto* responsibility for the present unsatisfactory situation lies, in consequence, with the police who are unable or unwilling to pursue only those cases which have some real prospect of ending in conviction. Once the police lay a charge, the case has sufficient momentum to carry it through to the Crown Court.

To return to our original point, we can see that it would be unsound to describe the criminal system as characterized by a series of obstacles that the prosecution must surmount before a case can reach court.[40] It is true that most of the weak cases examined ended in the acquittal of the defendants concerned. But this is little consolation to a defendant whose life may have been wrecked or irreparably damaged by the mere fact of being forced to stand trial and the fear of eventual conviction. The obstacles that have been erected to obviate this situation are ineffective, and prosecutions very rapidly develop a momentum of their own. When this happens, those features of the system which appear to represent obstacles to misconceived prosecution turn out to be no more than stepping stones.

[40] Our sample is, of course, confined to those cases which have passed earlier screening mechanisms, such as the charge sergeant, the prosecuting solicitor, or the magistrates' court. It is possible in principle for weak cases to be weeded out at any of these points, but in practice most cases survive these checks.

6

THE PROSECUTION CASE

INTRODUCTION

We have argued in the previous chapter that, whatever formal checks are provided by the criminal justice system, the police remain firmly the central figures in the prosecution process. And if weak cases limp forward to the Crown Court, this is primarily a consequence of decisions that have been taken by police officers, not by their legal advisers. Whether the police are adequately equipped to make informed judgments as to the sufficiency and quality of evidence is a matter of dispute and is a question to which we return in chapter 10. But this is only one aspect of the role that the police play in the prosecution process. They are responsible in addition for the gathering of evidence, interviewing suspects and witnesses, and collecting forensic evidence—in other words, assembling the prosecution's case. It is curious that, though much is written about this aspect of the police function (often in fact extremely critical of current police procedures), almost nothing of substance is known about what work the police do at this stage. Very little is known, for instance, about the frequency with which suspects make statements to the police or about what form such statements take, and nothing is known about the extent to which the police rely on civilian witnesses or the degree to which cases hinge upon what the police themselves offer in evidence. These are basic questions, yet their importance to the criminal process is inestimable since it is now generally recognized that it is how the prosecution uses information derived from the suspect's encounter with the police when he is arrested and interviewed in police custody that as a rule determines his eventual plea and the subsequent disposition of his case in court.[1]

We shall be particularly concerned in this and the following two chapters with the delicate question of police interrogation and with the sorts of evidence the police gather in a typical

[1] See, for example, Bottoms and McClean (1976) p. 230; Baldwin and McConville (1977a) pp. 91–2, 101–5; and Morris (1980).

cross-section of Crown Court cases. Before we deal with these matters and discuss our findings from the study we conducted in Birmingham and London, it is worth making a number of general observations which are suggested by the available research and writing on the subject of the police role in preparing cases for prosecution. These observations have a wider relevance than the interrogation of suspects or the gathering of evidence. Indeed, they touch upon the basic principles of adversary justice—principles which are at the very heart of the Anglo-American legal system.

THE POLICE IN THE ADVERSARY SYSTEM

It is becoming increasingly evident that the opportunity to operate the adversarial trial procedure, popularly regarded as typical of Anglo-American justice, rarely presents itself in criminal courts in England. Though this may seem at first sight a crude overstatement, more careful consideration reveals that these procedures apply only in exceptional circumstances. The emphasis of the adversary system is upon formal, combative trial proceedings in open court with a jury acting as the independent adjudicator of guilt or innocence, and the judge ruling on questions of law and ensuring that the procedural rules are followed. Whether this method of resolving issues of guilt works effectively or not, the underlying principles are scarcely relevant to most cases that reach the criminal courts. The great majority of defendants plead guilty and adversarial confrontation is absent from the court appearance but may have occurred privately outside the courtroom.[2] Furthermore, trial by jury—the very epitome of the adversary system—is a comparatively rare phenomenon with fewer than one in twenty defendants who could be tried by jury actually opting to do so.[3]

The resources of the system could not possibly provide jury

[2] There is a vast literature on the subject of guilty plea determination, particularly concerned with the practice of plea bargaining whereby defendants plead guilty in return for concessions offered with regard to charge or sentence: see, for instance, Newman (1966); Blumberg (1970); Heberling (1973); and Baldwin and McConville (1977a).

[3] In 1978, 85 per cent of those whose cases could have been tried by jury in England and Wales were dealt with in the lower courts and a majority of the remainder pleaded guilty in the Crown Court. On this, see Home Office *Criminal Statistics for England and Wales, 1978* Cmnd. 7670, Table 4.8, and Lord Chancellor's Department *Judicial Statistics, 1978* Cmnd. 7627, Table B7.

trial in more than a small minority of cases, but this can be regarded as only one factor in a much more complex equation. It is clear that many of the key exchanges between the various actors in the criminal process take place outside the courtroom in circumstances which correspond much more closely to French inquisitorial procedures than to the Anglo-American adversarial (or, as they are sometimes viewed, accusatorial) procedures. As far as out-of-court plea discussions are concerned, we can see a clear demonstration of a form of 'administrative' justice in which the central issues of adjudication are settled privately. It is easy to see in such dealings an erosion of the principles of adversarial procedure and their replacement by essentially inquisitorial procedures.[4] But an even closer parallel with inquisitorial procedures can be found when one examines the investigative role of the police. For the police in England (unlike the police in most other jurisdictions) have very considerable power and autonomy, not only in the investigation of crime but also in assembling the case for the prosecution. They make decisions about the appropriate charges to be preferred and even about whether the prosecution should proceed at all. Indeed, the police in England perform many of the central functions of public prosecutors in other countries—the procurator fiscal in Scotland and the *juge d'instruction* in France, for example.[5] Lord Devlin (1979a) has forcefully made the same point:

> What happens now is that the inquisitorial procedure is conducted, but by the police, and the collection of facts is done by the police; however rich you may be as a defendant, however powerful, you could not begin to have the resources of the police to collect your evidence for the defence. So we rely upon the police to do the job that the procurator fiscal or the *juge d'instruction* does abroad. And, to that extent, we have made the police inquisitors. (p. 442.)

It is perhaps not surprising that doubts have been raised about whether the training and outlook of police officers equip

[4] We have argued elsewhere that, in such dealings, the formal safeguards embodied in the concept of 'due process' are absent and the procedural protections associated with adversarial confrontation are lacking. Proof beyond reasonable doubt assumes a different meaning; there is no testing of witnesses in cross-examination; inadmissible evidence (particularly the accused's previous criminal convictions) may well be taken into account in the final determination, and the traditional remedies open to defendants on appeal are largely foreclosed. See further Baldwin and McConville (1979b).

[5] See the discussion of the attributes of French inquisitorial procedures in Sheehan (1975), particularly at pp. 24–30. For useful discussions of prosecution procedures in Scotland, see McCluskey (1975); Field (1970); and Wilcox (1972) at pp. 3–13.

them to make such decisions.[6] It would certainly be a little odd if police officers did not commonly develop a psychological commitment to securing a conviction, an attitude that may well be incompatible with objective and dispassionate decision-making. The point we wish to emphasize here, however, is the pervasive and multi-faceted nature of the police role at this stage in the criminal process—a role performed by a number of separate officials in most other jurisdictions.

It is commonly assumed that the gathering of information from suspects is central to this process. Yet, if one examines the massive literature on the role of evidence obtained by the police from the interrogation of suspects, one immediately encounters a great deal of rash and uninformed speculation based upon partial observation and narrow experience. The truth is that, in terms of empirical information, almost nothing is known about the importance of statements made to the police by suspects, and the available research evidence (largely American) is so fragmentary and limited in nature as to render generalization hazardous. It is worth pausing at this stage to consider the insights offered by the existing literature on the subject.

RESEARCH ON CONFESSION EVIDENCE

The literature on the role played by defendants' statements in the prosecution of criminal cases is characterized by dogmatic assertion presented as indisputable truth. Confident and largely unqualified statements are often made by writers without reference to the available empirical evidence. Such assertions must be treated with caution, if only because of our almost total ignorance of the frequency with which confessions are made by suspects, let alone their importance. A number of studies concerned with the role of confession evidence have appeared in the past few years, but all of them have been so limited in scope and so flawed by methodological weaknesses that doubts must be raised about their value.[7] Furthermore, since most of these

[6] Doubts have been raised, for instance, by JUSTICE (1970, 1979); Fisher (1977) at para. 2.45; and the Legal Action Group (1979).

[7] These weaknesses include a lack of standardization in the procedures adopted; a failure to take account of independent variables likely to affect the results obtained; evaluations of evidence conducted by parties who cannot be regarded as impartial or objective; the adoption of different definitions of what constitutes a 'confession'; and ambiguities surrounding the *locus standi* of those responsible for making the evaluation. These and other problems associated with research concerned with assessing the weight

studies have been carried out in the United States, the findings cannot be assumed to have any direct or necessary relevance to England.

Despite these difficulties, some limited observations seem reasonably well supported by a number of independent studies and to that extent a measure of consistency in the results is discernible. It is worth drawing attention to two findings in particular. First, it appears that a majority of suspects make a confession or some other incriminating statement when interviewed at the police station. This has been reported by several American researchers[8] and has also been noted in a number of English studies. Indeed the main English studies suggest that a higher proportion of defendants make such admissions in England than has been noted by researchers in the United States. Bottoms and McClean (1976), for instance, who interviewed a sample of defendants passing through the Sheffield courts, found that about 70 per cent stated that they had told the police from the outset that they had committed the offence in question, whereas Zander (1979), who relied upon the depositions relating to a sample of defendants involved in Crown Court trials in London, discovered that as many as 76 per cent of the defendants had made an oral or a written admission to the police. Irving (1980), who was able to observe the interrogation of sixty people suspected of criminal offences in Brighton, noted that thirty-five suspects made admissions during the course of the interview and four others made admissions subsequently—in all 65 per cent. Softley's (1980) similar observational study produced a comparable result with 61 per cent of suspects making a confession or other incriminating admission. All these studies indicate, then, that suspects frequently make admissions when they are interrogated.

Secondly, there is a good deal of evidence to suggest that the police can obtain incriminating statements from suspects without for the most part resorting to coercive or oppressive tactics. Most researchers who have been allowed to observe how interrogations are actually conducted by the police have found them to be generally of short duration and likely to produce material

to be attached to confession evidence in criminal cases are discussed at length in Baldwin and McConville (1980) at p. 3.

[8] See, particularly, Younger (1966a); Souris (1966); and Witt (1973).

that strengthens the prosecution's case.[9] It seems that, though police officers commonly warn suspects (if only perfunctorily) of their rights, most suspects are prepared to offer some explanation of their conduct to the police at this stage. Indeed, it appears that statements and confessions are so readily volunteered or extracted (or else are considered by the police to be irrelevant) that recourse to sophisticated interrogation techniques or coercion, even if contemplated, would be unnecessary. This finding has some extremely important implications because it bears upon the right of the suspect to remain silent in the face of police questioning, a right historically regarded as quite fundamental to the Anglo-American adversary system.[10] For a variety of reasons, the right to silence is rarely exercised by suspects. From the interviews we conducted with police officers about contested trials in Birmingham and London, it seemed that only about one defendant in ten attempted to exercise his right to keep silent while in police custody. One factor which produces this situation has nothing whatever to do with unfair pressure or trickery on the part of the police. It is simply that the subtle social and psychological pressures that operate in any human interaction make the maintenance of silence very difficult.[11] This was noted by Biderman (1960) in study of the psychological pressures that induced a sample of American prisoners of war to talk to their captors, even when only superficially interviewed and despite orders from their superiors to the contrary. The same phenomenon was noted by Griffiths and Ayres (1967) who discovered that even a sample of members of the University of Yale, who were not in any way subjected to oppressive tactics when interviewed by police officers, found it extremely difficult to maintain silence, if this meant appearing discourteous. 'The most striking lesson we learned', the authors write, 'is the point, obvious once noticed, that interrogation is a social situation, and suspects respond

[9] It is, of course, a major limitation of such observational studies that interrogators would be disinclined to resort to strong-arm tactics if an independent observer is present. Although all researchers concede this point, they nevertheless claim that it is one that can easily be overstated.

[10] The proposal by the Criminal Law Revision Committee (1972) to limit the accused's right to remain silent provoked such an outcry that it was rapidly dropped. On this controversy, see MacKenna (1972); Miller (1973); Zuckerman (1973); Cross (1973); Zander (1974b); Greenawalt (1974); and Heydon (1976).

[11] See generally Irving and Hilgendorf (1980).

according to the normal rules of social interaction in such a situation.' (p. 315.)

The difficulties surrounding the effective exercise of the right to silence have been dramatically illustrated in recent years in a number of studies conducted in the United States, where the courts have striven (to a much greater extent than courts in England) to protect the suspect while he is in police custody. In a series of highly controversial decisions in the 1960s, culminating in the case of *Miranda* v. *Arizona* (384 U.S. 436) in 1966, the U.S. Supreme Court sought to ensure that all suspects were warned of the risks of self-incrimination, their constitutional right to remain silent, and their entitlement to have a lawyer present at the interrogation, if necessary free of charge.[12] Many predicted that law enforcement would be severely impaired by these decisions, and one writer argued that 'if faithfully implemented, the dictates of *Miranda* can only result in the virtual disappearance of confessions' (Gorecki (1979) p. 86). The *Miranda* decision has stimulated a vast amount of empirical research, and over twenty different studies have now been conducted in an effort to evaluate the consequences of the decision.[13] What the studies demonstrate, with an astonishing degree of consistency, is that, even where the requirements of the *Miranda* decision are faithfully followed by the police, little or no change in traditional interrogation practices has been effected. The main reason for this is that the great majority of defendants waive their rights both to remain silent and to have a lawyer present, often, it must be said, because they fail to grasp the significance of what is being offered to them.

This examination of the available empirical information[14] illustrates the limitations of present knowledge about the results of police interrogation. The research is largely American in origin and its applicability to England is at best problematic. It is also the case that many key questions remain unexplored—little is known, for example, about the relationship between

[12] The Judges' Rules in England lay down similar, though much weaker, safeguards for the accused, but these have the status of administrative directions and lack the force of law.

[13] The most important studies are by Younger (1966a; 1966b); Wald *et al* (1967); Griffiths and Ayres (1967); Seeburger and Wettick (1967); Medalie *et al.* (1968); Leiken (1970); Milner (1971); Stephens *et al.* (1972); Stephens (1973); and Witt (1973).

[14] Other studies have been carried out on the importance of confession evidence in criminal cases, and these are discussed in chapter 7.

confession evidence and plea, though it is frequently assumed that a written or verbal confession is likely to lead to a plea of guilty.[15] What is clear is that confessions must be viewed within the context of the prosecution process as a whole. For some cases, where independent evidence is readily available, the police may actually regard the interrogation of suspects as superfluous. Indeed, they may even feel on occasions that interrogation might damage an otherwise strong case.[16] Furthermore, there now exists a considerable body of research concerned with the process of detection—what sociologists have termed the 'construction of conviction'[17]—and this research has raised doubts about many of the assumptions that have been made about the police role in the investigation of criminal offences and also the importance of police interrogation. It is now well established, for example, that many criminal offences are virtually 'self-detecting' in that clearance requires little effort on the part of the police. The research in question indicates how much police investigative work is 'reactive' in nature with more reliance being placed upon the evidence of victims and witnesses than upon interviewing the suspect himself.[18]

Before turning to the procedures adopted in our own study, it is necessary to make a few general observations which have direct relevance to the ensuing discussion. First, we must note that, even if it were established that confession evidence is rarely crucial to the prosecution's case, it would not follow that police interrogation is itself of little consequence. The simple point is that interrogation may be seen by the police as serving purposes other than the obtaining of a confession—for example, to obtain the names of accomplices, to recover stolen property, to solve

[15] The interesting study conducted by Neubauer (1974a) sheds some light on this question. He found that defendants who confessed rarely contested the case in court and that the existence of a confession often had a critical bearing on the process of plea bargaining. We ourselves examined this question in Birmingham in a limited way but concluded that the effect a confession had on plea negotiation was in most cases indirect and unpredictable. See further Baldwin and McConville (1977a) pp. 109–10.

[16] See, for instance, Devlin (1979b) who, writing about the difficulties facing an accused in establishing at trial that the police have behaved improperly, argues that, if the police do overstep the mark, 'the accused can hit the jack-pot: a case against him which is 90% sound can by exclusion of a small but vital admission be utterly destroyed' (p. 81).

[17] See the penetrating observations of Black (1970), and McBarnet (1976, 1978b).

[18] See particularly Bottomley and Coleman (1976); Vera Institute (1977); Greenwood *et al.* (1977); McCabe and Sutcliffe (1978); and Steer (1980). We discuss this question further at pp. 145–153.

other crimes, or to exonerate innocent suspects.[19] Secondly, the way in which confessions are viewed by the police, prosecutors, defendants, and their advisers is crucial in making sense of the role played by confessions in criminal trials. For it may well be that the assumptions that are made about the importance of confessions have more bearing upon the outcome of cases than any probative or evidentiary value they in fact possess. This is perhaps seen most clearly in relation to decisions made by defendants to plead guilty or not guilty at trial.[20]

OUR RESEARCH IN BIRMINGHAM AND LONDON

The conclusions we have drawn from earlier research about the role of confessions have not been made with much confidence. As we have noted, the research procedures adopted have commonly been flawed, the questions asked have been limited, and the available literature is largely American in origin. We therefore set out to provide further information about these questions, drawing upon samples of cases heard in the Crown Court.[21] All cases that reach the Crown Court must first be presented on paper before the magistrates can commit the defendant for trial. These committal papers provide excellent sources for the detailed analysis of the prosecution case that we had in mind. They present the details of the prosecution case and include, among other things, witness statements, details of forensic tests, reports of interviews conducted by police officers with defendants, and the statements made by the accused. Legally and sociologically, they are fascinating documents containing a wealth of information and detail about how the prosecution has assembled its case. The committal papers represent, in short, what sociologists would call the prosecution's 'con-

[19] Some of these purposes are discussed by Wald *et al.* (1967); Stephens *et al.* (1972); Witt (1973); Irving (1980); and Steer (1980). These 'collateral' purposes of interrogation are examined in greater detail in chapter 8.

[20] We discuss this question in Baldwin and McConville (1977a) and in the following chapter.

[21] The research on which this and the following two chapters is based was generously funded by the Royal Commission on Criminal Procedure. We wish to express our indebtedness to members of the Commission and particularly to its Secretary, Mr C. J. Train, for the advice and encouragement we received in conducting the research. Needless to say, the views expressed in these chapters are ours alone and are not to be taken as those of the Royal Commission.

struction of reality'.[22] They may or may not faithfully reproduce the reality they purport to represent, and they are at best truncated and severely edited descriptions of events that will often be hotly disputed at trial, but, as sources for research purposes, they provide insights into the way the prosecution has compiled and organized its case which could scarcely be obtained from any other source. It would certainly have taken us several years to gather the information we were able to obtain from committal papers had we been obliged to collect it from direct observation in the courtroom.[23]

We were able to carry out a detailed content analysis, using large samples of committal papers, to build up a picture of the sort of evidence contained in the prosecution case in relation to defendants involved in criminal trials heard in Birmingham and London. We wanted to find out whether defendants commonly confessed to the police. If so, what sort of statements did they make? Most importantly, how did the existence of a confession affect the plea that was tendered in court, or the outcome at trial? How significant was forensic evidence? These may seem curious questions to ask, so much having been written on the subject, but we re-emphasize the point that knowledge about the make-up of criminal cases is extremely limited. The second objective of our study was to assess the place and importance of confession evidence in a series of criminal trials, and this assessment forms the focus of chapter 7.

Before discussing the results of this exercise, it is worth saying a little about the method of content analysis and its usefulness in relation to the sort of information contained in the sets of committal papers that we examined. Berelson (1952) defines content analysis as 'a research technique for the objective, systematic and quantitative description of the manifest content of communication', and it has proved a useful tool in quantifying essentially qualitative material (such as newspaper editorials or historical records[24]) to a generation of social scientists. It has

[22] See further Berger and Luckman (1967); Cicourel (1968); Black (1970); and McBarnet (1976).

[23] Other researchers have attempted to collect comparable information by means of direct courtroom observation. See, for instance, Vennard (1980) who examined the role of confession evidence in a series of contested cases heard in the magistrates' courts.

[24] See particularly the classic studies conducted in the 1930s and 1940s by Lasswell and his associates: Lasswell (1942), and Smith, Lasswell and Casey (1946).

been used, for example, to reveal, in a systematic way, trends, biases, or other details of content which otherwise could only be the subject of hunch or impression. But it is a technique that can be inappropriate for certain types of material. For successful application of the technique to research materials, a number of conditions must be satisfied. One leading authority sets out three basic conditions: first, that the categories used to classify the content be made explicit so that others can replicate the analysis to verify the conclusions; secondly, that the analysis be based upon the methodical classification of all relevant material and not merely upon what strikes the particular researcher as interesting; and, thirdly, that some quantitative procedure be used to measure the importance and emphasis of material so as to permit comparison with other samples of material.[25] Committal papers, it seemed to us, provided excellent material for an analysis of this kind, and we found no real difficulty in fulfilling the basic conditions of its satisfactory application.

Relying upon this method, we carried out a descriptive analysis of the prosecution evidence in a series of Crown Court trials. The main source of material was the committal papers relating to our original sample of 500 contested trials heard in the Birmingham Crown Court in 1975 and 1976 (as described in chapter 2), supplemented by an equivalent number of cases in which there had been a guilty plea. The latter group formed a one in four sample of guilty pleas heard in the Birmingham Crown Court in the same time period. In addition to the Birmingham cases, we analysed a sample of 476 cases tried in the seven Crown Court centres in London over a three-month period in 1979.[26] Of the cases tried in London, 271 (57 per cent) were contested and 205 (43 per cent) involved guilty pleas.

The Birmingham and London samples provided altogether almost 1,500 run-of-the-mill Crown Court cases. About 90 per

[25] See Selltiz *et al.* (1965) pp. 335 42. Excellent discussions of the technique of content analysis are also given in Cicourel (1964) and Galtung (1967).

[26] The committal papers were collected for us by the Metropolitan Police as each trial was concluded in the seven court centres. Though a purist might argue that this method of collecting papers would not provide a truly representative sample of London cases, there is no doubt in our minds that the final sample supplied to us was not subject to any important distortions arising from the way the sample was drawn. We are indebted to the Metropolitan Police in allowing us to carry out this work, and in particular to Mr R. E. T. Birch of the Prosecuting Solicitor's Department who facilitated the collection of committal papers.

cent of the defendants in both cities were charged with property, violent, or sexual offences, predominantly of a serious nature. In confining our attention to Crown Court cases, we make no claim to be dealing with a representative cross-section of all criminal cases. Any generalizations we draw apply only to those cases tried in the Crown Court and may not have relevance to cases tried in the lower courts or to uncharged suspects interviewed by the police. It is important to note that the little evidence that is available on magistrates' courts suggests that the picture there may well be different. The research of Vennard (1980), though limited in nature, indicates that there may be a greater reliance upon the evidence of police witnesses in cases heard in the magistrates' courts than in those tried at the Crown Court, and that confessions as such may be of slight importance as far as the outcome in the magistrates' courts is concerned.[27] Rather than basing our analysis upon a representative sample of all criminal cases, we describe a sample of prosecutions drawn from the more serious end of the crime scale. It must also be remembered that the exercise is heavily based upon paper records, and whether committal papers can be viewed as accurate reflections of the exchanges between the police and suspects or witnesses is very much a matter of active public debate (not to say public concern). We shall discuss in chapter 9 the question whether statements of defendants contained in committal papers are likely to be fair reflections of what was actually said whilst in police custody. This consideration is, however, scarcely relevant to the issues with which we are concerned in this chapter.

THE FINDINGS

When we began to examine the committal papers for both

[27] Vennard confines herself to contested trials heard in the magistrates' courts, many of which involve non-indictable offences. For some reason, the overall acquittal rate in her sample is very low, even though the method of calculation she adopts (based upon charges, not upon defendants) inflates it. It would be unsafe to base generalizations about the importance of confessions on Vennard's work since one might expect that confession evidence would play a much greater role in those cases in which there is a guilty plea. Since the *Criminal Statistics* show that only about 10 per cent of all cases tried by magistrates are in fact contested, it is difficult to know what weight should be given to her finding that in only 8.9 per cent of all cases was a written confession or other incriminating written statement relied upon by the prosecution. As we shall see in due course, our own results relating to Crown Court cases demonstrate the central importance of plea in examining this question.

Birmingham and London, it became immediately apparent that statements made by suspects while in police custody form part of the case for the prosecution in the vast majority of trials. These statements do not by any means always represent a crucial element in the case: indeed they frequently consist of simple denials of the charges in question or are in other ways of a non-incriminatory character. Before examining the sorts of statement made by defendants, it is worth discussing the extent to which cases revolved around the evidence of police officers, of independent witnesses, or of the defendant himself. Any discussion of this question inevitably involves a subjective assessment of the relative importance of different items of evidence, and the evaluation that we carried out is subject to this limitation. For most cases, however, the position was perfectly clear: either a case depended on the ability of the police, and the police alone, to supply incriminating evidence and to rebut the defendant's explanation, or else the police were acting more in the role of agents in the prosecution of cases than as initiators of the process. In this latter group, it was apparent that, although police officers may have carried out some investigation and interviewed suspects or witnesses, the cases boiled down essentially to private disputes between citizens in which the police played only a subsidiary role in assisting the prosecution. Domestic violence and shoplifting are good examples of this kind of case.

Our assessment of the part played by the police in the prosecution of cases at trial is, therefore, to a degree subjective, but classification of the great majority of cases presented no real ambiguity. Table 4 indicates the extent to which cases depended upon police and/or civilian witnesses and to which this evidence was coupled with a written confession from the defendant in question.[28] The figures are also broken down according to the outcome at trial.

It is apparent from this table that, in about 40 per cent of all cases within each sample, the evidence directly implicating the accused came exclusively from the police,[29] and, in almost a

[28] In Table 4, and in several subsequent tables, allowance has been made for the different sampling fractions as between guilty and not guilty pleas in Birmingham.

[29] In these cases, civilians often provided evidence of an offence as victims or as witnesses without implicating the particular defendant. They may even on occasions have been able to offer a vague description of those responsible. But even here it was clear that the essence of the case was the evidence of the police.

TABLE 4

The extent to which reliance was placed upon police or civilian witnesses according to the availability of written confessions

(a) *Birmingham cases*	*Not guilty pleas, defendants acquitted*	(%)	*Not guilty pleas, defendants convicted*	(%)	*Guilty pleas*	(%)	*Overall* (%)
No written confession: case dependent upon police not civilian witnesses	57	25.3	75	28.8	95	19.5	21.0
No written confession: case dependent upon civilian witnesses	62	27.6	61	23.5	83	17.0	18.7
No written confession: case dependent upon both police and civilian witnesses	83	36.9	64	24.6	95	19.5	21.6
Written confession supported by strong civilian evidence	10	4.4	35	13.5	102	20.9	18.6
Written confession made: in other ways case dependent upon police not civilian witnesses	13	5.8	25	9.6	113	23.1	20.1
No information or not codeable	5	-	10		12		–
	230	100.0	270	100.0	500	100.0	100.0

further quarter of cases, police witnesses were major components in the prosecution's case. The police were also involved in the taking and reporting of statements made by defendants in about 40 per cent of all cases in Birmingham and in about 30 per cent in London. This shows how central the police are to the prosecution case. The picture is not changed much when forensic evidence is taken into account. No forensic evidence of any kind was presented in 80 per cent of cases and, in those cases in which it was used, it rarely assumed much significance. Indeed, in no more than 5 per cent of all cases did important forensic evidence (such as fingerprints, or blood and urine tests) directly implicate

Table 4 (*cont.*)

(b) London cases	*Not guilty pleas, defendants acquitted*	(%)	*Not guilty pleas, defendants convicted*	(%)	*Guilty pleas*	(%)	*Overall* (%)
No written confession: case dependent upon police not civilian witnesses	53	42.0	43	29.7	41	20.0	28.8
No written confession: case dependent upon civilian witnesses	34	27.0	33	22.8	19	9.3	18.1
No written confession: case dependent upon both police and civilian witnesses	32	25.4	44	30.3	42	20.5	24.8
Written confession supported by strong civilian evidence	2	1.6	16	11.0	57	27.8	15.7
Written confession made: in other ways case dependent upon police not civilian witnesses	5	4.0	9	6.2	46	22.4	12.6
No information or not codeable	0	–	0	–	0	–	–
	126	100.0	145	100.0	205	100.0	100.0

the defendant,[30] and even in these cases it was buttressed by other incriminating evidence.

The table shows, interestingly, no relationship between the reliance on police evidence and the outcome at trial. But it does

[30] The forensic evidence in most other cases was either of a technical nature (to establish the extent of a person's injuries in violent or sexual assaults) or used to show that a defendant could have committed the offence charged because he fell within a particular group in the population (as, for example, where he belonged to a specific blood or hair grouping). A similar picture emerged in the study of Greenwood *et al.* (1977) concerned with 200 house-breakers. In each of three cities, it was found that, even though fingerprints were often recovered, in only about 1 per cent of all cases did an identification result (p. 153).

reveal a much more important relationship—that between the existence of a written confession and the probability of conviction (either by plea or after a full trial). Over 90 per cent of defendants who made written confessions to the police in Birmingham, and 76 per cent in London, pleaded guilty at trial. Indeed, no more than 23 defendants who had made written confessions in Birmingham (2.4 per cent) and 7 in London (5.2 per cent) were eventually acquitted at trial.[31] The same appears to be true of verbal confessions, though care is needed here since about two-thirds of all verbal confessions were accompanied by a full written confession. However, it was apparent that over 90 per cent of those making full verbal confessions in Birmingham, and 87 per cent in London, were eventually convicted, with the majority in each city actually pleading guilty.[32] There can be no doubt, therefore, of the close correspondence between confession evidence, whether written or verbal, and conviction. When present, acquittal at trial is extremely unlikely—a fact which is not of course lost on police officers, lawyers, or defendants themselves.[33]

Since the existence of confession evidence is so closely associated with the eventual conviction of defendants, it is important to examine the nature of statements that are made to police officers or are at least contained in the committal papers at the end of the day. Much has been written about interrogations and much concern expressed about the circumstances in which they take place. It is not often appreciated, however, that defendants make a great variety of statements when interviewed, and it is wrong to assume that these are invariably of an incriminating nature. Even cursory inspection of a small number of committal papers reveals a bewildering range of statements. As we noted above, we found that approximately a third of defendants within the samples of London and Birmingham committal papers had made written statements which could be regarded as full confessions. Though verbal statements were much more

[31] The acquittal rate in those cases in which a written confession was made and which were contested was also lower than in other contested cases. 28.4 per cent of such cases in Birmingham and 21.9 per cent in London ended in acquittal compared with 50 per cent for other cases in each city. In both cities, these differences reach a level of statistical significance.

[32] Of those defendants who had made verbal confessions and who had contested their cases in court, 34.7 per cent in Birmingham and 36.5 per cent in London were acquitted.

[33] See further Baldwin and McConville (1977a) chapters 2, 3, and 6.

common, a surprisingly high proportion took the form of denials or in other ways fell short of full admissions. Very few defendants in either sample made no statement whatever to the police. Table 5 gives the overall picture that emerged in Birmingham and London. This table presents a number of important findings. As was noted earlier, full confessions were a comparative rarity and even verbal confessions featured in only about a half of all cases. As far as the frequency of different sorts of statement is concerned, it is apparent that the overall proportions are remarkably similar in each city. More significantly, the table provides further information on the question of plea, and shows that the committal papers contained many more confessions, both written and verbal, in the cases of those defendants who pleaded guilty at trial. Although about a quarter of those who pleaded not guilty had written or verbal confessions recorded against them, such statements were recorded against 88 per cent of those who pleaded guilty in Birmingham and about two-thirds in London.

Written statements can of course provide cogent evidence against the defendant, and it is interesting to examine the extent to which these are in the accused's own handwriting or written down by a police officer and signed by the accused. The conduct of interrogations is governed by the Judges' Rules and these provide in rule IV that, where a person says that he wants to make a statement 'he shall always be asked whether he wishes to write down himself what he wants to say; if he says that he cannot write or that he would like someone to write it for him, a police officer may offer to write the statement for him'. It might be expected from this that a not inconsiderable number of defendants choosing to make a statement would elect to write it themselves,[34] and one police officer, writing about the reformulation of the Judges' Rules in 1964, went so far as to say that 'a great many more prisoners will find themselves writing their own statements whether they wish to or not'.[35] What emerged from our own analysis was entirely contrary to this picture. We were able to examine the question in some detail

[34] The majority of the Criminal Law Revision Committee, in their report on *Evidence* (1972), assumed that many defendants preferred to write their own statements (para. 50), but the minority asserted that 'most written statements produced in evidence are not in the suspect's handwriting' (para. 52).

[35] A Police Officer 'The Judges' Rules and the Police' *Criminal Law Review* (1964) at p. 175.

TABLE 5
Statements made by defendants

(*a*) *Birmingham cases*

	Not guilty pleas	(%)	*Guilty pleas*	(%)	*Overall* (%)
No statement of any kind	17	3.5	19	3.9	3.8
Full written confession only	5	1.0	9	1.9	1.7
Full written and full verbal confession	62	12.8	144	29.5	26.2
Full written confession and other verbal statement	17	3.5	61	12.5	10.7
Full verbal confession only	39	8.0	42	8.6	8.5
Written statement not a confession, but full verbal confession	20	4.1	7	1.4	2.0
Written statement not a confession	93	19.2	47	9.6	11.5
Damaging verbal statement only	96	19.8	85	17.4	17.9
Verbal denial only	124	25.6	55	11.3	14.1
Other kind of statement	12	2.5	19	3.9	3.6
Papers missing, incomplete, or no information	15	-	12	-	-
	500	100.0	500	100.0	100.0

(*b*) *London cases*

	Not guilty pleas	(%)	*Guilty pleas*	(%)	*Overall* (%)
No statement of any kind	22	8.1	9	4.4	6.5
Full written confession only	2	0.7	5	2.4	1.5
Full written and full verbal confession	25	9.2	80	39.0	22.1
Full written confession and other verbal statement	5	1.9	18	8.8	4.8
Full verbal confession only	48	17.7	52	25.4	21.0
Written statement not a confession, but full verbal confession	1	0.4	2	1.0	0.6
Written statement not a confession	9	3.3	4	1.9	2.7
Damaging verbal statement only	72	26.6	16	7.8	18.5
Verbal denial only	78	28.8	11	5.4	18.7
Other kind of statement	9	3.3	8	3.9	3.6
Papers missing, incomplete, or no information	0		0		
	271	100.0	205	100.0	100.0

in relation to the sample of Birmingham cases, since officers of the West Midlands Police Force completed for us formal questionnaires on aspects of the pre-trial preparation (details of which are set out at p. 25 on every case committed for trial during the study period. Since 99.6 per cent of the 2,406 questionnaires were returned by the police, we were able to ascertain how many handwritten statements had been obtained overall. No more than seven confessions of this nature were made, and almost all written statements of a non-incriminating character were written out by a police officer. This pattern, which held good for the London sample of cases as well, provides one reason why disputes as to the completeness or accuracy of written confessions can arise.

These difficulties apart, it is perhaps easy to understand how a suspect who signs a written statement might consider it fruitless to fight the matter in court. Verbal evidence is different, since it consists of the unverified (indeed unverifiable) word of the police officer against that of the defendant, and we have found in our earlier research that defendants complain more frequently, and more vehemently, about police 'verbals' than about any other aspect of their experiences.[36] Yet most defence lawyers will advise defendants (often for sound tactical reasons) against challenging verbal evidence in court or at least point out to them in no uncertain terms the serious risks they run in attempting to contradict such evidence. Most defendants, it seems, concede and plead guilty. We pursue in chapter 9 some of the dangers in this situation; here we examine more closely qualitative aspects of verbal evidence, and discuss the variety of statements that are commonly subsumed under the general category of police 'verbals'.

As we have already noted, by no means all statements of defendants to be found in committal papers constitute full confessions or are in other ways damaging to the defendant. Over a quarter of all written and verbal statements could be considered non-incriminatory in nature. These proportions were somewhat lower in London than in Birmingham, particularly in relation to written statements.[37] The effect of a written denial to an offence may, however, be undermined by an accompanying verbal statement, and it is not without significance that only about a quarter of all defendants in the samples actually reached court without a damaging statement of some kind having been recorded against them. It might be noted in

[36] See Baldwin and McConville (1977a) at pp. 68–70.

[37] In Birmingham, about 4 per cent of all defendants made statements to the police in which they admitted the *actus reus* only. In London, the corresponding proportion was about 2 per cent. It is worth noting in passing that over 90 per cent of all such statements were buttressed by damaging verbal admissions attributed to the defendant.

this context that other damaging material may emerge as part of interrogation evidence. This relates not to what the defendant allegedly said but to how he is reported to have reacted when questioned. Where the interviewing officer has put some pointed question, the defendant is sometimes reported as having 'looked dejected', 'buried his head in his hands', or responded in some other way that is thought to convey culpability. Observational descriptions of this kind may have an effect as potent as a statement of admission.

It is worth pausing at this point to consider in some detail the sort of verbal statements that we commonly encountered in the committal papers we examined. We discuss such statements under three headings: (i) full confessions; (ii) damaging verbal statements; and (iii) verbal denials.

VERBAL STATEMENTS

(i) *Full confessions*

Full verbal confessions were attributed to 37 per cent of all defendants in the Birmingham sample, and to 44 per cent of those in London. The frequency with which they are encountered in the committal papers, together with the fact that they are strongly associated with the guilty plea and with outcome at trial, underlines the importance that such statements assume. The category 'full confessions' may appear at first sight to be self-explanatory, but there are in fact a variety of statements subsumed under this broad heading. Some statements are straightforward admissions to a particular offence, but many serve to indicate in addition that the defendant has a criminal record or is in other ways involved in serious criminal activity. Many of the reported conversations are liberally spiced with criminal argot, and this represents one way in which a criminal record or deep involvement in serious criminality might be inferred from the papers or conveyed to the court.[38]

Case 8 (*Birmingham*) Has she really fingered me? It's right what she's said. I punched her in the face, but I won't make a statement. I'll put my hands up when I get to court. I love the girl, I can't believe that she's fingered me.

[38] Other examples of verbal confessions are given in Baldwin and McConville (1979d; 1980). In all the quotations that follow, any detail that might identify an individual has been disguised. In certain cases, heavy swearing has been moderated—purely in the interests of propriety.

Case 23 (*Birmingham*) Yes, I know about the burglary, but you must let me out, I want to find out who put me here . . . Yes, it was me. I'll be fair, but can I have bail?

Case 131 (*Birmingham*) Fair enough, I knew the stuff was bent, it had to be. Leave it at that. I want to see my solicitor. I am saying nothing else till then.

Case 170 (*Birmingham*) It's a fair cop.

Case 202 (*Birmingham*) Yeah! O.K.! I put the window in but I couldn't get it open. I was out for cash. It was a big house and I thought there would be some there. I'm not making a statement—I've only just come out.

Case 320 (*Birmingham*) You've got to believe me. I was wound up and went berserk, that's the truth. I've never hit a copper before—I don't know what came over me. I did it without thinking. It's the first and last time. I'm very sorry for doing the copper and I'll plead guilty.

Case 364 (*Birmingham*) I had better make a statement as well in case Alan puts all the blame on me. I only helped to nick it.

Case 620 (*Birmingham*) I thought the car was nicked but I only had a lift in it.

Case 781 (*Birmingham*) I don't know why I did it. I just had a flash of temper. I have been taking tablets but my wife hid them.

Case 784 (*Birmingham*) I won't be having the stealing but I'm guilty of handling.

Case 807 (*Birmingham*) I can only admit it.

Case 859 (*Birmingham*) O.K. The job's down to me. Let the others off, they're only helping me out. They don't know anything. I screwed the pitch and that's all you need to know.

Case 865 (*Birmingham*) I don't know what came over me. I got in scraps but its the first time I've smashed a copper. I've given up smoking, I think I'll give up boozing as well . . . I expect I'll go down for this.

Case 24 (*London*) Someone was taking the mickey out of me, so I chucked the stool. You'll have to find out who was with me—I'm putting no one in the frame.

Case 340 (*London*) All right, I know what it's about. I've been expecting to get nicked. I'm the one you want.

(ii) *Damaging verbal statements*

Almost as common as full verbal confessions are those statements which, though falling short of complete admissions, show the defendant in an unfavourable light. About a quarter of all defendants in each city had statements of this kind recorded against them in the committal papers. Many such statements involved, for example, extensive use of criminal jargon or swearing; others merely suggest that the defendant must be of dubious character, or has a lengthy criminal record. The following provide examples:

Case 11 (*Birmingham*) When Bob gave me a lift, I knew he hadn't got a car of his own but I didn't ask him where he'd got it from. I'm not saying any more at all. You seem to know all about it. Charge me if you want to but you'll have to prove it.

Case 67 (*Birmingham*) I know you bastards, once you take me away from here, I'll never come back. Why can't you bloody well leave me alone? I suppose you are going to plant me.

Case 96 (*Birmingham*) You will never prove that I had those keys to steal cars. I'm going to say I collected them over the last few months and needed them to start my car because I lost my keys.

Case 109 (*Birmingham*) As far as I'm concerned, I've never seen anything. It's your word against mine. You never saw me at any house. Another thing, we are not that stupid to get followed by you lot.

Case 205 (*Birmingham*) I bet you can't prove it. I'm pleading not guilty to that lot.

Case 209 (*Birmingham*) Look, I'm not the main one.

Case 329 (*Birmingham*) No way was it rape. She was with me all the way. If she wants to stitch me up, I'll sort her out in my own way.

Case 415 (*Birmingham*) [The witness] is lying. I can bring twenty witnesses to say it wasn't me. I'm signing nothing. The bastard. I'll get him. You'll be doing me for murder next.

Case 637 (*Birmingham*) You don't believe me? Please yourself. That's what I'm saying, now it's up to you to prove something different.

Case 736 (*Birmingham*) You can't arrest me. I ain't been doing any screwing. I didn't screw the place this time, so you can't prove it.

Case 975 (*Birmingham*) I don't make statements to the police until I've seen my solicitor.

Case 109 (*London*) You know I can't make a statement. If I was on my own, it would be different.

Case 221 (*London*) Well, that's not me. It's not my game, cheques. Ask anyone, they'll tell you I don't do cheques.

(iii) *Verbal denials*

It is often overlooked, in discussions of so-called police 'verbals', that many verbal statements attributed to defendants consist of non-incriminatory material. In the present samples, we found that almost a fifth of all defendants in both cities were said to have made statements to the police which amounted to complete denials of the charges in question and, moreover, they were stated in language which casts no shadow over the defendant's character (as do several of the denials included under category (ii)). Verbal denials are usually short, simple, and direct, as the following examples demonstrate:

Case 231 (*Birmingham*) No, I didn't hit him. He must have hit his head on the ground. I've got nothing else to say.

Case 242 (*Birmingham*) I fully deny the allegation made against me.

Case 303 (*Birmingham*) No, it wasn't me. I had nothing to do with it. I don't want to make a statement. I've said it once and I'll say it again, I didn't do it.

Case 962 (*Birmingham*) I didn't take the car. I'll bring witnesses to say I wasn't in Green Street when the car was taken. I know nothing about it.

Case 2 (*London*) I've nothing to say except not guilty.

Case 43 (*London*) I didn't do it. The man is trying to cause me trouble.

OTHER ISSUES

Before we turn our attention to the question whether the committal papers accurately reflect what took place between the defendant and the arresting or interviewing officer, it is important to examine a few general questions concerning the circumstances in which statements are reported to have been made. As we have already stated, very few defendants appear to exercise their right to silence in the face of police questioning, and Table 5 shows that fewer than one defendant in twenty had no statement of any kind recorded in the committal papers. When we carried out interviews in Birmingham and London with police officers responsible for handling each contested case, it became apparent that only about 10 per cent of the defendants involved in these trials had exercised their right of silence either at the police station or at court. A further 10 per cent in Birmingham, and 13 per cent in London, had advanced major new explanations at their trial that they had not previously mentioned when being interviewed by the police.[39] This latter point had been taken up by the Criminal Law Revision Committee in their report on evidence (1972). One of the Committee's most contentious proposals was that:

> the law should be amended so that, if the accused has failed, when being interrogated by anyone charged with the duty of investigating offences or charging offenders, to mention a fact which he afterwards relies on at committal proceedings or the trial, the court or jury may draw such inferences as appear proper in determining the question before them. The fact would have to be one which the accused could reasonably have been expected to mention at the time. (para. 32.)

This immediately raises the question of how successful are such defendants in gaining acquittals. Is the springing of a late defence particularly effective in bringing about the perverse acquittal of the defendants in question? The answer from our research in both Birmingham and London strongly suggests that it is not. There were 38 defendants in Birmingham who introduced at their trials major new evidence which, in the view of the police officers involved, they might reasonably have been expected to mention when they were being interviewed in police custody if only to establish their innocence and so eliminate themselves from the enquiry.[40] Altogether 26 of these defendants (68 per cent) were eventually convicted at trial and, of the 12 who were acquitted, there were only 5 cases in which it appeared to the police officers concerned that the new explanation itself brought about the acquittal. In the remaining cases, there were, in the view of the officer concerned, other strong reasons why the defendant obtained his acquittal. Furthermore, the 5 cases

[39] These proportions relate to the 370 cases that were contested before juries in Birmingham and to the 358 cases contested before juries in London. We excluded the cases that ended in ordered or directed acquittals because, in almost all these cases, the trial was terminated before the defendant had been given the opportunity to give evidence and to put his side of the story.

[40] It is clear from the observational studies of police interrogation practices that have been carried out in this country that one objective of the police at this stage is simply to establish whether or not the suspect can provide a satisfactory explanation of his conduct and so be eliminated from the enquiry. See, for instance, Irving (1980); and Softley (1980).

in which a belated defence was successful were not the sort of cases which led the Criminal Law Revision Committee to make the proposal they did. Three were cases of shoplifting, one was of unlawful sexual intercourse, and in the fifth a man had been charged with stealing a quantity of scrap metal—hardly the sort of cases which involve professional crooks who represent a serious threat to members of the general public. A similar picture was obtained from the interviews that we conducted with police officers in London about the outcome of cases that had been tried by jury in 1975. In 41 of these cases (13 per cent), defendants had, in the view of the police officer interviewed, introduced major new explanations at the trial. Of these, 21 (51 per cent) ended in the conviction of the defendant concerned, and in only 2 of the 20 other cases did the officer view the acquittal as primarily explicable in terms of the late explanation advanced. One of these cases involved the theft of £250 worth of equipment from a building site, the other making an untrue statement to obtain a passport. Again neither case could be viewed by any stretch of imagination as posing a threat to public safety.

A related question as to the relevance of a disposition to commit certain offences seriously exercised the minds of members of the Criminal Law Revision Committee. Defendants may at trial admit that they have carried out the act alleged but deny that they had the necessary guilty mind, as for example where a defendant claims that he removed goods from a supermarket by oversight or claims a girl consented in a rape case. Where a defendant had on an earlier occasion been convicted of a similar type of offence, the Committee took the view that this fact (which, they argued, tended to 'show that he has a disposition to commit the kind of offence charged') would be very relevant in deciding whether the defendant had committed the offence with which he was now charged. Choosing as one example the case of a man with ninety convictions for pickpocketing who is identified by a total stranger at a football match as a thief, the Committee argued that it would be 'a great strain on human credulity to be asked to suppose that so confirmed a pickpocket ... would have been wrongly pointed out as the thief' (para. 72). They thus recommended that:

where the defence admit that the conduct in respect of which the accused is charged occurred (but deny that the accused was guilty of an offence in respect of it), then evidence of other conduct of the accused tending to show in him a disposition to commit the kind of offence charged should be admissible for certain particular purposes. The purposes would be (i) showing that the accused possessed the state of mind necessary to make him guilty in respect of that conduct; (ii) proving that the conduct was not accidental or involuntary or (iii) proving that there was no lawful justification or excuse for it. (para. 92.)

Members of the Committee were satisfied that evidence of previous convictions should be admitted in the circumstances envisaged notwithstanding the prejudicial effect it might have.

Earlier research has suggested that the impact of the proposed change might be substantial. McCabe and Purves (1972b), for example, in a study of defendants acquitted in contested cases, found that 63 per cent of defendants admitted taking part in the conduct in question but denied the necessary *mens rea*. Similarly, Zander (1974a) reported that, of the cases in which details of the defence were ascertained, no fewer than 81 per cent rested upon a defence of this nature. Neither study reveals how many defendants running this defence would have been affected by the implementation of the Criminal Law Revision Committee's proposal. We were able to examine this question in some depth for both the Birmingham and London samples, drawing upon interviews we had conducted with police officers involved in those trials. Our analysis strongly suggested that the effect of such a fundamental change to current practice would be so limited as to make worthless any attempt to introduce this proposal. In approximately 40 per cent of cases in each city, the defence consisted of an admission of the act alleged and a denial of the *mens rea*. But in about 7 out of 8 of these cases, the accused either had no similar previous convictions or else he was nevertheless convicted at trial. Taking all cases together, no more than about 1 in 20 cases could, therefore, have been affected by the Committee's proposals. Furthermore, it was apparent that only 7 defendants in Birmingham and 5 in London in these kinds of cases had secured acquittals to which, in the view of the principal participants in the trial, they were not entitled.[41] We cannot know, of course, whether the 12 defen-

[41] We were able to obtain the views of trial judges, defence and prosecuting solicitors, and police officers about jury verdicts for all Birmingham cases, and we attempted to build up a rounded view of each verdict in this way. We conducted a partial replication

dants acquitted in allegedly questionable circumstances would have been convicted had the Criminal Law Revision Committee's proposals been enacted, but the possible prejudicial effect of the proposed change does not seem to be offset by any real compensating benefit.[42]

A separate matter which has given rise to concern in some quarters has been whether certain groups or types of individual may be more vulnerable in the stressful situation created by interrogation than are others. There is now a considerable body of research and writing, produced primarily by psychologists, which suggests that certain groups in the population may be particularly suggestible (and therefore at greater risk as far as false confessions are concerned) or readily exploited by a heavy-handed or tricky interrogation.[43] We could examine this question only from the standpoint of the information contained in the samples of committal papers at our disposal, and these of course give no impression of the sort of interviewing tactics employed by interrogators, but we were able to determine the frequencies with which different groups of defendants made confessions. It is important to bear in mind, however, that it is possible that different results might have emerged from a study involving suspects (whether or not proceedings were eventually instituted) or from a study of all defendants (regardless of the court of trial). We wished to investigate the extent to which younger defendants and those without prior criminal experience were more likely to confess than were their older and more experienced counterparts.[44] It might be hypothesized, for instance, that more experienced defendants would be better able

---

of this exercise in London, based upon the opinions expressed by police officers. Further details of this research are given in Baldwin and McConville (1979c).

[42] On this point, the Committee state somewhat equivocally:

> We are all satisfied that, on the assumption (as to which some members of the committee do not agree) that the proposals ... will prove to be of sufficient practical value to justify the additional complication in the law which it involves, it would be consistent with the interests of justice to enact the proposal. (para. 93.)

[43] See particularly Horowitz (1956); Sargant (1957); Reik (1959); Sterling (1965); Driver (1968); Deeley (1971); and Kellam (1980). For good reviews of this evidence, see Teh (1973), and Irving and Hilgendorf (1980).

[44] We also examined the committal papers to find out whether confession rates varied according to the defendants' sex and race. We found that, although certain differences emerged as far as sex was concerned (women being somewhat less likely to make written and verbal statements), the numbers were too small to reach a level of statistical significance.

to withstand the pressures and inducements to confess and better placed to understand and assert their rights.[45]

As to age, the hypothesis was in fact strongly supported by the material we collected both in Birmingham and in London. The younger the defendant, the more likely he was to confess. This trend was statistically highly significant in each city.[46] A more surprising result emerged from our examination of the criminal records of those who made confessions to the police, because it became apparent that, for London cases, recidivists were more likely than others to make written and verbal confessions.[47] We were able to examine this question in greater detail in relation to the Birmingham sample because we were given information by the West Midlands Police not only on each defendant's criminal record but also on the extent to which he was suspected by the police of being involved in uncharged criminal activity or in organized crime, of the extent to which he was seen as making a living out of crime and of the extent to which he was viewed as skilful in his criminal activities and prepared to use every means (legal and illegal) to avoid apprehension. In short, we were told whether the police regarded each defendant as a professional criminal.[48] It might be supposed that those defendants viewed by the police as professionals would be less likely than others to make confessions when interviewed, but this turned out not to be the case: the 'professionals' confessed at about the same rate as others within the sample, as far as both written and verbal statements were concerned. Thus, those regarded by the police as the least profes-

[45] This is suggested by some of the research conducted in the United States. Leiken (1970), for instance, found that many more young defendants made confessions to the police than did older. He suggested that older defendants were 'better equipped psychologically to cope with the interrogation situation, or experience or temperament may have been a significant factor' (p. 19). Although Leiken produced no comparable results for those with prior contacts with the police, Neubauer (1974a) showed, in a more extensive examination of cases, that those with prior experience of the criminal system were more likely to resist police pressures to make a confession.

[46] A linear trend test of significance was used to measure these trends: see Armitage (1955). The detailed results on the question of the association between the age of defendants and their propensity to confess are given in Baldwin and McConville (1980) pp. 23–4.

[47] This trend was statistically significant as far as London cases were concerned. Full details of the results are set out in Baldwin and McConville (1980) pp. 24–5.

[48] For further details of the methods we adopted in classifying defendants as 'professionals', see Baldwin and McConville (1979c) at pp. 110–11. We are indebted to Inspector Stuart Harris of the West Midlands Police who organized the collection of this material.

sional made written confessions in 43 per cent of cases and written or verbal confessions in 56 per cent of cases, whereas the comparable figures for those viewed as the most professional were 36 per cent and 56 per cent. It is not easy to draw inferences from these figures. They may mean, on the one hand, that the non-professional recidivists are more willing than others to talk to the police about their involvement in criminal activities or are less skilful in covering up their participation. Alternatively, it may be that police officers are more ready to attribute verbal admissions to those who are least able to and least likely to challenge them. This is a point to which we return in chapter 9, though one must note that, in the present state of knowledge, deciding between these competing interpretations is a matter of speculation, given the fact that police interviews are not independently monitored in England.

Related to the question whether certain types of defendant are more likely than others to make confessions when interviewed is that concerning the sorts of case in which confessions are commonly made. There is some evidence from American studies (notably Medalie *et al.* (1968), and Neubauer (1974a)[49]) that the confession rate varies according to offence type. The evidence is, however, far from clearcut because so many other variables complicate the picture. Perhaps the most important of these variables is the strength of the other evidence against the accused. Neubauer, for instance, found that a key factor in inducing defendants to confess was the existence of other incriminating evidence (such as stolen goods or fingerprints), and Sobel (1966) put the point in this way:

> experience (as well as common sense) establishes that the overwhelming percentage of confessions are obtained under circumstances where because of other evidence it is futile and pointless for the defendant not to confess. To put it affirmatively most confessions are obtained precisely because the defendant is already 'hooked' by the other evidence. (p. 137.)

This pattern did not emerge in our analysis of Birmingham and London cases, and we found in both cities no significant differ-

[49] Medalie *et al.* (1968) found that the rate of confession varied according to the offence charged though no clear pattern was apparent. Neubauer (1974a) produced a much clearer result—that defendants accused of property offences confessed at a much higher rate (56 per cent) than those accused of crimes against the person (32 per cent). See also Seeburger and Wettick (1967) and the Vera Institute (1969).

ences in confession rates according to type of offence.[50] In other words, the confession rate for property offences corresponded closely to that for offences against the person.[51]

CONCLUDING COMMENTS

We have attempted in this chapter to make sense of the mass of information and detail that is contained in a large sample of Crown Court committal papers by applying to them the rigorous quantitative technique of content analysis. Whatever difficulties of interpretation this exercise may have produced, we can claim for the results that they provide some insights into the way prosecution cases are assembled and, more specifically, into the role of confession evidence in Crown Court trials. In the next chapter, we re-examine the question of confession evidence when we attempt to evaluate its *significance* to the outcome of the trials in question.

It is appropriate in conclusion to relate the findings discussed in this chapter to the broader context of the complex role of the police within the adversary system—a subject to which we referred at the beginning of this chapter. Our examination shows that the police role in providing the evidence necessary for conviction is in most cases absolutely central. It is clear that the evidence that comes from the police (either in the form of material adduced directly from their own investigation and observations or from their reports of interviews they have conducted with defendants) forms part of the prosecution evidence in the great majority of cases. Some indication of the importance of the police role in this respect is given, for instance, by the finding that only about a quarter of all defendants reached trial without damaging statements of some kind being recorded against them. Lord Devlin (1979b) has referred to the 'quasi-judicial' role of the police and describes it as 'theoretically unsound'. The police are, on the one hand, committed to detecting and investigating crime but, on the other, required to make what amount to judicial decisions about whether there is sufficient evidence to warrant prosecution. Devlin argues that

[50] The detailed figures on this are set out in Baldwin and McConville (1980) at pp. 26 7.

[51] We return to the question of the relation between offence type and confession evidence in the following chapter when we examine the bearing that confessions have on the outcome of cases in court.

this means that the adversary system 'drifts' towards the inquisitorial system. He writes:

> We leave the inquisition to the prosecution, administering to them one of our favourite nostrums by exhorting them to act fairly. Would it not be better to impose an undisguised judicial figure between the prosecution and the defence? ... He should be ... a single figure of standing and accountability ... so as to ensure that his decision to drop a prosecution is accepted as authoritative and impartial. (p. 78.)

The results of the present chapter, which serve to illustrate the critical role of police evidence in the prosecution's case, bear out Lord Devlin's point that the roles currently played by the police in the English prosecution system make their position unsound.

7

THE IMPORTANCE OF CONFESSION EVIDENCE

INTRODUCTION

In both England and the United States in recent years, there has been considerable disquiet about the rights of suspects in police custody, for it is at this stage in the criminal process that the suspect is most vulnerable. The right of a suspect to remain silent in the face of police questioning has traditionally been regarded as a fundamental protection, enshrined in the common law and in the rules that exist to govern interrogation. Attempts to whittle down or abolish this right have met with unrestrained hostility from many quarters. At the same time, the importance attached by the police to interrogation has led them stubbornly to resist efforts to monitor the conduct of interviews and helps explain why they view the introduction of any independent scrutiny of existing practices as a retrograde and dangerous step. All this suggests that the initial encounter between the suspect and the police officer is a key exchange in the criminal process and that evidence obtained from interrogation is critical to the ultimate disposition of cases in court. In the present chapter, we critically examine this assumption and attempt to assess the significance of confessions and more generally of interrogations in criminal cases heard at the Crown Court.

Although in legal theory a confession is not of itself conclusive of guilt and may always be explained away, there can be little doubt that a statement of admission by an accused person may be a devastating piece of evidence against him. It may on its own be sufficient to convince a jury or a bench of magistrates of his guilt, and it will invariably be difficult for the defendant to retract. One indication of the importance of a confession can be seen in the way the courts have historically viewed such evidence.[1] At one time courts were so suspicious of confessions that there was a tendency to exclude them on the slightest

[1] The attitude of the courts to confession evidence is traced in 3 Wigmore (1970) paras. 817 20.

pretext. The present position is that a confession, though a species of hearsay, is admissible in evidence provided that it has not been obtained by pressure or inducement.[2] The rules governing these matters are complex and many of the distinctions fine,[3] but the very cogency of this type of evidence has meant that special care has been needed in dealing with it.

Even if it is accepted that a confession may tell heavily against the accused, it does not necessarily follow that the prosecution relies to any great extent upon such evidence. Many commentators, however, have asserted that confessions are not only deadly in their effect but that they constitute an essential part of the case for the prosecution in a majority of criminal trials. Some have contended that, without confessions, a great number of cases simply could not continue. The following quotations, from English and American writers, illustrate the sort of assumptions often made about confessions in criminal cases:

> admissions in a written statement signed by the accused form a significant part of most cases for the prosecution and in many an essential part. (Devlin (1979b) p. 79.)

> more than 80 per cent of all criminal cases are solved by confession. A defendant is seldom acquitted once his confession is admitted as evidence during his trial. Thus, for a majority of defendants, trial is but a mere formality. (Zimbardo (1967) p. 17.)

> Today the importance of confessions ... cannot be over-emphasised ... In many cases there would be no trial without them, for many times the state has no other evidence implicating the defendant. (Schafer (1968) p. vii.)

> How else can [crimes] be solved, if at all, except by means of the interrogation of suspects or of others who may possess information? Absent a confession, the guilt of the offenders in most of these cases could not be established (Inbau (1968) p. 274.)

If, as these quotations suggest, the prosecution routinely relies upon confession evidence to prove its case and could not in many cases otherwise proceed, it would be necessary to reassess the fundamental principles upon which Anglo-American criminal procedure is grounded. For underlying that procedure is

[2] The Criminal Law Revision Committee (1972) recommended that the rules governing admissibility of confession evidence should be changed, and a minority of three members went so far as to recommend that all restrictions on admissibility should be abolished.

[3] The whole question is discussed in Cross (1979) chapters 3 and 20.

the principle that it is for the prosecution to establish its case and that it is no part of the defendant's duty to supply the necessary evidence.

The quotations given above not only conflict in principle with the adversarial model, but they have also been made in ignorance of the available empirical evidence. Indeed, such research as has been conducted on these questions tends to show that on the contrary the prosecution is not to any marked extent dependent upon the confession of the person charged. It is. already clear, for example, from the details of our own research provided in chapter 6, that full confessions, written or verbal, were made in no more than a half of the cases in the Birmingham and London samples; and it must follow from this that the reliance of the prosecution on such evidence is far from total. But there is other research (all of which comes from the United States) bearing upon this question and, in attempting to assess the role of confession evidence in the prosecution's case, it is useful to examine this material first.

THE AMERICAN RESEARCH

Contrary to what many people have assumed, there is in fact a sizeable body of research material bearing upon the significance of confession evidence in criminal cases. Before discussing the major findings that have emerged, it is important to set out some of the limitations that make assessment of its value problematic. First, since the research is exclusively American in origin, it cannot of course be taken to have any necessary or direct relevance to the situation in England. Secondly, many of the enquiries have been primarily concerned with other questions (such as police interrogation methods and the sufficiency of the warnings given to suspects) and only incidentally with the role of confessions. One result of this has been a lack of standardization in approach and a consequent difficulty in comparing the findings of different researchers. Some, for example, have regarded confession evidence as necessary to the prosecution if, without it, the defendant would secure an acquittal, whereas others see it in this way only if the prosecution would not otherwise be able to institute proceedings.[4] Thirdly,

[4] Similar problems arise with the meaning given to 'confession evidence' for some writers have not confined it to statements of admission but extended it to include any statement made during interrogation.

a number of the evaluations have been conducted by people whose connection with the criminal process hardly gives an impression of detachment. Prosecutors, defence lawyers, judges, and even serving police officers have carried out evaluations of confession evidence, alongside academic researchers. Notwithstanding these and other limitations, the findings must be considered seriously for they show a remarkable degree of consistency and, interestingly, a consistency that appears to be directly at variance with many of the opinions cited above.

The earliest research was conducted by Sobel (1965, 1966), a judge of the New York State Supreme Court, who examined a sample of cases tried in Kings County, New York. The cases consisted of the first 1,000 indictments returned in the County following the establishment of a rule that the District Attorney was required to serve a pre-trial 'notice of intention' on defendants where the prosecution intended to use a confession at trial.[5] Sobel discovered that notices of intention had been filed in only 86 of the cases examined. He concluded that

> it is safe to estimate that confessions constitute part of the evidence in less than 10 per cent of all indictments . . . That confessions are essential to conviction in any substantial number of cases is simply carefully nurtured nonsense . . . From a practical perspective the value of confessions in law enforcement has been grossly exaggerated. (1965, pp. 4–5.)

This firm conclusion has, however, been called into question on a number of grounds.[6] The major weakness is that the District Attorney, under the new rule, was not required to file a notice of intention in guilty plea cases or in cases in which the defendant's confession had led the police to other convincing evidence of guilt which rendered the subsequent confession at trial unnecessary. At best, therefore, Sobel's conclusions relate only to those contested cases in which the prosecution needed to rely directly upon a confession.

Other evaluations, of an equally subjective nature, quickly followed this early study and not all produced findings entirely consistent with those of Sobel. In a survey conducted by the Detroit Police Department and reported in Souris (1966), for example, investigating police officers were interviewed to de-

[5] The rule was established in *People* v. *Huntley*, 15 N.Y. 2d 72; 204 N.E. 2d 179 (1965).
[6] For detailed criticisms, see Inbau (1966), and Wald *et al.* (1967) at p. 1642.

termine the proportion of felony prosecutions in which a confession was essential. In line with Sobel's findings, confessions were deemed to be essential in only 11 per cent of all cases.[7] A very similar result was obtained by Younger (1966a, 1966b), the District Attorney of Los Angeles County, who found that 'in only 67 instances, or 10 per cent of the 649 defendants having trials or who had pleaded guilty, did the [deputy District Attorneys] feel that the confession or admission was necessary for conviction' (1966a, p. 39). But other studies of this kind have come up with somewhat different conclusions. In an analysis of pending homicide cases in New York County, for example, the District Attorney reported that 27 per cent of the indictments could not have been obtained without the evidence of confessions made to the police,[8] and prosecutors and police departments in other regions have asserted that confessions are very important items of evidence.[9]

The general conclusion to be drawn from these early studies is that confession evidence is not nearly as crucial as many writers have assumed, and the more rigorous studies that have been conducted subsequently have not affected this conclusion. Three of these later studies are worth mentioning. In the study of Wald *et al.* (1967), police interrogations were observed and the files that the police compiled were scrutinized. The observers assessed whether the evidence that was essential to the prosecution in each case could have been obtained by means other than interrogation of the suspect. Interrogation was considered necessary only where there was little or no evidence against the suspect and where alternative investigative methods were nonexistent or probably inadequate. The main findings were that confessions were necessary in at most 13 per cent of cases, and that in almost all the cases observed the police had enough evidence to convict without the need even to question the suspect.[10] The second study, which was conducted by Seeburger and Wettick (1967) in Pittsburgh, was based solely upon an examination of police files. A confession was considered to be

[7] The detailed findings show differences according to offence type, with about a quarter of robbery and burglary cases dependent upon confession evidence.

[8] The study is reported in Kuh (1966), and Inbau (1966).

[9] For details of these, see Kuh (1966) at p. 245, and Seeburger and Wettick (1967) at pp. 25 6. Impressionistic evidence of the way in which confessions are viewed is given in Rogge (1972) at p. 85.

[10] See Wald *et al.* (1967) at pp. 1584–8; and Reiss and Black (1967).

essential if a conviction was unlikely without it. On this basis the researchers concluded that in approximately 20 per cent of all cases a confession was needed to ensure conviction.[11] Finally, the study by Witt (1973)—himself a former police officer—showed, on the basis of an examination of 478 police files in a major metropolitan area, that confession evidence was necessary in 24 per cent of all cases. He concluded that 'it appears that in most cases interrogation was not needed to solve the immediate crimes for which the suspects were accused' (p. 324).

This brief review of the American literature[12] suggests that claims that confession evidence forms an essential part of the prosecution case in the majority of criminal trials are without empirical foundation. It appears that in most cases the prosecution can get by without such evidence. But this conclusion must be treated with caution. As we have noted, all of the research is subject to severe methodological limitations and all of the studies rest upon subjective evaluations. More importantly, there is no reason to believe that the findings have direct relevance to the situation in England. Greenawalt (1974) sets out in the following succinct passage a number of factors which might lead one to anticipate a different outcome in England. He writes:

> The percentage of 'necessary' confessions is affected by the kinds of crimes committed, the methods of investigation other than interrogation, the willingness of witnesses to testify and the willingness of the police to use certain witnesses, such as informers. A correspondence on these matters cannot be assumed for different areas within one country, let alone different countries. The *Miranda* warning is more thorough than the warnings of the Judges' Rules; and the right of a suspect to counsel is absolute in the United States but not in England. On the other hand the American police probably have more latitude in interrogating suspects who have waived their right to silence than the English police have. (p. 252.)

Although the existing studies strongly suggest, therefore, that the importance of confession evidence has been greatly exaggerated by many commentators, it would be wrong to infer

[11] The value of the study is reduced by the fact that the information in the police files was often inadequate and that the researchers consequently had to rely to some extent upon guesswork: Seeburger and Wettick (1967) at p. 15.

[12] For other discussions of this body of evidence see Pepinsky (1970); Rogge (1972); and Gorecki (1975, 1979).

from the American research that the picture in England is necessarily comparable.

THE SITUATION IN ENGLAND

In England, unlike the United States, there is an almost complete lack of evidence on the significance of confessions in criminal trials,[13] although it might appear from the information already given in chapter 6 that material derived from interrogations is of great importance in English trials. Of particular relevance here is the striking association between confession evidence and conviction, only about 3 per cent of those making written confessions and 9 per cent of those making verbal confessions being acquitted at trial. It would, however, be wrong to infer from this that confession evidence *per se* is vital to the prosecution's case, for it may be that defendants made confessions in those cases in which the prosecution already had an overwhelming body of incriminating material. This latter hypothesis was put forcibly by Sobel (1966) in the following passage:

> experience (as well as common sense) establishes that the overwhelming percentage of confessions are obtained under circumstances where because of other evidence it is futile and pointless for the defendant not to confess. To put it affirmatively most confessions are obtained precisely because the defendant is already 'hooked' by other evidence. (p. 137.)

In order to tease out the actual weight assumed by confessions we therefore had to use other methods of independent assessment. To carry out this kind of qualitative assessment, every thing hinges upon the soundness of the judgment of those responsible for making the evaluations. We have already hinted, in our discussion of the American research, that one's confidence in the studies is diminished by the lack of independence from the prosecution of many of those involved. For our purposes, we decided to use the services of our two assessors, both of whom had had considerable experience of the prosecution process although both, being retired, could be considered quite independent of it. Their work in relation to the pre-trial identification of weak cases, described in chapter 4, strongly suggested that

[13] The only exception concerns a study carried out by Hadden and Wright (1979) into the trials of terrorist offences in Northern Ireland. In these cases, it appeared, most of the trials revolved around the alleged confession of the defendants in question.

they were able to assess the strength of the prosecution's evidence with considerable accuracy. Given their success in that exercise, we asked them to evaluate the importance of the different items of evidence upon which the prosecution was intending to rely in the series of 1,000 cases tried in the Birmingham Crown Court, as described in the previous chapter. To this end, two approaches were adopted: one a subjective evaluation of the importance of any statement made by an accused to the strength of the case as a whole; and the other a comparison between their predictions of the likelihood of a case ending in conviction based upon the whole of the evidence and their predictions (made two years later) based upon the same body of evidence but leaving out of account any statements made by the accused. We consider the outcome of each of these approaches in turn.

THE VIEWS OF THE ASSESSORS

(i) *Subjective evaluation*

This approach was the more straightforward of the two, and in essence involved asking each assessor to give his opinion of the weight to be given to defendants' statements in relation to other evidence presented by the prosecution. This kind of assessment is similar to that adopted in many of the American studies and is subject to the sorts of limitation mentioned earlier. One advantage of this approach was that, since the assessors were operating wholly independently of each other, comparisons could be made between them. Although the opinions of the assessors did not correspond for every case, there was a high level of correspondence in their overall results. In over 60 per cent of cases their views were entirely consistent and serious disagreements occurred in fewer than 10 per cent of all cases. In about half of all cases, statements by accused persons were seen as largely immaterial to the strength of the case and they were of critical importance in less than a third. Table 6 presents the detailed results on this.[14] The findings presented here are broadly in line with those that have emerged from American studies and provide further, if limited, support for the view that,

[14] In Table 6, the figure in which no assessment was made includes fourteen cases in which the assessors knew the outcome at trial because of national publicity that had earlier been given to the cases.

TABLE 6

The views of the assessors on the importance of the accused's statements in the prosecution case as a whole

(a) Birmingham not guilty pleas

	Assessor A	(%)	*Assessor B*	(%)
Accused's statements made all the difference between a strong case and no case	139	29.5	150	31.8
Accused's statements important but not crucial	85	18.1	87	18.5
Accused's statements relatively unimportant—largely immaterial to strength of prosecution case	230	48.8	217	46.1
No statement made by the accused	17	3.6	17	3.6
No information or no assessment conducted	29	–	29	–
	500	100.0	500	100.0

(b) Birmingham guilty pleas

	Assessor A	(%)	*Assessor B*	(%)
Accused's statements made all the difference between a strong case and no case	158	32.4	134	27.5
Accused's statements important but not crucial	98	20.1	144	29.5
Accused's statements relatively unimportant—largely immaterial to strength of prosecution case	213	43.6	191	39.1
No statement made by the accused	19	3.9	19	3.9
No information or no assessment conducted	12	–	12	–
	500	100.0	500	100.0

in a majority of cases, the prosecution does not rest heavily upon the confession of the defendant.

(ii) *Comparative assessment*

This method was more complex, though we think that it is at least as reliable as any alternative method. In the course of conducting our research on juries in Birmingham in 1975 and 1976, we had submitted hundreds of sets of committal papers to our two assessors and asked them, *inter alia*, to give their opinions of the likelihood of each case ending in a conviction or an acquittal. In all cases, the assessors were unaware of the result of the trial and in most cases they were in fact making their assessments even before the trial had started. They were in addition making their assessments wholly independently of each other. We have described in chapter 4 the outcome of one aspect of this exercise—that concerned with the pre-trial identification of weak cases. The success of that exercise suggested to us the possibility of undertaking a similar assessment of the extent to which the case against the defendant in 1,000 Crown Court trials heard in Birmingham hinged upon confession evidence. We found ourselves, quite fortuitiously, well placed to do this for we were able to re-submit to the two assessors the same case papers and to seek their opinion on whether the decision to prosecute would have been justified had written and/or verbal evidence of the defendant been excluded. This exercise enabled comparisons to be made with the assessors' original evaluations which had been made on the basis of the whole of the evidence (including the defendants' statements), and in this way to tease out the weight to be attached to confession evidence in the prosecution's case. Putting it in another way, comparison of the two sets of predictions allowed us to measure the extent to which the case for the prosecution would be weakened by the exclusion of verbal or written statements.[15] Table 7 sets out the results on whether there remained a *prima facie* case[16] when defendants' statements were excluded. Although, as Table 7 shows, there were some differences between the assessors, the overall picture that emerged was remarkably similar.[17] Considered separately, each assessor felt that approximately a fifth of all cases were

[15] Discussion of the procedures adopted, the schedules used as well as the limitations of the exercise itself, is given in Baldwin and McConville (1980) at pp. 8–11, 28–34.

[16] A *prima facie* case is one in which there is sufficient evidence, if uncontradicted, which would justify a reasonable jury in convicting the defendant.

[17] When we compared the predictions of each assessor with his prediction made two years earlier, some anomalous results became apparent. The most peculiar concerned those cases in which an assessor had earlier predicted an acquittal and, on re-examination, had been confident of a conviction even without interrogation evidence. Some apparently anomalous predictions were easily explained since they related to cases in which the only statements were the accused's denials. In such cases, the exclusion of statements would actually have assisted the prosecution and weakened the defence. There remained, however, a group of cases which could not be explained away in these terms and which had to be put down to inconsistency on the part of the assessors. Happily, from the point of view of interpretation, these inconsistent results were rare, occurring in less than 4 per cent of all cases that the assessors examined.

TABLE 7

The views of the assessors on whether the evidence disclosed a *prima facie* case

(*a*) *Birmingham not guilty pleas*

	Assessor A	(%)	*Assessor B*	(%)
No case on the whole of the evidence	7	1.5	35	7.4
No case if verbal statements excluded	38	8.1	38	8.1
No case if written and verbal statements excluded	54	11.4	45	9.6
Still a *prima facie* case after written and verbal statements excluded	372	79.0	353	74.9
No information or no assessment conducted	29	-	29	-
	500	100.0	500	100.0

(*b*) *Birmingham guilty pleas*

	Assessor A	(%)	*Assessor B*	(%)
No case on the whole of the evidence	6	1.2	7	1.4
No case if verbal statements excluded	8	1.6	27	5.6
No case if written and verbal statements excluded	89	18.4	63	13.0
Still a *prima facie* case after written and verbal statements excluded	382	78.8	388	80.0
No information or no assessment conducted	15	-	15	-
	500	100.0	500	100.0

either inherently weak or would be fatally weakened if confession evidence was taken away. If, therefore, the confessions had been excluded, about 20 per cent of all cases would not have survived full committal proceedings or a submission of no case to answer at trial.

These results, however, relate only to the lowest threshold that the prosecution must cross—ensuring that there is sufficient admissible evidence to get the case before a jury. It is equally important to know how many cases surviving this test would be so weakened that an acquittal becomes probable. This would provide a much fuller appreciation of the extent to which the prosecution relies upon confession evidence and of the effects produced by its exclusion. When we compared the results of the two sets of predictions, we found that each assessor, considered independently, thought that about a fifth of all cases would be destroyed by the absence of confession evidence and that a further group (3 per cent in the view of one assessor, 11 per cent in the view of the other) would be undermined to the extent that an acquittal would be the probable outcome. The value of the exercise is considerably enhanced if we ascertain the extent to which the assessors *agreed* that certain cases would be fatally

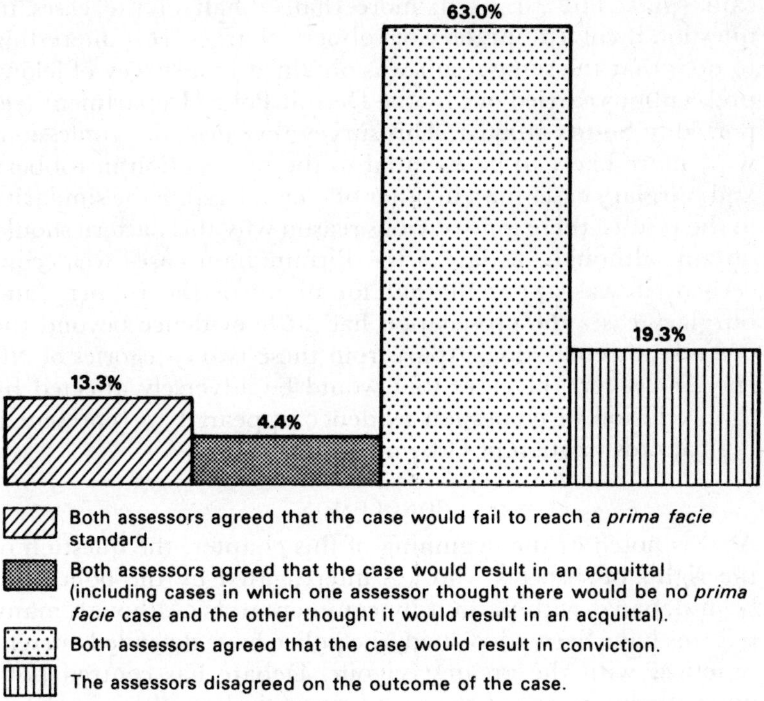

FIGURE 2

The predicted outcome of all cases when confession evidence was not taken into account the extent of agreement between the assessors on individual cases

weakened. We examined the extent to which they were in agreement in individual cases, and we present the results relating to the cases examined in Birmingham in Figure 2.

It is clear from the figure that there was a close correspondence between the assessors on individual cases. They were agreed that about one case in eight either disclosed no sufficient evidence to put the defendant on trial or, without the evidence of confession, would have failed on a submission of no case to answer. They were also agreed that a further group of about 4 per cent would have been so weakened by the removal of confession evidence that an acquittal was the likely outcome. An analysis of the types of case that fell within these categories produced a surprising finding—that the removal of confession evidence would bear disproportionately upon burglary and robbery offences. This pattern was statistically highly significant ($p. < .001$). Indeed, more than a half of the cases in question involved burglary or robbery charges. It is interesting to note that the same result was obtained in a survey of felony prosecutions carried out by the Detroit Police Department (reported in Souris (1966)). This survey revealed that confessions were more likely to be essential to the prosecution in robbery and burglary cases than in other offences. Despite the similarity in the results, there is no obvious reason why this pattern should obtain, although, as far as the Birmingham cases were concerned, it was apparent that for many of the robbery and burglary cases the prosecution had little evidence beyond the defendant's confession. Apart from these two categories of offence, however, the cases that would be adversely affected by the exclusion of confession evidence appeared to represent a typical cross-section of Crown Court business.[18]

CONCLUSION

As was noted at the beginning of this chapter, the question of the rights of suspects who are interrogated by the police has been debated with passion by commentators. Although many reforms have been advocated, the police have defended current practices with the greatest vigour. Debate has centred both upon the adequacy of the protections given to those in police custody and upon the consequences that would follow further checks being placed upon existing police powers. Yet the findings that we have presented in this chapter suggest that the actual evidentiary significance of confessions, viewed in relation to a large number of Crown Court trials, has been greatly overplayed by a good many writers. Confession evidence, it seems, is not in most cases of fundamental importance to the prosecution, and assumes a vital role in only about 20 per cent

[18] The defendants involved were, for instance, in most respects comparable to defendants concerned in other cases. The great majority were seen by the police as petty offenders and few were viewed as professional criminals.

of all cases heard in the Crown Court. This conclusion contrasts strongly with the confident assertions that we quoted earlier on p. 127 and, indeed, with the views often expressed by police officers.

The New Haven researchers compared their own evaluations of the importance of interrogation with those of detectives involved in the individual cases that fell within their sample. The researchers' assessment—that confession evidence was generally not necessary to the prosecution—was amply supported by the opinions of the detectives.[19] But when asked whether interrogation could in general be replaced by other methods of investigation, the vast majority of detectives thought that it could not.[20] Other research carried out in the United States has tended to confirm this finding[21] and in England, Irving (1980) concluded that interrogation is 'regarded by all C.I.D. officers as of central importance to criminal investigation'—a view echoed by the Association of Chief Police Officers (1978) which has asserted that 'if suspects did not confess to crimes whilst being interrogated, many offences would not be detected as there is often no other evidence to show their involvement' (para. 7.4). Insofar as such beliefs are founded upon an assessment of the evidentiary value of confessions in securing a conviction, we would argue on the basis of the findings presented in this chapter that they cannot be supported. There are now a number of empirical studies that suggest that confessions are numerically of slight significance to the outcome of criminal trials, both in England and in the United States. But this is not the end of the story, for the police *do* regard interrogation as an integral part of their work, and it would be naive indeed to assume that the findings of researchers will have much effect upon that. An

[19] Wald *et al.* (1967) at pp. 1591–3. Detectives considered that interrogation was important in 13 cases and unnecessary in 57, and interrogation was considered necessary by the researchers in 10 of the 13 cases.

[20] 71 per cent of detectives felt that interrogation was indispensable, 19 per cent thought it not absolutely necessary but considered alternative methods too costly in terms of time and resources, and only 10 per cent thought that interrogations could be eliminated without any great loss to law enforcement effectiveness (Ibid. at pp. 1591–2).

[21] See, for example, Witt (1973) who, in a similar exercise to Wald *et al.*, asked detectives in Los Angeles whether they believed that interrogation of suspects could possibly be replaced by other methods of criminal investigation. His findings corresponded closely to those of the New Haven research: only 7 per cent thought that interrogation could be eliminated without loss and 65 per cent believed that no alternative methods could remove the need for the interrogation of criminal suspects.

important question, therefore, is why the police perceive interrogation as essential and what consequences flow from this attitude. For some cases, of course, the police might properly attach significance to a confession as, for instance, where there is little or no other evidence of guilt or where the evidence which is available is weak and unsatisfactory. But this can at best be only a partial explanation, for it is now clear that the police attempt to obtain confessions in cases where, as the police know full well, an admission is not needed in evidentiary terms.[22] It would, however, be wrong and foolish to dismiss the views of the police on the grounds that they are generalized, impressionistic, or inconsistent with the sort of quantitative assessments that have been set out in this chapter. The research that we have discussed has been primarily concerned not with the role of interrogation but with the much narrower question of the part confession evidence plays in the case for the prosecution. The simple point is that the existence of a confession may be unrelated to the need for interrogation. In order to discover how important interrogations are in crime detection in general, it is necessary to examine other purposes that may be served by interrogation, and it is with this subject that the following chapter deals.

[22] See, for example, Softley (1980) and Irving (1980).

8

THE COLLATERAL PURPOSES OF INTERROGATION

INTRODUCTION

Police interrogations serve a variety of purposes in addition to that of obtaining a confession. Interrogations may be helpful in obtaining evidence against alleged accomplices, in recovering stolen property, in 'clearing the books' of offences, and in many other ways. But the main justification for the interrogation of suspects by the police is almost invariably discussed in terms of the desirability (if not the necessity) of obtaining a confession from guilty suspects at an early stage. No one has seriously suggested that detectives attempt to obtain confessions at any price, and the research evidence clearly shows that in some cases at least a genuine effort is made to allow the suspect to offer an explanation to exonerate himself.[1] This consideration apart, there can be no doubting the considerable advantages to the police—and indeed to the smooth operation of the whole criminal system—of a confession from a suspect at that stage. For good reasons, detectives simply do not like having to appear in court and they particularly dislike contested trials. It is not merely that the experience may be stressful and profoundly disagreeable for them; it is also likely to be extremely time-consuming.[2] Obtaining a confession from a defendant is viewed by the police as a very useful way of alleviating this inconvenience and, to the extent that defendants who have made confessions to the police only infrequently contest the case in court, the police view is an entirely realistic one. On the other hand, the available research indicates that the police overestimate the advantages of a confession, and that they obtain them primarily in those cases in which the prosecution evidence is already strong. Thus, it is argued, defendants tend to plead guilty be-

[1] This concern was noted in the two observational studies of police interrogations in England by Irving (1980) and Softley (1980).

[2] Laurie (1972) writes that 'it would not be unreasonable to say that every contested case involves a detective in an average of two weeks' extra work' (p. 216).

cause of the strength of the other evidence against them, not because they have made a confession.

But it would be misleading to suggest that police interviews are inexorably directed towards the gaining of a confession, and other purposes have to be considered when assessing the value of interrogations. The main thrust of each encounter between the suspect and the interviewing officer reflects, and is shaped by, the information about the incident or about the suspect that the police already possess when he is first taken into custody. This point can be illustrated simply with reference to a hypothetical case of burglary. If two men are caught by the police in the vicinity of a shop that has recently been broken into, the questioning might at first be directed to establishing whether they were in fact the culprits. If one suspect is found in the building, his interrogation will probably be designed to identify and implicate the accomplice. If both are caught in the act, the police might still wish to obtain a written confession to seal the case and prompt a guilty plea. In each instance, questioning may not be confined to the burglary offence itself but may be concerned with other offences of a similar nature that have occurred in the locality on previous occasions. Some interrogations will be designed to amplify what the police already know, others to clarify what the police merely suspect, and others to produce information about matters of which the police are wholly ignorant. Although the literature and public discussion has properly tended to focus upon the role of interrogations in producing confessions from suspects, there is a body of evidence which provides limited insights into other purposes of interrogation, and it is important to discuss such 'collateral' purposes here.

COLLATERAL PURPOSES OF INTERROGATION

One subsidiary purpose of interrogation, identified by many writers, is to obtain information from the suspect about accomplices. Of the 90 cases observed by Wald *et al.* (1967), 36 involved offences committed by more than one person. In the majority of these cases, the accomplices had been arrested together but in 13 cases the police knew only that another individual was involved. Taking the sample as a whole, the researchers concluded that interrogation was necessary in 12 per cent of cases to identify accomplices, and in almost 18 per cent of cases to provide incriminating evidence against accomplices.[3] In these cases, therefore, the researchers were of the opinion that the police either had no other ways in which they could establish the identity of the accomplice or lacked sufficient independent evidence to convict him. Witt's (1973) analysis also showed that the police were able to use interrogation to obtain evidence to implicate accomplices in only 12 per cent of the cases examined.[4] It is important to bear in mind, however, that both of these studies are limited in value and that they were carried out in the United States. Moreover, the few studies that have been conducted in England have failed to uncover much information on this question. Irving (1980) observed the interrogation of 60 suspects, but none of the suspects was arrested on the basis of evidence supplied by an accomplice and none apparently gave information which implicated others. In the majority of cases, the suspect and the crime had been simultaneously identified, and in most other instances the arrest was based either upon information supplied by witnesses or informants or else upon the suspicious actions of the suspect himself. The other relevant study is that by Softley (1980) but this is less illuminating. In this study, members of the Home Office Research Unit observed the conduct of police interviews with 187 suspects. Softley simply asserts that, of those interrogated, '43 per cent gave information about other persons' (p. 87). There is no analysis of the nature of this information, of its value, whether it related to the commission of offences, whether it concerned known or unknown individuals, or whether it was acted upon by the police. In the absence of details of this kind, it is not possible to make sense of the finding.

Apart from the possibility of obtaining information about accomplices, an interrogation may provide the police with the opportunity to clear up other offences committed by the suspect. In the New Haven study, Wald *et al.* (1967) found that, when detectives questioned suspects about other crimes, only three suspects out of 90 admitted that they had committed further offences. The small number of admissions did, however, result

[3] Wald *et al.* (1967) at pp. 1593–4. Although questioning was deemed necessary, it was not always successful.

[4] Witt (1973) Table 5 at p. 328. No details were given about whether the information in question identified unknown accomplices or whether it implicated known or already apprehended accomplices.

in the clearance of about a dozen previously unsolved crimes. Other American studies have confirmed that the clearance of other crimes may be a useful by-product of interrogation,[5] and, in England, Softley (1980) reports that 17 per cent of suspects, having confessed to the offence under consideration, were 'persuaded to admit other offences' and that the number of offences involved was often 'impressive.'

In addition to the obtaining of a confession (to a particular offence or to others committed at an earlier date) and the identification of accomplices, interrogations can be employed to recover stolen goods, to identify drug suppliers, to remove weapons, and to exonerate innocent suspects. A few empirical studies (e.g. Wald *et al.* (1967); Stephens *et al.* (1972); Witt (1973); Irving (1980); and Softley (1980)) have confirmed that, to a limited extent, interrogations do fulfil purposes of this nature. The police themselves appear to value interrogation as part of their general criminal intelligence network, as a means of finding out more about the suspect's habits and life-style, as a way of keeping themselves abreast of what is happening in their locality, and, in general, as an aid to updating their files and records. But it is possible to overstate the importance of interrogation for these purposes.[6] Some of these purposes are of their nature problematic and unquantifiable. Stephens *et al.* (1972), for example, found that police officers preferred to speak of the value of interrogation in vague terms such as 'filling of information gaps'.[7] The equivalent English studies, carried out by Softley (1980) and by Irving (1980), though at various points advancing claims of a similar nature, have failed to produce much evidence to support them.

[5] See, for example, Seeburger and Wettick (1967); Stephens *et al.* (1972); and Witt (1973).

[6] It is necessary to express a degree of scepticism about some of the research that has been conducted. Much of it has been carried out in the United States and has involved, in the main, small samples of cases. Furthermore, the methods employed have often produced findings that are no more than the subjective opinions of the researchers themselves or the equally subjective claims of the officers questioned.

[7] Stephens *et al.* (1972) write:

> In stating their reasons for regarding interrogation as essential, the officers were conspicuously reluctant to make direct references to the obtaining of confessions. They tended to prefer such ambiguous substitutes as 'the filling of information gaps' or 'the implication of other suspects'. Clearly much of what they said implied the obtaining of incriminating statements, but there was a tendency to explain the purposes of interrogation in terms that de-emphasized the direct confrontation of the arrested person by officers presumably inclined to regard him as guilty. (pp. 421 2.)

THE POLICE ROLE IN THE DISCOVERY AND DETECTION OF CRIME

There is, however, a quite separate body of writing and research—concerned broadly with the meaning and construction of crime rates—which sheds some light on these questions. The primary focus of this literature has been the extent to which the discovery and detection of crime is a result of initiative on the part of the police as opposed to members of the public: whether, to use the terminology of Reiss and Bordua (1967), the police role is a 'proactive' or a 'reactive' one.[8] Bottomley and Coleman (1976), for example, showed, as have several researchers in the United States,[9] that the police play a surprisingly minor role in discovering criminal incidents that later form the substance of official crime reports. In their study, the main discoverers of crime were victims, and the police themselves discovered no more than 13 per cent of all incidents the authors analysed. Three other English studies, conducted by Chatterton (1976), by Mawby (1979), and by Steer (1980) strongly confirm the view of police operations as essentially reactive in nature.

Even when researchers have moved beyond the discovery of crime to the processes of the detection of offenders and conviction at trial, the picture changes little. In his study of policing in Sheffield, Mawby (1979, pp. 109–32) carried out a painstaking analysis of the way that individual crimes are cleared up by the police. Although he found that an extraordinarily high proportion of crimes were cleared up 'indirectly' (following the routine questioning of those already apprehended for other offences), about 60 per cent of all other offences were detected on the basis of evidence given to the police by civilians. The police role in detection was not therefore primarily concerned with determining the identity of offenders or with tracing them; rather it was one of eliciting information from victims, witnesses, and other civilians and, more generally, assembling the prosecution's case for trial. Similarly, in Softley's study of police contacts with criminal suspects, it was apparent that the overwhelming majority of suspects had been seen committing the act, appre-

[8] The police role is characterized as 'reactive' where members of the public are responsible for bringing matters to the attention of the police. The reference to policing as 'proactive' relates to police officers acting upon their own initiative.

[9] See particularly Sellin and Wolfgang (1964); Black (1970, 1971); Greenwood *et al.* (1977); and Vera Institute (1977).

hended near the scene of the crime, identified by witnesses or victims, found in possession of stolen goods, or been seen in the company of persons suspected of committing offences. Of the 218 suspects in question, only three had been identified by forensic or other physical evidence found at the scene. Finally, mention should be made of Zander's (1979) research, which is the only study based upon a court, not a police, sample. He examined the files relating to 150 cases tried at the Old Bailey in 1972. Of the 133 cases for which information was available, he found that the police had in the majority of instances discovered the identity of the defendant from information supplied by the victims or other members of the public. In over 80 per cent of cases, it was clear that the police knew the name of the person responsible from the outset or had arrested one or more defendants at or near the scene of the crime.

These studies demonstrate that the police role in the actual discovery and detection of crime is a comparatively minor one. In most cases which are eventually cleared up, the identity of the offender is known at the outset, and the task of the police is confined to tracing and apprehending the individual identified and collecting the evidence against him.[10] In the United States, for example, Greenwood *et al.* (1977) concluded from a study of cleared serious crime in several police departments that about 80 per cent of cases were cleared by on-the-scene arrests or the initial identification of the offender, and that most of the remainder were solved without recourse to any special investigative techniques.[11] The studies bear out one American writer's stark contention that 'the police are able to solve a crime if someone tells them who committed it; if no one tells them, it is unlikely they will make an arrest' (Silberman (1978) p. 218[12]).

[10] One main reason for this is that the complainant and the offender are often well known to each other. This applies particularly in offences involving violence against the person. See, for instance, Wolfgang (1958); McClintock (1963); and Vera Institute (1977).

[11] The findings are summarized in Greenwood *et al.* (1977) at pp. 226–7 where there is also a useful discussion of the comparable results of other researchers.

[12] Silberman also argues that 'when policemen catch an offender on their own, it is more likely to be the result of chance, or the criminal's incompetence than of their own investigative efforts' (p. 204). A similar point is made by Greenwood *et al.* (1977) who argue that, with the possible exception of homicide, 'if investigators only performed the obvious and routine tasks needed to clear the "easy" cases, they would solve the vast majority of crimes that now get cleared. All their efforts in relation to other cases have a very marginal effect on the number of crimes cleared'. (p. 141.)

A somewhat different picture emerges when minor offences are considered. Mawby (1979), for instance, in an examination of non-indictable offences committed in Sheffield, found that the police role was much more pronounced than it was in relation to more serious indictable offences. Bottomley (1979) also argues that police operations are of a more 'proactive' nature in minor offences.[13] He writes:

> It must be stressed ... that the roles of the police and the public are reversed in certain offences where there may be no specific victim or where the law is enforced almost entirely on the initiative and at the discretion of the police—ranging from motoring offences and breaches of public order, to prostitution, drug-taking and pornography (p. 28).

Nevertheless, as far as serious criminal offences are concerned, the available empirical evidence overwhelmingly shows the police as an essentially reactive organization. It is clear that most serious offences are discovered and cleared up without much investigative effort on the part of the police. Victims and members of the public witnessing criminal incidents supply information which is crucial in solving most crimes, and few infractions are cleared by special investigative methods or on the basis of sophisticated forensic techniques. All this suggests that the role of interrogation itself in the detection and solution of crime is of little overall importance. But it must be emphasized that some of the studies have dealt with small samples of cases, and many of them have been primarily concerned with other issues, throwing up information on interrogation only as a by-product of the main focus of the research.

We decided, therefore, to use the material that had been made available to us by the Crown Court authorities in Birmingham to examine whether interrogation of defendants produced material other than confessions which assisted police investigations. The description of each case in the committal papers is generally very detailed and includes information on the time and place of the alleged offence, how the police come to learn of its existence, the evidence of victims and witnesses, details of the time and place of the defendant's arrest, and a record of any interrogation carried out. For most cases, a reader of the committal papers can readily build up a picture of the

[13] Support for this view comes from other sources both in England and the United States: see particularly Foote (1956); Skolnick (1966); Bittner (1967); Young (1972); Chatterton (1976); and Steer (1980).

police investigation, and only rarely are gaps apparent and questions left unanswered. Using this information, we attempted to find out how each offence had come to the notice of the police in the first place and how the police came to apprehend a particular defendant. Were the police themselves, for example, the prime movers, having witnessed the incident or having been called to the scene before the perpetrator could make good his escape? What information were the police given by victims and witnesses, and was it specific enough to lead them directly to a particular suspect? Did the police, in the absence of leads from witnesses, use forensic evidence to identify the defendant? Where only one of several involved was arrested, did interrogation serve to identify accomplices?

While examining these and similar questions generally presented no difficulty, it is necessary to spell out some of the limitations of the exercise. Sometimes the account contained in the prosecution's case does not reveal the whole course of the investigation, particularly those parts of it which proved unproductive. Moreover, the record of the interview with the defendant that is contained in many committal papers is obviously a highly condensed and selective rendering of events. This 'construction of reality' by the police may be, if only unconsciously, at variance with what was actually said and what actually occurred and, where this happens, it is impossible for the researcher (and, we would argue, for the courts as well) to detect it. Again, it is likely that in some instances part of an interrogation might take on the character of an off-the-record conversation and contain information useful to the police but not for wider consumption. Whilst such instances are believed to be infrequent, no doubt they do occur and are not revealed in the papers. These limitations must be borne in mind in the following discussion.

In line with what other researchers have found, our detailed examination of committal papers revealed that the apprehension of most defendants rested heavily upon the evidence of victims or other civilian witnesses, that forensic evidence was rarely important, and that the police were directly responsible for the detection of the defendant in only a minority of all cases. Table 8 (in which account has been taken of the different sample fractions as between not guilty and guilty pleas) presents the broad findings on these questions.

TABLE 8

The source of evidence linking the defendant to the alleged offence for all Birmingham cases

	Not guilty pleas	(%)	*Guilty Pleas*	(%)	*Overall* (%)
Police caught defendant in act	75	15.5	89	18.0	17.5
Victim or other civilian caught defendant in act	40	8.2	27	5.4	6.0
Police caught defendant in possession of stolen goods or in other suspicious circumstances	65	13.4	88	17.8	16.9
Victim or witness named or otherwise directly identified defendant	235	48.5	193	39.0	40.9
Defendant identified through interrogation of alleged accomplice	16	3.3	43	8.7	7.6
Defendant apprehended by other means	54	11.1	55	11.1	11.1
No information	15	-	5	-	-
	500	100.0	500	100.0	100.0

As one would expect, the pattern set out in the Table differed markedly according to the types of offence involved. Where the police said that they had actually witnessed the commission of the act, the charges in question related mainly to motoring offences, assaults on the police, and incidents (such as affray or a burglary) to which the police had been summoned by members of the public whilst the offence was still in progress. Most cases in the second category (defendants who were caught in the act by victims or other civilians) involved shoplifting offences, though a few were cases of assault or robbery where the victim or passers-by had apprehended the defendant. Here, the police were called to the scene, heard the complaint, and then facilitated, or took upon themselves, the prosecution of the person apprehended. The third group comprised for the most part cases in which the police had stopped the defendant on suspicion and found stolen goods or drugs in his possession, or else they were cases in which the police, having been called to an incident, caught the defendant running away from the scene without seeing him commit the alleged offence. The largest group involved cases in which the victims or witnesses supplied direct evidence against the defendant and our classification was restricted to cases in which the defendant was clearly identified, as by name, nickname, or address. Violent offences (particularly those occurring in a domestic setting), and sexual offences predominated in this group. Indeed, victims or witnesses supplied the police at the outset with direct information about the defendant in 66 per cent of all cases of violence, whereas the equivalent figure for burglary offences was only 15 per cent.[14] The next category concerns cases in which the interrogation of one defendant produced information which led to the apprehension of an alleged accomplice. In many of these cases, the police already had some information about the others involved, as where the victim or witnesses gave a description of the perpetrators, and it is likely that in some cases the police could have picked up the accomplices without interrogating the individual first apprehended. Nevertheless, we can say that, at the least, the interrogation produced material which implicated the accomplice in all these cases and that, for some, the accomplice would otherwise have remained at large. The final category is a miscellaneous group, including arrests based upon tip-offs, undisclosed sources ('acting upon information received'), forensic evidence, arrests based upon the investigative work of enforcement agencies other than the police, and evidence supplied by victims or witnesses which, though not directly identifying the defendant, assisted the police in making the ultimate arrest.

Table 8 provides some fascinating material concerning the police role in the discovery and detection of crime, and it presents a view of police operations which is markedly at variance with the popular image. There are two points which emerge from this analysis to which we wish to draw particular attention. The first is that in about a half of those serious offences which led to prosecution in the Crown Court, victims and civilian witnesses played a crucial role in supplying direct evidence against the individual finally charged. In the present samples,

[14] Similar proportions have been unearthed by researchers in the United States: see particularly Vera Institute (1977) and Silberman (1978) at pp. 218–23. Cases in which victims and offenders are known to each other are, of course, greatly overrepresented in court. Thus, for instance, researchers of the Vera Institute found that, although only about 7 per cent of victims of robbery offences in New York City knew their assailants, nevertheless such cases represented no less than 36 per cent of all robbery arrests. Similar patterns obtained for other types of property offence. On this, see Vera Institute (1977) at pp. 3–19.

victims alone supplied such evidence in 26 per cent of all cases.[15] Secondly, claims that interrogation plays a major role in identifying alleged accomplices have been greatly exaggerated. In only 7.6 per cent of all cases within the present sample did the interrogation of a defendant produce such information. Nor did it appear that interrogation was particularly productive in other ways. There was little evidence, for example, that much effort was spent in using interrogation to trace stolen goods. The question did not arise in 49 per cent of property offences because the defendant had been caught in the act of taking, or found in possession of the stolen goods, or had been apprehended before any property was taken. In most other cases, particularly those involving small amounts of cash or items already disposed of, there was obviously no point in wasting time trying to trace the items in question.

There is, however, one purpose served by interrogation which appears to be much more productive than the others that we have discussed. This concerns the practice of ascertaining from suspects whether they have been involved in other criminal activity for which they have not been charged. The incentive for the suspect to do so is quite high since he can make a clean breast of any earlier uncharged criminal activity (and so avoid the risk of subsequent prosecution), and will probably be able to have the offences 'taken into consideration' by the court which will not as a rule involve any great accretion to his sentence. This practice, which is apparently pursued with varying degrees of enthusiasm by different police forces,[16] has little relevance to those defendants who plead not guilty at trial.[17] However, 106 of the defendants who pleaded guilty (21 per cent) asked for a total of 610 other offences to be taken into consideration when they appeared in the Crown Court. This

[15] Other studies carried out in England have produced even higher proportions. In Bottomley and Coleman's study (1976) of indictable offences reported to the police, for example, victims initiated the crime complaint in 45 per cent of cases, and Zander (1979) found that the police first heard of the offence from the victim in 43 per cent of cases.

[16] Less enthusiasm for the practice was shown by the West Midlands Police Force than appears to be shown by certain other forces. On this, see McClintock and Avison (1968) at pp. 113-16; Baldwin and Bottoms (1976) at p. 53; and Mawby (1979) at pp. 109-10.

[17] It is technically possible for defendants who plead not guilty to have other offences taken into consideration if convicted. Within the present sample of 500 contested cases, there were only four defendants who asked for offences to be taken into consideration by the court.

may seem at first glance an impressive return for interviewing the defendants concerned, even though we know little about the nature of the offences involved,[18] and it is possible to discuss the matter only speculatively. There is, however, more than a suggestion from some writers that the procedure is used by some police forces primarily to raise detection rates rather than to ensure that justice is done.[19] Little has been written about the topic but the available research suggests that the procedures commonly adopted are unregulated and haphazard and that, despite the strictures of the Courts,[20] much of the prosecution's work in this regard is casual, if not sloppy.[21] Whitaker (1964), for example, notes that: 'Not all police officers are as particular as others when they attribute "crimes to be taken into consideration" to the correct defendant: some have been known to agree to put in a good word in return for help in clearing up their books.' (p. 142.)

There are, of course, considerable incentives held out to all defendants by the judicial system to induce compliance, if not co-operation. Assisting the police in this way is one obvious manifestation on the defendant's part of a wish to be co-operative.[22]

In one sense, it can be argued that no one suffers from the

[18] The information on offences taken into consideration that was available to us was not sufficiently detailed to allow further analysis. We did not know, for example, whether the offences admitted were ones not previously recorded or whether the police already had a record of their commission.

[19] On this, see particularly McClintock and Avison (1968); Lambert (1970) at pp. 42–3; White *et al.* (1970); Baldwin and Bottoms (1976); Bottomley and Coleman (1976); Mawby (1979); and Steer (1980).

[20] These are briefly summarized by Thomas (1979) at pp. 374–5.

[21] There is evidence that some defendants have asked for offences to be taken into consideration that they could not possibly have committed. In the case of *Forbes*, (1968) 52 Cr. App. R. 585, for example, the defendant asked for 145 offences to be taken into consideration, at least 88 of which he had not committed. Cavenagh (1967) notes that younger offenders are particularly susceptible to pressure on the part of police officers. Writing about children in remand homes, she notes that

> an appreciable number do not understand the significance of offences taken into consideration . . . some children do have the feeling that they are pressed by the police to admit offences which they have not always committed, and on other occasions they have not understood what the offence was supposed to be. There is always a risk with a child that he may not pay enough attention to exactly what the alleged offences are but may admit them more in a spirit of co-operation than with a proper understanding of what he is doing. (p. 218.)

[22] On this, see particularly, Skolnick (1966) pp. 174–86; Laurie (1972) pp. 215–19; Bottoms and McClean (1976); and Baldwin and McConville (1977a).

casual approach adopted in dealing with these offences. The defendant is said to benefit, because he can make a clean breast of his earlier misdeeds, without a corresponding penalty being imposed, and avoid the risk of subsequent re-arrest and prosecution; the police can clear their books and maintain higher rates of detection than would otherwise be the case; and the courts can deal expeditiously with long lists of criminal infractions at one sitting.[23] Though this process might be viewed as operating to the detriment of the wider community since offenders are not receiving their just deserts, even this point can be overstated because it is doubtful whether the prosecution could produce sufficient evidence in court to secure a conviction in the case of all offences taken into consideration.[24] But it is at this point that the argument runs out of steam, and it becomes apparent that the benefits to which these practices supposedly give rise are simply not sufficient to outweigh the costs which they inevitably incur. For the procedures do not square with even minimal requirements of 'due process' of law. What we see instead is an extreme demonstration of Herbert Packer's (1968) Crime Control Model, where the routine processing of cases assumes ascendancy over the safeguarding of individual rights. Indeed, we would argue that current procedures designed to gain admissions to other offences from defendants while they are in police custody, far from providing a justification for police interrogation, merely serve to reinforce the concern that has been expressed in many quarters about the lack of safeguards at that stage to protect the rights of innocent suspects.

CONCLUDING COMMENTS

We have argued in this chapter that many of the collateral benefits assumed to be gained from interviewing suspects while in police custody are in important respects illusory. Our own examination of the available evidence suggests that the principal benefit deriving from police interrogation is the alleged confession of the accused, but even the value of this can be easily exaggerated. Our research showed that such confessions assumed a vital significance in only about 20 per cent of all cases,

[23] An editorial in the *Justice of the Peace* (vol. 142 (1978) at p. 592) referred disapprovingly to a practice that had been adopted in some busy courts of putting large numbers of offences to be taken into consideration *en bloc*. This, it was argued, might lead to the sentence being quashed on appeal.

[24] For a good discussion on this point, see White *et al.* (1970).

and there is a good deal of other evidence available which demonstrates the relatively minor role played by interrogation in the discovery and clearance of serious criminal offences. We also found that the importance of collateral products of interrogation was slight. Some indication of the minor role played by interrogation is provided in the Home Office observational study in which Softley (1980) noted that in only 8 per cent of cases would the police actually have dropped the case had the suspect refused to answer questions. Softley concluded from this that, though increased curbs on police powers to question persons in custody would tend to increase the numbers of offenders who escape conviction and reduce the detection rate, these effects 'would not necessarily be dramatic in terms of rates' (p. 94). The combined effect of all the studies on reported as well as detected offences, whether based upon police files, case papers, or observational exercises, is that, in relation to indictable crime, the police are in essence a reactive organization and that interrogation is in fact a relatively unimportant part of the total law enforcement picture.

But whatever conclusion one may draw about the evidentiary value of confessions, it can be argued that it is the *effect* that a confession has upon the defendant concerned and upon his lawyer that is of much greater import. It is a sociological truism that what people believe to be real is real in its consequences, and the wisdom of this aphorism is strikingly demonstrated in relation to confession evidence. Confessions are notoriously difficult to retract, and the perceived futility of future denials may induce in defendants a fatalistic and resigned outlook, the culmination of which may be a guilty plea.[25] As we discussed earlier, the great majority of defendants making full confessions at the police station pleaded guilty, though about a quarter of those who had made written confessions and who contested their cases were eventually acquitted. Legal advisers tend to view any attempt to rebut an earlier confession as hopeless and may, without much effort, convince the defendant of the prudence of a guilty plea.

This emphasis upon the perceptions of defendants and their lawyers can, however, provide no more than a partial explanation of the importance placed by police officers upon the

[25] We discuss this proposition at some length in Baldwin and McConville (1977a).

interrogation of suspects. There are other psychological and sociological factors that have to be considered. For instance, it is clear that a great many activities which eventually become the subject of criminal charges are not susceptible of easy classification—the defendant may or may not himself have committed the act in question; his state of mind, if he did commit it, may be difficult to ascertain; and the victim or others may have contributed to or even precipitated the final deed. These, and a range of other possibilities, may create unsettling doubts in the minds of investigating officers, doubts which a confession can erase.[26] Furthermore, as Pepinsky (1970) argues, the police may use interrogation as a means both of creating and of reinforcing society's norms. The function of the police is designed to uphold norms which are openly dignified by the whole apparatus of the legal machinery and, in particular, by the trial itself.[27] A confession makes the suspect reveal the illegal nature of his own conduct, confirming the image the police have of him and setting himself apart from the police themselves and from the general public.[28] From this perspective, Pepinsky concludes that

> the police generally are more strongly motivated by their desire to develop and to maintain a stable identity as individuals and as a group than by a fear of harm to society at large. The obtaining of confessions specifically and the interrogation process generally serve to create and to stabilize this identity by establishing the police as followers and upholders of societal norms. In fact, in this process the police define who does and who does not live up to the norms and by this act seek to define the norms themselves. (p. 288.)

[26] This is seen even more forcefully where the confession leads to a guilty plea, as Laurie (1972) notes in the following passage:

> The detective's *amour-propre* is involved. A guilty plea recognises the rightness of his case and the soundness of his judgment . . . The detective is as much a prisoner of the judicial system as the man he arrests. A guilty plea unties his hands and helps create a good relationship between them. As well as saving him a great deal of physical work, the guilty plea relieves him of a lot of worry and thought. (pp. 218–19.)

[27] As Pepinsky notes, building on the work of Garfinkel (1956), the extraction of a confession may be an important factor in producing a successful status-degradation ceremony in court. Also of relevance here is Carlen (1976) who adopts the same perspective in her analysis of trials in the lower courts in England.

[28] The French sociologist, Emile Durkheim (1933), identified the functions performed by crime (and other forms of deviance) in drawing the community together in a common posture of outrage and indignation. See the excellent illustration of this by Erikson (1966).

A number of important consequences result from this police perception of the centrality of interrogations. First, as we have seen in chapter 5, the police choose in the overwhelming majority of indictable offences to proceed by way of arrest rather than by way of information and summons. Arrest, and sometimes less than arrest,[29] allows the police to take the suspect to their own territory and sets the interrogation in motion. Secondly, the importance the police attach to the interrogation makes it essential for them to conduct their business in private. Outsiders wishing to view interrogations are accordingly rebuffed and, even when it would be impolitic for the police to refuse, they may still successfully control the conditions under which the outsider can operate.[30] Thirdly, the police might be expected to show scant regard for the rights of suspects when these might impede them in gaining a confession. This expectation is indeed amply confirmed by research. In the United States, Wald *et al.* (1967) found that, even with observers present, the detectives 'cannot be trusted to give warnings [of suspects' rights] consistently and conscientiously' (p. 1614) and Medalie *et al.* (1968) reached similar conclusions. In England, there is a considerable body of legal and social scientific research which demonstrates that the safeguards provided for suspects in the Judges' Rules are very often flouted. Somewhat surprisingly, the most revealing study on this is that carried out by researchers of the Home Office Research Unit (Ditchfield (1979); Softley (1980))—research which is often assumed to demonstrate the basic fairness and moderation of current interrogation practices. The presence of Home Office observers during police interrogation might be thought (to put it at its lowest) to create optimum conditions for strict compliance with the Judges' Rules, and Ditchfield's report acknowledges that some observers formed the impression that certain officers 'might have made a particular effort to observe the formalities in their

[29] There appears to be an increasing number of cases in which the police detain suspects for questioning without arresting them and blandly announce that the suspect is 'helping them with their enquiries'.

[30] When the Royal Commission on Criminal Procedure asked the Home Office to conduct an observational study of police interrogations, the research that followed did not cover the interrogation of persons suspected of having committed serious crimes. The reason given for this omission was that some senior police officers had said that 'they would not wish independent observers to be present at such interrogations not out of concern over possible police improprieties, but out of regard for the particularly sensitive nature of the offences' (Softley (1980) p. 58).

presence' (p. 38). Nevertheless, in Softley's final report it is apparent that the police 'sometimes omitted to caution suspects when they questioned them' (p. 94), and that in several cases the way in which the caution was delivered or the manner of its phrasing 'seemed to present the right to silence as an option which the suspect was not seriously expected to entertain' (p. 74). Other researchers have shown that a more flagrant disregard of suspects' rights has occurred in relation to access to legal advice. In England, suspects have under the Judges' Rules a general right to communicate and to consult privately with a solicitor, provided that no unreasonable delay or hindrance is caused to the processes of investigation or the administration of justice by their doing so. The police are required to inform the suspect of this right orally and by notices.[31] Our own study in Birmingham (Baldwin and McConville (1979d)), like the earlier study by Zander (1972), showed that in practice few suspects are allowed to consult a lawyer before or during interrogation, and that the controlling provisions are easily evaded by the police. Softley has argued that these studies take no account of the possibility that allowing access to a solicitor might have hindered enquiries. But Softley (1980) appears not to have appreciated the significance of his own findings which, far from contradicting the earlier studies, strongly reinforce them. In his study, solicitors were present in only 2 of 168 interrogations, and in 141 (84 per cent) the subject of a solicitor was not even raised despite the provision in Administrative Direction 7(b) that persons in custody should be informed orally of the rights and facilities available to them. When it is recalled that Softley's study was concerned almost exclusively with less serious offences (serious offences having been specifically excluded at the request of the police), and that, as the police themselves conceded to the researchers, there was in a majority of cases sufficient evidence prior to interrogation to proceed and in very few cases would the enquiry have been dropped had the suspect refused to answer any questions, the inconsistencies in Softley's argument become apparent. For, in most of the cases in question, the qualification to the right of access to a solicitor (i.e. that this might hinder the conduct of the investigation) manifestly did

[31] The principles and duties involved are set out in the Judges' Rules of 1964 and the accompanying Administrative Directions, and in section 62 of the Criminal Law Act, 1977.

not apply. All these factors strongly imply that the police were being observed under unduly favourable conditions, yet even under these conditions they commonly disregarded the rights of suspects. Softley's study can be seen, therefore, to reinforce the picture presented by earlier research, and to demonstrate that the attachment the police have to interrogation will lead them to violate the rights of persons in custody, even where the enforcement of those rights would not thwart investigations.[32] Fourthly, the subjective reliance upon interrogation and confession, the desire to lay the foundations for a guilty plea, and the wish to save time and avoid administrative complications can produce, as Greenawalt (1974) points out, 'a tendency to overbear suspects rather than establish guilt by independent means' (p. 265). This goes beyond the mere denial of rights (though this is surely in itself serious enough), and can include the offer of bargains and inducements, subterfuge, threats, and other excesses.[33] Softley himself found that some suspects had been given 'more encouragement to make verbal or written confessions than the strict criteria of voluntariness allow' (p. 94) and that threats (particularly of detention for a long period) were employed where this was felt useful or necessary.

It is clear from the foregoing that any new restrictions placed upon the power of police officers to question persons in custody would have some bearing upon the detection, conviction, and clearance rates, but that it would not be very great. For the purposes of criminal justice, however, the actual evidentiary importance of interrogation may be much less significant than the subjective evaluation of it by police officers and others. Police officers attach considerable weight to the products of interrogation, and this commitment in turn has a major impact upon the way in which they carry out their day-to-day business. When a suspect is in police custody, the police appear to behave as if they were a 'proactive' organization, and their attitude appears to be unaffected by the relatively meagre fruits that interrogations bear. Whether these fruits have to be treated with caution on other grounds is a question to which we turn in the following chapter.

[32] In some cases it appears that the police are actually ignorant of the suspect's rights: see Fisher (1977), and Thomas and Smith (1978).

[33] For discussion of these points see Dell (1971); Laurie (1972); Herberling (1973); and Baldwin and McConville (1977a).

9

VERIFYING CONFESSION EVIDENCE

INTRODUCTION

We noted in chapter 6 the close relationship between the existence of a confession and the eventual conviction of defendants at trial. The chances of obtaining an acquittal where there is a confession are slender indeed. To repeat the proportions: we found that only about one defendant out of every thirty-five who had made a written confession to the police was acquitted at trial, and only about one in ten who had made a verbal confession. In this chapter we argue that these findings make it imperative that evidence of this kind be collected under conditions that make reliance upon it much safer than at present. The existing system in England is little concerned with establishing such conditions, and instead puts trust in the integrity of police officers and in the sharpness of their memories in reporting accurately what a defendant has said. The safeguards provided at trial, where the accused can complain about such evidence, are in our judgment unrealistic and at best provide what Lord Devlin (1979b) has called 'a hit-or-miss procedure'. The other protections, enshrined in the Judges' Rules, are similarly ineffective. They do not have the force of law, they have been emasculated by the interpretations placed upon them by the courts,[1] and, as a considerable body of research evidence demonstrates, police officers during interrogation are able to disregard them if they choose.[2]

[1] See, for example, *Elliot* [1977] Crim. L. R. 551 and *Lemsatef* [1977] 2 All E.R. 835. In *Stepehen King* [1980] Crim. L. R. 40, the Court of Appeal considered the meaning of paragraph 7 of the Administrative Directions appended to the Judges' Rules. They held that, the word 'allow' in sub-paragraph (a) ('A person in custody should be allowed to speak on the telephone to his solicitor ...') presupposes an initial request and, in the absence of the suspect first raising the matter, questioning may proceed without the police informing him of this 'right'. Sub-paragraph (b), however, provides that suspects 'should ... be informed orally of the rights and facilities available to them ...'. The Court of Appeal dealt with this by saying that 7(b) does not specify when the obligation to inform the prisoner of his right arises, and this may therefore be delayed until after questioning. This line of argument bankrupts comment.

[2] See, particularly, Laurie (1972); Dell (1971); Zander (1972); Bottoms and McClean (1976); Baldwin and McConville (1977a, 1979d); Cox *et al.* (1977); Thomas and Smith (1978); and Smith (1979).

It is now clear that confessions have to be viewed with considerable circumspection. Despite the acute difficulties in establishing innocence in cases in which the accused has made a confession to the police, a disquieting number of such instances have been recorded in recent years. Brandon and Davies (1973), for example, in a study restricted to known cases of wrongful imprisonment, discovered that confessions and statements alleged to have been made by the accused were one of the most common causes of wrongful imprisonment. Moreover, they found that eight of twenty-two defendants given free pardons had actually pleaded guilty.[3] Other evidence of this kind is scattered throughout the literature.[4] Commenting upon the problem of false confessions, Williams (1979) has written:

> To the ordinary person it must seem baffling why a man or woman, apparently of sound mind and understanding, should, when under suspicion of a serious crime, make to the police a full and circumstantial yet false confession of the crime. Occasionally there may be understandable motives, as to shield a lover, but in other cases there seem on the surface to be none. The reason may sometimes be found in the very efficiency of the police methods of obtaining confessions. There are perhaps persons of such mentality and temperament that in order to end an atmosphere of suspicion and hostility they will say and sign anything that seems to produce for the moment a more favourable feeling. (p. 8.)

The available research, drawn primarily from the field of psychology, lends weight to this conclusion.[5]

There will no doubt always be instances in which innocent people for no obvious reason seek to confess to crimes. On occasions, particularly where notorious offences are involved, the police are put to considerable trouble by individuals claiming responsibility for incidents with which they have no connection. And sometimes, despite the thoroughness of the investigation, innocent volunteers of this kind succeed in getting the police to believe them. But our concern in this chapter is not with such cases. It is that the way in which interrogations are carried out and the ineffectiveness of the rules which exist to

[3] See Brandon and Davies (1973) at pp. 47–65.

[4] See, for example, Borchard (1970); Cox (1975) at pp. 171–92; and Price and Caplan (1977).

[5] See particularly Sargant (1957); Reik (1959); Deeley (1971); and the literature review of Irving and Hilgendorf (1980).

regulate police practices provide sound reasons for viewing confession evidence in general with some suspicion.

THE PROBLEMS INVOLVED

The first problem relates to the manner in which statements, and reports of statements, are compiled. Written statements, as we have seen, are rarely in the defendant's own handwriting and, though he may sign them, do not always faithfully record the way in which they were made. The interrogating officer does the writing but the words used will often represent a collaborative effort between the police and the suspect, and in some cases will be the work of the police alone. As Lord Devlin (1960) puts it:

> statements have sometimes been put in evidence which have been said to be the prisoner's own unaided work as taken down by the police officer and in which the prisoner has recounted in the stately language of the police station (where, for example, people never eat but partake of refreshment and never quarrel but indulge in altercations) the tale of his misdeeds. (p. 39.)

Evidence of this kind of intervention is to be found in the observational studies of police interrogations recently conducted by English researchers. Softley (1980), for example, found that, in the vast majority of cases in which there was a written statement, the police had given some assistance in its preparation. In most cases, this assistance was of a neutral character, relating to matters such as spelling and relevance, but in about 14 per cent of cases the police role was 'much more active', including instances in which the words were entirely those of the police. Moreover, statements are usually set out as if they were a straightforward narrative, thereby disguising the true manner in which they are elicited. For the obvious point is that the interchange between police and suspect is one of question and answer, and the answers are often nothing more than a simple acceptance or non-acceptance of material contained in a leading question.[6] None of this appears in the final statement. These difficulties are compounded where the suspect has not made a written statement but is reported by

[6] Statements taken in such circumstances are reported in Irving (1980).

the police as having made only verbal replies to their questions. After the interrogation is finished, the police will prepare an account of what was said. In constructing this account, the interviewing officers are allowed to collaborate with each other and may draw upon any notes taken at the interrogation.[7] The police rarely take a verbatim record during an interview,[8] and the final record is at best an attenuated version of what was said, coloured, and distorted by the frailties of human memory. The end product is an account that, though perhaps containing inaccuracies and misunderstandings,[9] will nevertheless be virtually unchallengeable in a court of law.

A second difficulty concerns the period and character of the questioning involved. Though interrogations are usually concluded within a relatively short period of time, many involve detention for long periods, and in some the questioning may be prolonged or take place at night or at other stressful times. Generally speaking, the courts do not regard confessions obtained in such circumstances as involuntary and accordingly admit them in evidence at trial.[10] The manner in which the interrogation is carried out is also very important. Questioning may be directed towards placing the suspect under stress, and this in turn may produce mental deterioration and increased suggestibility. The suspect may face persistent and unremitting accusation in which incriminating evidence, if it exists, is emphasized and bluff is used where it does not. The authority and control of the police is constantly at the forefront of the encounter, and this may be reinforced by returning the suspect to the cells for temporary periods of confinement. The use of such tactics is much more highly developed in the United States,[11] where the courts have been prepared to recognize (as courts in England have refused to do) that, no matter how interrogations are conducted by the police, the setting remains 'inherently coercive', and that the suspect in this

[7] *R.* v. *Bass* [1953] 1 Q.B. 680; see the critical comment of Cooke (1954).

[8] In none of the interrogations observed by Irving (1980) was a verbatim note taken.

[9] On the question of misunderstanding, see Brandon and Davies (1973) at p. 61. For attempts to test the trustworthiness of confessions by linguistic analysis, see Svartvik (1968) and Niblett and Boreham (1976).

[10] See, for instance, *R.* v. *Prager* [1972] 1 All E.R. 1114; Cross (1979) at p. 544; and Williams (1979) at p. 10.

[11] See, for example, Inbau and Reid (1967); Griffiths and Ayres (1967); O'Hara (1970); Van Meter (1973); Morris (1980); and Irving and Hilgendorf (1980).

situation is likely to be at a very considerable disadvantage.[12] For many suspects, indeed, the experience is likely to be a thoroughly frightening one. In England (even with a Home Office observer present), Softley (1980) found that, although the police never resorted to the use or threat of physical violence, they frequently applied what amounted to psychological pressure on the suspect, and Irving (1980) reported that the available repertoire of tactics described in the psychological literature was widely used by police officers. It is at least arguable, therefore, that, given the secrecy which surrounds interrogations, the reliability of any confession produced by such tactics may be called into question.

But the major problem is the extent to which it is safe to rely upon 'verbals'—oral statements said to have been made by suspects, the only evidence for which is the testimony of police officers. It has been alleged that the police sometimes 'fit up' innocent suspects and, more frequently, that certain officers, being satisfied that a defendant is guilty, falsely bolster the evidence to support this view. As Morton (1975) puts it:

> any experienced [solicitor] will tell you that the police off duty and perhaps off guard—will admit to 'gilding the lily' where they *know* the defendant is guilty. What makes life more worrying is that a number of officers will tell you they have never arrested anyone whom they have not *known* to be guilty. (p. 830.)

This is, of course, a serious charge, yet perhaps the most surprising point that one can make about it is that its accuracy is now taken for granted by most commentators. The Royal Commission on the Police (1962), for example, referred to

> a body of evidence, too substantial to disregard, which in effect accused the police of stooping to the use of undesirable means of obtaining statements and of occasionally giving perjured evidence in a court of law. Thus the Law Society suggested that the police sometimes use guile, and offer inducements, in order to obtain confessions, in the belief that irregular means of securing the conviction of a person whom they believe to be guilty are justifiable in the public interest, and that occasionally police officers colour, exaggerate, or even fabricate the evidence against an accused person. (para. 369.)

[12] See, particularly, *Miranda* v. *Arizona*, 386 U.S. 436 (1966). *Miranda* and other important cases which have had a bearing upon the conduct of police interrogations in the United States are discussed in Milner (1971) at pp. 13–47.

In a similar vein, the General Council of the Bar (1973), commenting upon the proposals of the Criminal Law Revision Committee (1972) to abolish the suspect's right to silence, argued that it 'would add to the current prevalent mischief of the invention of false oral admissions, known universally in the criminal courts as "verbals"' (para. 28). More recently the legal reform group, JUSTICE (1979), asserted that: 'The files of hundreds of cases brought to our notice over the years and the experience of our members who practise in the criminal courts indicate that police malpractice is far more widespread in some forces and crime squads than police spokesmen would have us believe.' (p. 4.)

Statements of this kind from judges, Members of Parliament, and others could easily be multiplied,[13] but they do not in themselves make out a case. Nevertheless, the secrecy with which interrogations are conducted readily creates a suspicion that the rules are not merely being broken but that the practices used are unfair and coercive. Allegations of misconduct, trickery, or even violence are commonplace, as are the vehement denials of the police that accompany them. The statement made by Lord Devlin in 1960, that 'it is only because there is a general sense among policemen that the accused ought to be fairly treated that the English system works at all' (p. 22), could not be made with the same confidence today. There are simply too many disturbing and well-documented instances of police malpractice to warrant any complacency.[14]

We have argued elsewhere (Baldwin and McConville (1977a) pp. 68–70; (1979d)) that there is reason to suppose that verbal statements are sometimes falsely attributed to defendants, and that unfair pressures are in some cases brought to bear to induce suspects to make admissions to the police. In the course of interviewing hundreds of defendants who passed through the

[13] See, for example, Sir Brian MacKenna (1970) at pp. 688–9; Viscount Dilhorne, 338, *House of Lords* (*Debates*), cols. 1550–1; Lord Reid, 338, *House of Lords* (*Debates*), cols. 1612–13; Alex Lyon, MP, 868, *House of Commons* (*Debates*), col. 909; Peter Archer, MP, 868, *House of Commons* (*Debates*), col. 935; Criminal Law Revision Committee (1972) para. 52; Devlin (1960, 1979b); Whitaker (1964); Williams (1960, 1979); Fisher (1977); Price and Caplan (1977); and Hain *et al.* (1979).

[14] A recent example, discussed by Hansen (1980), concerns the case of George Lindo, who was convicted of robbery and sentenced to two years' imprisonment on the basis of a disputed confession and verbals. It came to light belatedly that one of the police officers involved had fabricated evidence in this and in other cases.

Birmingham Crown Court in 1975 and 1976, we were made aware of the acute sense of grievance that many defendants felt in confronting verbal confessions which they could not rebut in court. We have seen in chapter 6 that the great majority of defendants who make statements to the police do not challenge them in court but instead plead guilty. A broader based survey conducted in London by the Home Office in 1973 and 1975 produced an even more convincing picture.[15] The figures collected by the Home Office are interesting; they are reproduced in Table 9.

TABLE 9
Metropolitan Police Survey

	March–May 1973 (All Courts)	
	Defendants : all courts	*Defendants : Crown Courts*
Defendants prosecuted	136,811	4,488
Written or verbal statements challenged	2,275	944
% of defendants making challenges	1.7%	21.0%
	May 1975 (Selected Courts)	
	Defendants : all courts	*Defendants : Crown Courts*
Defendants prosecuted	1,938	279
Written or verbal statements challenged	25	25
% of defendants making challenges	1.3%	9.0%

Source : Home Office, *The Feasibility of an Experiment in the Tape-recording of Police Interrogations, Cmnd.* 6630 (1976)

Other information collected by the Home Office in South Wales and Kent on the frequency of challenges to written statements demonstrated that such challenges were rare, occurring in no more than 2.4 per cent of cases in which such statements were made.

It is tempting to draw the inference from these figures that written and verbal statements must be reliable if defendants do not bother to challenge them. But this inference is based upon a fallacy, and it is in our view precisely because such statements

[15] The details of this survey are given in the Home Office feasibility study of the tape-recording of police interrogations (1976) at pp. 28 30.

present acute difficulties to defendants who wish to dispute them that the present lack of safeguards surrounding the taking of statements by the police is so dangerous. Indeed, from a strategic standpoint, defendants are usually foolhardy to attempt to challenge a statement made to the police and they will often be advised by their own lawyer to refrain from doing so. That counsel will probably be prudent in most cases in offering advice of this nature is in itself a demonstration of a grave weakness in current procedures.[16] The inability of counsel (and for that matter of anyone else) accurately to determine the truth of what took place during the defendant's interrogation at the police station is bound to colour the sort of advice that can realistically be offered at court.

The problem of determining what took place creates severe difficulties for all parties, and justice is a likely casualty. For, if the statements contained in the committal papers are inaccurately reported, the defence case will be prejudiced. Equally, if the statements are in fact well-founded but subsequently challenged at trial, the prosecution case may well be unfairly weakened. No one can possibly know on which side the balance comes down, and it may well be that more police officers are unfairly pilloried in the witness box than defendants are convicted on the basis of false or inaccurately reported statements. Even so, the ease with which a false verbal confession can be attributed to a defendant, whether guilty or innocent, by police officers who are overzealous (or worse) is extremely disturbing. We have ourselves often encountered in off-the-record conversations with police officers open acknowledgement of the existence of the practice of 'verballing'. We even came across references to this in the course of formal tape-recorded interviews conducted with police officers in connection with our research into the outcome of contested trials in the Birmingham Crown Court (Baldwin and McConville (1979c)). It was, of course, rare for an officer to admit that evidence had been fabricated in relation

[16] There are several reasons why such advice may well be prudent. Legal advisers will, for instance, point out as a rule that the evidence given by police officers will usually be preferred to that of a defendant; that a defence based upon mud-slinging is to be avoided if at all possible, and that an attack on police witnesses may well merely antagonize the judge and lead to a heavier sentence. That heavier sentences are indeed imposed on defendants who unsuccessfully contest cases than on those who plead guilty is demonstrated by a number of studies conducted in England and in the United States: see particularly Mileski (1971); Shin (1973); and Baldwin and McConville (1978b).

to specific defendants,[17] but occasionally officers were more forthcoming, as in the following two cases:

Case 67 (*Birmingham*) [A case in which the defendant was charged with going equipped for theft and acquitted]

Police officer: The defendant was seen at night loitering near some shop doorways. He had two keys in his possession. When challenged, he said 'You try and prove it'. So we did but it backfired at the trial. I was the first witness and was unshaken in my evidence. The other police officer got in the witness box and swore that the defendant had tried several doors. He started to get nervous and shaky and he didn't have time to collect his thoughts. The prosecution barrister said to me afterwards 'He has given evidence of a different deposition completely'. We had got our stories together beforehand and if he had stuck to what we agreed it would have been all right. The defendant had tried the door of one shop so we had him admitting it. You have to use a bit of verbal but there was no need for [the other officer] to talk about several doors. I could have cried.

Case 482 (*Birmingham*) [A case in which a defendant, charged with burglary of a shop, was acquitted]

Police officer: It is difficult for me to put this as a police officer. The witnesses were police witnesses; the case rested entirely on police evidence. The defendant's written statement [taken during police questioning] was not very good and well, in these circumstances, you use your imagination—verbals and that. Well, the officers weren't convincing and their verbals weren't good enough—they didn't have good imaginations. You see, when you know a bloke has done it, and I know [the defendant] was guilty, you sometimes have to resort to verbals. It happens all the time and usually it comes off, but here the verbals weren't good enough. When you've been in the force as long as I have, over twenty years, I know, or at least I think I know, when the bloke is guilty, and if the evidence is not there, you have to use your imagination.

It would be foolish to set too much store by the observations of individual officers, and we cannot hazard any guess at how frequently 'verballing' takes place. But that leads to another problem, a problem that was referred to by the distinguished

[17] No less an authority than Lord Devlin (1960) has made the following penetrating observation: 'Lawyer-like tendencies flourish to an even greater extent among the police than they do at the Bar or on the Bench. The police have sometimes seemed to treat the Judges' Rules as if they were a drill manual and to be unwilling to admit to the slightest deviation from the text.' (p. 39.)

Law Lord, Lord Reid, when he spoke of the public disquiet with regard to the conduct of a few members of the police force. He said: 'the trouble is that, although there are very few, one never knows who they are or what is happening in a particular case. I think that one can say that juries are becoming a little suspicious of "verbals" and things like that' (338, *House of Lords* (*Debates*) col. 1612). Such suspicion of verbal evidence is surely welcome. Scrutiny of a police officer's report of what a defendant said may uncover inaccuracies and falsifications. By the same token, it may lead to a rejection of true and accurate accounts. Where such evidence is not accepted, it is usually impossible to discover the reason which led to its rejection. A few defendants do, of course, manage to rebut statements that they are alleged to have made to the police. Thus, in the present sample, there were cases in which the written or verbal confessions in the prosecution's case *were* successfully challenged by the defendant. In Birmingham, 23 cases containing full written confessions and 23 others containing verbal confessions resulted in the acquittal of the defendant.[18] It would be a mistake to assume that all of these acquittals could be equated with innocence and, on the basis of the information that we collected about each case from the trial judge, the defence and prosecuting solicitors, and the police officers involved, we classified 14 out of the 46 acquittals as questionable in nature.[19] In a further 15 cases, the acquittal was at the direction of the trial judge, in almost all instances for reasons unrelated to the reliability of the alleged confession. But there were 17 cases in which the trial judge or the jury rejected the police accounts or were not persuaded by them and acquitted the defendant concerned. We cite below a few of the admissions in these cases:

Case 144 (*Birmingham*) [Verbal admission by a defendant charged with housebreaking]

Defendant: Look, I'll tell you that we had a try at a house, but don't say anything to the other two about it.

[18] In 19 of the 46 cases, the defendant had both a full written and a full verbal confession recorded against him in the committal papers.

[19] We classified acquittals as 'questionable' where the trial judge and one other respondent expressed strong and unambiguous disagreement with it. The procedures we adopted in this classification, together with details of the sort of comments made by trial judges and other respondents, are given in Baldwin and McConville (1979c) at pp. 52–67.

Case 258 (*Birmingham*) [A defendant, charged with another, acquitted of robbery.[20]]

Defendant: (verbal confession) I suppose I was keeping watch for him. It's not the first time we've done it. Jack has never got any money, so he asks people for it and if they don't give it, he threatens to punch their heads in. We only say we will beat them up, we have never done it.

Case 360 (*Birmingham*) [A defendant acquitted on a serious robbery charge]

Defendant: (verbal confession) Look, it's up for me. I did it but I'm no grass. You can't expect me to say who was with me. I'm taking it on my own. You can talk until you're blue in the face but you're not getting me to grass. Unless, of course, I get bail.

Police officer: You're a fool to yourself. I can't make deals about bail.

Defendant: Well, that's up for me. Don't ask me any more times—if you won't give me bail, forget it.

Police officer: Do you wish to make a written statement about what you have said? It is only putting in writing what you have already said.

Defendant: No, I am not making a written statement, things are bad enough as they are. I don't think you can have that much on me except the verbals which I would deny.

Case 381 (*Birmingham*) [A case in which a defendant was charged with stealing a credit card and attempting to use it to obtain money. He was acquitted on both counts]

Defendant: (from his written confession) There's not much I can say really. I met Terry and we had a few drinks. I was a bit down and he chatted to me, and in the course of our conversation the credit card came up and it was suggested that he use it to try to get us some money. It appeared to me to be a very good idea at the time so I went along with it and I gave Terry the card. If Terry had got money it was going to be a two way split.

Case 495 (*Birmingham*) [A defendant acquitted with others in a case involving a serious assault on a police officer]

Defendant: (verbal confession) It should never have happened. We all seemed to go mad for nothing. But I'm sorry I hit the policeman, that was stupid.

These quotations would seem to indicate that something is seriously amiss. If these confessions were proven accurate reports

[20] Despite the fact that a verbal confession was contained in the prosecution's case, the police officer who was responsible for the conduct of the case described the evidence against this defendant to us as 'very, very thin'.

of what defendants said when interviewed by the police, one would expect the trial judge, defence and prosecuting solicitors, or the police to comment adversely on the acquittals. The important point is that, just as we have no way of knowing what is the truth in these statements, neither does a court nor jury. The only persons who know what actually took place are the participants themselves. This being so, subsequent conflicts in the different versions given to the court may give rise to doubts, doubts which can destroy well-founded and ill-founded cases alike.

That doubts might reasonably be raised is already clear from the discussion earlier in this chapter. It is easy to see how, where there is a dispute, interrogations that are conducted in the absence of an independent person, in which the suspect is encouraged or assisted in making a confession or in which the only evidence of an admission is what the interviewing officers have written down after the event as a collaborative effort without the benefit of complete or contemporaneous notes, may contain the seeds of their own destruction. And the difficulties are magnified if the reported conversations (whatever their veracity) stretch the imagination because of the character of the narrative or the circumstances in which it was made. Consider, for example, the following conversations, again extracted directly from the Birmingham and London committal papers:

Case 67 (*Birmingham*)
Defendant: Why can't you leave me alone? . . . I suppose you are going to plant me.
Police officer: I resent that allegation. You have made it, not me, and at no time while I am here will anyone plant you. It is a thing that is talked about, and which I will not tolerate.

Case 319 (*Birmingham*)
Police officer: I am of the opinion that to a certain extent you have been most truthful. However, I am most desirous of recovering the property you bought from this man ... You must surely have suspected that this property was stolen?
Defendant: Yes, I did, but that's the game.

Case 370 (*Birmingham*)
Police officer: Eric, you are being arrested for a burglary.
Defendant: Nothing to do with me, Tony, I don't know about that.
Police officer: Eric, you know me. This is my mate Sergeant Stevens. I told you why you were arrested.

Defendant: Fair enough, this had to come sooner or later. But how do you know its down to me? Bloody hell, your information is red hot . . .

Case 58 (*London*)

Defendant: Listen, I'll put my hands up in court if you'll give me and my mate bail.

Police officer: We don't make threats or promises, but we'll take note of anything you want to say.

Defendant: If I don't get bail, I'm saying nothing.

Case 108 (*London*)

Defendant: Look, if I do get bail, you'll get the gear. You'll get a phone call where it is over the weekend.

Police officer: Well, Phil, I can't bargain with you over bail. That's a matter for the court tomorrow.

Case 221 (*London*) [The defendant denied any involvement with the offence when interrogated at the police station. Subsequently, when the defendant appeared at the Magistrates' Court for remand, he met a police officer in the court precinct when the following conversation is reported to have taken place]

Police officer: What is happening today?

Defendant: I'm going to plead guilty.

Police officer: Oh! you are now admitting you did it?

Defendant: Well, yes. [After being reminded that he was still under caution.] You know the story, it's like [the victim] said . . . I don't know why I did it, it was so stupid, I didn't even need the money.

Case 303 (*London*) [The defendant was interviewed at length in the presence of his solicitor. He made no admissions. The solicitor then left]

Defendant: Sorry, I can't say it in front of him, can I? I took it all.

Police officer (after cautioning the defendant): Do you want to recall your solicitor?

Defendant: No, you understand, don't you, I've got to lie for the children.

Police officer: Are you admitting to me that the property I have questioned you about was stolen by you?

Defendant: Yes, you know that anyway. No one can hear me, can they? This place isn't bugged, is it?

Police officer: No, but I will record this conversation.

Defendant: You can do what you bloody well like.

It would be surprising if the defence did not challenge evidence of this kind, and it is all too easy to see how a court or jury might be sceptical of the authenticity of the accounts in question. We re-emphasize the point that we are not arguing that these conversations did not take place or that the reports of them were embroidered or concocted. Perhaps some conversations of this kind represent nothing more that what Lord Devlin (1960) has called translations into 'official' vocabulary. But more may be involved. All these statements must surely represent highly truncated renderings of delicate and complex conversations, with the police officer concerned being responsible for what is included in the case papers. And they are all at the very least the sort of exchanges that would raise an eyebrow in court and outside. As one experienced criminal court solicitor puts it; 'it is mildly surprising that a man with many years of experience of police questioning and the courts, when approached, at the drop of a handkerchief makes such damning admissions of guilt'.[21]

Since there is no independent check on the conduct and reporting of interviews with defendants, there is a danger both that correctly recorded verbal evidence will be dismissed by a jury and that incorrectly recorded verbal evidence will be accepted. For any given case there is at present no way of knowing for certain whether the confessions or other statements contained in the committal papers were involuntary, whether they were voluntary but obtained in breach of the Judges' Rules, whether they were fully or accurately reported, or indeed whether they were made at all. A better approach would be to ensure that any confession evidence is obtained under conditions that remove or reduce such uncertainty.

POSSIBLE SOLUTIONS

How can this be done? Several approaches, which have been adopted in other jurisdictions,[22] have been canvassed in this

[21] Morton (1975) at p. 830. And compare Mr Justice Cave in *Thompson* [1893] 2 Q.B. 12, at p. 18:

> I would add that for my part I always suspect these confessions, which are supposed to be the offspring of penitence and remorse, and which nevertheless are repudiated by the prisoner at the trial. It is remarkable that it is of very rare occurrence for evidence of a confession to be given when the proof of the prisoner's guilt is otherwise clear and satisfactory; but, when it is not clear and satisfactory, the prisoner is not infrequently alleged to have been seized with the desire born of penitence and remorse to supplement it with a confession—a desire which vanishes as soon as he appears in a court of justice.

[22] A useful summary of the rules governing police interrogation in Canada, France, Germany, Israel, Japan, and Norway is given in the Note, *Journal of Criminal Law, Criminology and Police Science* (1961); the position in Italy is described in Scaparone (1974); and Ashworth (1976) discusses reforms proposed in Australia and Scotland.

country, and a Royal Commission is at the time of writing examining the various possibilities. We start from the bald assumption, with which many will disagree, that present procedures in England, as enshrined in the Judges' Rules, offer no real protection to innocent suspects, that the Rules are widely disregarded, and that some form of independent monitoring of police interrogations is urgently required. Ashworth (1976) argues that: 'A legal system which proclaims rules which it is not prepared to uphold is indulging in a dangerous form of hypocrisy. Thus, once an acceptable framework for criminal investigation is settled, it must be reinforced by safeguards and sanctions.' (p. 609.) There appear to have been four principal methods which have been seriously advocated in England, all of which would, if adopted, provide only partial solutions, but all of which represent in our judgment improvements over the present situation. We shall say a little about each of these methods in turn.

(i) *Conducting police interviews in the presence of the accused's solicitor*

In England, suspects in police custody have the right to consult a solicitor with the major qualification that, as the Preamble to the Judges' Rules states, this causes 'no unreasonable delay or hindrance ... to the processes of investigation or the administration of justice'. What this qualification means is open to considerable differences of interpretation, although it must be said that the courts have themselves shown the greatest reluctance to exclude evidence obtained from a suspect who has been denied access to a solicitor.[23] In practice, however, it is apparent that police officers routinely refuse access to a solicitor because they feel it will indeed hamper their enquiries.[24] We found in our own study in Birmingham (Baldwin and McConville (1979d)) that 77 per cent of defendants who asked to see a solicitor said that they had been refused, and this closely accords with the proportion given by Zander (1972) of 74 per cent. Even the few defendants who were able to see a solicitor at police stations in Birmingham often said that this was only after prolonged questioning and then grudgingly. Perhaps as a conse-

[23] On this, see Baldwin and McConville (1979d) at pp. 146–7.

[24] This is clear from the various studies conducted in England in recent years. See particularly Zander (1972); Bottoms and McClean (1976); Baldwin and McConville (1977a, 1979d); and Softley (1980).

quence of this, it was not surprising to find that those who managed to see a solicitor while in police custody fared no better at trial than did those who were refused. Of the 32 defendants (9.1 per cent of those we interviewed) who said that a solicitor had been present, 20 were convicted at trial. We found that the absence of a solicitor for at least some part of the interrogation period (as well as at the time of arrest, of course) led to the same kind of disputes over the accuracy of verbal admissions that we had noted in other cases. In other words, as a protection for suspects in police custody, the right of access to a solicitor is at present of limited value.

A similar conclusion has emerged from the corresponding body of research carried out in the United States where a suspect's right of access to a lawyer is far more comprehensive, and subject to far fewer qualifications, than in England. The great number of so-called *Miranda* impact studies[25] have demonstrated that, even where police officers observe the letter (if not the spirit) of the *Miranda* ruling by informing suspects in custody of their right to have a lawyer present, the effect of this upon the conduct of police interrogations is slight. In most cases, suspects choose to waive their rights, either because they regard them as unimportant or because they do not appreciate the significance of what is being offered or because they cannot realistically enforce those rights in a situation firmly under the control of the police. To imagine that a suspect in police custody, after a grudging warning, emptied of meaning by the tone and manner in which it is given, can voluntarily and knowingly exercise or waive his rights is, as Wald *et al.* (1967) rightly observe, 'to engage in fiction'.

If, therefore, suspects in police custody are to be in a position to make informed decisions about their rights, it is not sufficient to administer mere warnings. It is necessary instead to ensure that they be given access to their lawyer before interrogation commences and that the lawyer be present throughout the period of questioning. To admit in evidence reports of conversations alleged to have taken place before the arrival or after the departure of the solicitor would invite abuse and render nugatory the formal protections. The major obstacle to reforms of this kind, however, comes from the police themselves. The

[25] The most important empirical studies are cited above at p. 101.

Association of Chief Police Officers (1978), for example, has argued that solicitors generally impede the conduct of interrogations by advising suspects to remain silent, and, as was clear from the interviews we carried out (Baldwin and McConville (1979d)), individual police officers are as a rule strongly opposed to the presence of solicitors. It is unhappily the case, therefore, that any rule requiring full access to a solicitor during interrogation could not be introduced with the consent of the police.

(ii) *The mechanical recording of police interviews*

Many of the disputes that arise in the courtroom about what was said during the course of interrogation could be removed if the interrogations with suspects were recorded on video-tape. In that way, courts could see for themselves whether, for example, a particular statement was or was not made. Although video-tapes have been used (apparently with enthusiasm) by some police forces in the United States,[26] the idea has never got off the ground in England, primarily for reasons of cost and policy. For present purposes, we shall concentrate on the tape-recording of police interviews which is the more realistic political possibility. Discussion on even this limited basis is a depressing business since, after years of debate, and procrastination in official circles, very little indeed has been achieved.

The idea of tape-recording police interrogations in England has been advocated for many years, and was given impetus by the Criminal Law Revision Committee in their ill-fated report on evidence (1972). A minority of three members of that Committee recommended that police interrogations in large centres of population should be mechanically recorded and that, if a confession was not recorded when it could have been, it should not be admitted at trial. The majority, however, took the view that, although careful consideration ought to be given to the possibilities of using tape-recorders, the time was not right to make their use compulsory. The result has been, as a distinguished member of the minority (Williams (1979) p. 6) has put it, 'a bipartisan policy of defensive inactivity' on the part of

[26] It is interesting to note that in the United States video-recordings have tended to be viewed primarily as aids for the prosecution rather than as means of protecting the accused. Gebhardt (1975), a senior police officer, saw video-tapes as 'one of law enforcement's newest technological advances in the fight against crime' (p. 10). For similar views, see Barber and Bates (1974), and Eisman (1977).

successive Home Secretaries exemplified in a note, containing 'the usual lugubrious list of reasons why tape-recording is impracticable', recently sent by the Home Office to the Royal Commission on Criminal Procedure. The evident lack of enthusiasm for the use of tape-recording is indicated by the fact that, although the Criminal Law Revision Committee's report was published in 1972, it was not until 1975 that the Home Office set up a committee to look into the question. Moreover, the terms of reference of that committee were confined to a consideration of whether an *experiment* along these lines would be feasible, and they were not asked to consider whether tape-recording (or even an experiment) would also be desirable. It took the Home Office Committee a further eighteen months to decide that a limited experiment would be feasible, as long as it was confined to the taking of any statement at the end of an interrogation. What had now become an almost absurdly narrow exercise nevertheless met with 'total opposition' from the Police Federation (*The Times* 20 October 1976). The matter was then handed to the Royal Commission on Criminal Procedure under whose auspices certain experiments were eventually set up. At the time of writing, neither the results of the experiments nor the outcome of the Commission's deliberations are known.

Some of the objections that have been made to the use of tape-recorders can be briefly enumerated. They relate to cost, the storage and transcription of tapes, the inhibition of suspects, and the fact that it is impracticable to record conversations which take place outside the police station. No evidence as to the importance of the last point has ever been gathered, but the Home Office Committee (1976) listed in Appendix D examples of cases in which, they said, it would have been difficult, if not impossible, to record important admissions. It is clear, however, from the examples they give that either the admissions in question were of no real value or the questioning could readily have been conducted at the police station.[27] The other argument that

[27] Thus one case involved a neighbour witnessing a man breaking into a house. She called the police and the man was arrested as he climbed through the window. On being arrested, he admitted burglary but refused to repeat the admission at the police station. It cannot seriously be argued that, in such circumstances, there was any real value in the admission and that without it the prosecution's case would have been seriously weakened.

is sometimes put forward (as, for example, by the Association of Chief Police Officers (1978))—that evidence not supported by a tape-recording would inevitably be regarded by juries as of inferior quality—was given short shrift by the Thomson Committee (1975), reporting on criminal procedure in Scotland. They wrote:

> The question arises whether or not an account of any recorded interrogation given by a police officer from memory and notes made at the time or immediately afterwards, should be admissible in evidence. We consider that it should not be admissible, as we feel strongly that particularly accurate recording of interrogation in a police station is essential as a safeguard to all the persons concerned. (para. 7.23.)

Moreover, although we could not ourselves investigate the administrative and economic objections to tape-recorders, we can provide information, extracted from the Birmingham and London committal papers, on the frequency with which important statements are made by defendants outside the police station. We found that most statements—88 per cent in Birmingham and 78 per cent in London—were made or repeated at the police station. If one examines the cases in which statements were made only outside the station (as, for instance, on arrest, in the police car, or in the corridors of the court), it becomes clear that their value to the prosecution case was, in the great majority of instances, slight. About 60 per cent of them in Birmingham and over 70 per cent in London did not even consist of admissions at all, and others were admissions to some charges only.[28] Taking these findings together, we can conclude that there were very few cases in which the prosecution was assisted much by evidence obtained from conversations held with defendants outside the police station.[29] These findings have, we believe, a significant bearing upon the question of the feasibility of monitoring interrogations by means of tape-recorders. They indicate that contemporaneous supervision of police interrogations would be much easier to achieve than many critics have contended, a conclusion that is strengthened by the

[28] Further details of these results are given in Baldwin and McConville (1980) at pp. 21–2.

[29] There were, of course, some occasions on which the prosecution case was enhanced by such evidence, but in the overwhelming majority of cases interrogation evidence of importance was obtained at the police station itself.

short duration of most police interviews with defendants. We found that the total length of most interrogations was less than two hours and that only about 2 per cent continued beyond four hours. When it is remembered that our analysis was confined to offences of some gravity and that the indications are that most interrogations are completed much more speedily in less serious cases,[30] it is clear that the cases we examined served to magnify rather than minimize the difficulties that would be encountered.

Other objections to the introduction of tape-recorders can be seen on analysis to be grossly exaggerated or misplaced. Williams (1979), in a careful review of the arguments raised by the Home Office with regard to cost, the transcription and editing of tapes, the inhibition of suspects and the protraction of trials, provides a convincing rebuttal. He concludes that: 'One cannot help wondering whether the real objection of the police to tape-recording (though it is never avowed) is their fear of the consequences of public inspection of what happens in the interviewing of suspects.' (p. 22.) It does not follow, of course, that tape-recording would solve all problems surrounding police interviews with suspects or that it would guarantee an accurate record of what took place. Indeed, there are dangers that it might present a distorted picture of the encounter between the suspect and the police, and it is arguable that the greater readiness of courts and juries to rely upon the tape-recording might make the truth even more difficult to uncover.[31] But we would argue that it nevertheless represents a considerable advance on current procedures, and amply justifies the resources currently devoted to experimentation and assessment.

[30] The study of Irving (1980), for example, revealed that, although the length of interviews varied from five minutes to over six hours, the average duration was little more than half an hour.

[31] The way in which this can happen is illustrated in Milner's study (1971) of tape-recording in Wisconsin. He found that, if the suspect waived his rights, the interrogation proceeded without the tape-recorder being activated. After this dress rehearsal came the final tape-recorded performance but this

> recorded none of the methods used to obtain the confession. What emerged on tape was a cut-and-dried version of the detective's merely asking questions he wishes to have answered and the suspect responding in a manner at least informally determined by the earlier interrogation. The confession was later signed by the suspect. Instead of furnishing an accurate account of the interrogation process, the tape presents a *fait accompli*. (pp. 211–12.)

(iii) *Judicial supervision of police interviews*

The idea that suspects should be interviewed or statements taken in the presence of a magistrate or somone of similar standing has been widely discussed in England in recent years, notably by the organization JUSTICE (1967, 1972, 1979). The proposal has taken several different forms. Some proponents would be satisfied with nothing less than full judicial supervision of the whole interrogation; others with ensuring that a magistrate be present when any statement is taken; and yet others with the simple judicial validation of statements elicited in an earlier interrogation. The Thomson Committee (1975) in Scotland recommended that the prosecution or the defence should be allowed to ask for a judicial examination of the accused as soon as possible after arrest. The Committee saw three advantages in this course:

a. to afford to an accused at the earliest possible stage in the judicial process an opportunity of stating his position as regards the charge against him . . .;
b. to enable the procurator fiscal to ask an accused questions designed to prevent the subsequent fabrication of a false line of defence, for example, alibi; and
c. to protect the interests of an accused who has been interrogated by police officers and who has given answers or made statements to the police, so as to ensure as far as possible that any such answers or statements which are to be used as evidence at the accused's trial have been fairly obtained and are not distorted or out of context. (para. 8.14.)

But there have been many objections to proposals of this kind. The Criminal Law Revision Committee (1972), for example, considered that the formality of the procedure would often defeat its own purposes by discouraging suspects from answering questions; that magistrates would be opposed to the idea; that its implementation would impose severe administrative problems; and that it would not necessarily end disputes as to what was said during the interrogation or how it was conducted (para. 47).

Much hinges upon whether the accused would at this stage be obliged to answer questions that are put to him (or face the consequences later at trial). A trenchant critique of such compulsory powers has been delivered by Sir Brian MacKenna (1970), who objects to them on the grounds that

> they would give a great power to the police, exercisable in every indictable case, for use against the innocent as well as the guilty, and capable, like all powers, of abuse, because they would alter our settled accusatorial procedure in a fundamental respect, and lastly because they are put forward without any proof that they are necessary for the containment of crime or that they would be likely to reduce it to any considerable extent. (p. 666.)

Objections of this kind would probably be removed if the compulsory element in the proposals were abandoned, and any new rule simply required that the defendant's answers or statements be inadmissible in evidence unless repeated before a magistrate or other judicial figure.

(iv) *Restrictions on the admissibility of confession evidence*

Under English law, no statement by an accused is admissible at his trial unless it is shown by the prosecution to be voluntary. This means broadly that it should not have been obtained by oppression or as a result of any threat or inducement made by a person in authority.[32] If a confession is voluntary although obtained in breach of the rules governing interrogation, the trial judge has a discretion to admit it in evidence. In practice, however, this discretion has not been exercised to protect the rights of suspects in police custody, and statements obtained in breach of the Judges' Rules are almost invariably admitted at trial.[33] Although courts in many other jurisdictions operate much stricter exclusionary rules,[34] English courts will as a rule

[32] *Ibrahim* v. *R.* [1914] A.C. 599; *D.P.P.* v. *Ping Lin* [1976] A.C. 574. See generally Cross (1979) pp. 535 46.

[33] There are a few isolated exceptions to this. Thus, for example, in *Allen* [1977] Crim. L.R. 163, Mr Justice MacKenna exercised his discretion to exclude evidence of statements made by an accused after he had been denied access to a solicitor, and made the following observations:

> if the police are allowed to use in court evidence which they have obtained from suspects to whom they have wrongly denied the right of legal advice, they will be encouraged to continue this illegal practice ... Complaints against the police of their refusing prisoners access to a solicitor are numerous. If there is substance in them, as I believe there often is, the exercise of the court's discretion in the manner I am exercising it may do something to put an end to an undesirable practice.

But this lead has not been followed by other judges and, to take the more typical example of *Elliott* [1977] Crim. L.R. 551, Mr Justice Kilner Brown refused to exclude evidence obtained in breach of the Judges' Rules, saying 'If the impression should be gained that the judges ought to punish police officers for breaches of the Judges' Rules that clearly and plainly begs the proper question and it is not the proper test.'

[34] See the discussions in Heydon (1973) and Inman (1979).

admit evidence that has been obtained by improper or unlawful means,[35] and admissions obtained in consequence of serious breaches of the Judges' Rules (such as being kept in isolation for long periods or being repeatedly denied access to a solicitor) will be accepted.

The attitude of the English courts to these questions has led to calls for the introduction of stricter exclusionary rules. Price and Caplan (1977), for example, have proposed that there should be some independent corroboration of all interrogation and that, in its absence, evidence of any written or oral statement should be inadmissible.[36] Similarly, Sir Henry Fisher (1977) has suggested that any confession obtained in breach of the Judges' Rules (as well as an oral confession made at a police station which is not tape-recorded) should be inadmissible unless supported by evidence not obtained in such circumstances (para. 2.26). The principal effect of such suggestions would be to cut down or eliminate the reliance placed upon judicial discretion by English law. Whether any other purposes would be achieved is, however, problematic, but a number of possibilities can be considered.

One of the proclaimed purposes of exclusionary rules relating to illegal search and seizure in the United States is that they operate to deter the police from engaging in improper behaviour. Even if one regards the adoption of this 'disciplinary principle' in England as desirable, it has to be recognized that the effect of an exclusionary rule on police conduct is likely to be small.[37] The main reasons for this are that interrogation practices may be less influenced by rules and pronouncements of courts than by the competing norms of police behaviour,[38] that the effect of the exclusionary rule would be felt only when

[35] The House of Lords decided recently that

> save with regard to admissions and confessions and generally with regard to evidence obtained from the accused after the commission of the offence, [a trial judge] has no discretion to refuse to admit relevant admissible evidence on the ground that it was obtained by improper or unfair means. The court is not concerned with how it was obtained. (*R.* v. *Sang* [1979] 2 All E.R. 1222, at p. 1231.)

[36] Price and Caplan (1977) at p. 127. In Scotland, a confession alone is insufficient for conviction, and there must also be evidence which incriminates the accused from another witness. *Connolly* v. *H.M. Advocate* [1958] S.L.T. 79; and see Renton and Brown (1972) p. 393.

[37] See, for example, LaFave and Remington (1965), and Oaks (1970).

[38] Skolnick (1967) found that 'norms located within police organization are more

there is an attempt to introduce evidence obtained in breach of it to secure a conviction,[39] and that, since the vast majority of defendants do not contest their cases but plead guilty instead, the opportunity for scrutinizing police behaviour is very limited, a fact that is likely to be apparent to the police. It is also apparent that the effectiveness of the rule would be reduced by difficulties in establishing what took place when the alleged breach occurred. In other words, if no further changes were made to existing interrogation procedures, the application of a rule designed to control police behaviour would be largely dependent upon the testimony of the police themselves. For these reasons, therefore, even a strict exclusionary rule (considered in isolation) would be only an imperfect means of controlling police behaviour.

But we would argue that the exclusionary rule need not be seen in terms of the disciplinary principle, and that the introduction of a strict rule in England would be a welcome advance in securing just dealing with individuals and in better ensuring the integrity of the judicial system as a whole. At present English courts are prepared to recognize that suspects have rights but readily admit evidence obtained in breach of them. In so doing, the courts in effect nullify those rights and at the same time disregard (if they do not actually condone) illicit police behaviour. If meaning is to be given to the rights of those in police custody, then some measurable penalty must be imposed where these are shown to have been infringed. Although, as we have argued, an exclusionary rule cannot by itself be other than an imperfect remedy, its implementation would formally recognize the importance of suspects' rights and demonstrate that courts are not willing to abdicate responsibility for the proper and fair administration of the law.

---

powerful than court decisions in shaping police behaviour' (p. 219). But compare Sir Rupert Cross (1979):

> Is it to be supposed that, when the Lord Chief Justice said [in *R.* v. *Mills and Lemon* [1974] K.B. 297, 299] 'The sooner the Bristol police study, learn and abide by the Judges' Rules, the better', the conduct of the police of Bristol was unaffected because his lordship admitted a confession obtained in consequence of a breach of those rules? (p. 328).

[39] Oaks (1970) argues that the exclusionary rule is not likely to be an effective deterrent against official misconduct if that misconduct is not directed toward acquiring evidence or if it is not likely to result in a prosecution' (p. 720).

CONCLUSION

We have seen in earlier chapters that, in objective evidentiary terms, the products of police interrogation do not represent significant elements of the vast majority of criminal cases. However, police officers, defendants, and lawyers do regard confessions as important, but this does not alter the fact that the prosecution can as a rule get by without such evidence. Inevitably, many decisions are made more on the basis of a subjective evaluation than upon an objective assessment of the probative value of different items of evidence. This consideration is of great significance in relation to the material discussed in the present chapter because no one knows what reliance courts or juries place upon confession evidence.[40] They may set great store by confessions, and the fact that few defendants making confessions to the police are acquitted at trial is perhaps an indication of this. If this is so, the findings discussed in the present chapter suggest that any such faith in the accuracy and veracity of confession evidence is misplaced. Some confessions are both accurate and true, and others no doubt are inaccurately recorded but substantially true. Equally, many statements do not properly reflect what was actually said during interrogation, and some are untrue or falsely attributed to the defendant. Existing procedures in England make it impossible to distinguish the accurate from the inaccurate, the true from the untrue. Moreover, it is a dangerous delusion to imagine that creating sophisticated procedures at the trial, or strengthening existing ones, can solve these problems. An inquiry after the event can produce unambiguous and final answers but, however searching it may be, it cannot reconstruct with accuracy what happened at a private encounter, particularly where the participants themselves may wish to conceal what took place. The partial solutions that were discussed above have one common purpose, which is to ensure, by contemporaneous supervision and scrutiny, that a fair record of interrogation is available to the court of trial, and that, at the same time, those in police custody are protected from false witness and oppression. The

[40] There is some evidence that magistrates tend to assume, somewhat uncritically, that police testimony is to be trusted, and criticisms are frequently made of the inability of magistrates to spot the exceptions. On this see Release Lawyers Group (1973) and Burney (1979) pp. 180–98. We have warned against taking this argument too far: Baldwin and McConville (1978c).

police may resist such changes,[41] but we would argue that the effectiveness of the system in achieving justice is a more important value and one that should direct any reform.

[41] Kettle (1979), for example, refers in this connection to 'the stiffening, increasingly public and outspoken hostility of the police at all levels'. An indication of the unwillingness of the police to contemplate major changes in this area is provided by the blunt statement of the Association of Chief Police Officers (1978) that 'no further safeguards to the rights of suspects need be given'.

10

THE STRUCTURE OF THE CRIMINAL PROCESS

INTRODUCTION

If we review the findings presented in this book, it becomes clear that English criminal procedure contains numerous elements of conflict, unfulfilled expectations, and a gap between beliefs and realities. Though claims are made that proceedings are instituted only against those who have at least a case to answer, some defendants against whom the prosecution has little or no incriminating evidence are nevertheless arrested, charged, and placed on trial. Suspects are given protections, if imperfect and qualified, yet for a variety of reasons do not and cannot exercise their rights in any meaningful way. The right of the accused to remain silent in the face of police questioning has given rise to disquiet in some quarters, but few defendants reach court without some kind of statement having been recorded against them. The police present themselves as an organization discovering and investigating crime largely on their own initiative, yet closer examination has shown that the organization is essentially reactive in nature, much more often responding to information that is supplied by members of the public. Furthermore, despite the great store that defendants, lawyers, police, and courts set by confessions, it is clear that for the most part the prosecution case is not much assisted by such evidence and could succeed without it. The heavy reliance that the police place upon interrogation as a means of solving crime, recovering stolen goods, implicating suspects, and the like, is accompanied in the real world by small pay-offs. And most important of all, it is readily apparent that the theory of justice which emphasizes challenge, confrontation, and conflict is barely evident, since the overwhelming majority of defendants in criminal cases plead guilty at trial.

LIMITS OF ADVERSARIAL THEORY

For two principal reasons, however, little of this should cause great surprise. Firstly, the adversarial model of criminal procedure does not describe actual behaviour of the various participants within it; and secondly, the model is ambiguous in its goals and ambivalent in its prescriptions and does not comprise a set of clear and certain rules, rights, and responsibilities. It is useful to say a little about each of these matters in turn.

Broadly speaking, in analysing the administration of criminal justice, researchers and other commentators have adopted explicitly or implicitly one of two general approaches, what Feeley (1973) has termed the 'rational goal' model and the 'functional systems' approach. The former implies, in Feeley's words,

> an elaborate apparatus which processes arrests according to highly defined rules and procedures undertaken by 'experts' who perform the functions ascribed to them by highly defined formal roles, under a rigorous division of labour, and who are subject to scrutiny in a systematic and hierarchical pattern. (p. 410.)

Those who have adopted this approach have focused upon the way in which the behaviour of participants in the various stages of criminal procedure diverges from the formal goals—in other words, they have concentrated upon discrepancies between the 'law in the books' and the 'law in action'. But there are problems with this approach, particularly because it assumes the formal goals to be self-evident and fails to take into account the fact that the behaviour of individuals may be more influenced by group interests than by the formal goals of the system however these may be defined. The functional systems model, on the other hand, while recognizing the influence of the legal rules and procedures, pays greater attention to the informal factors that shape decisions and behaviour. Under this approach, as Feeley (1973) puts it,

> the 'rules' the organization members are likely to follow are the 'folkways', or informal 'rules of the game' within the organization; the goals they pursue are likely to be personal or sub-group goals; and the roles they assume are likely to be defined by the functional adaptation of these two factors. (p. 413.)

Adopting this perspective, a number of writers have identified various interests and pressures that drive out notions of conflict and confrontation and replace them with relationships based upon exchange and co-operation.[1] The factors which lead to

[1] See particularly Skolnick (1966, 1967); Blumberg (1967); Cole (1970, 1979); Neubauer (1974b); and Nardulli (1978, 1979).

the displacement or modification of formal goals are not, however, agreed.[2] There has been little discussion of conflicts of interest within the different groups themselves, and the possibility of conflict between different groups is on the whole played down.[3] But there can be no doubting the fundamental contribution to our understanding of the operation of the procedures of criminal justice that writers adopting this approach have made. Although it may not be possible to predict the way in which behaviour will be at odds with the organizational goals, the functional systems model does at least indicate that a correspondence between actual behaviour and formal goals is unlikely, and that it is more important to explain the activities of individuals and groups by examining their working philosophies and the environment in which they conduct their business.

The second point, relating to the construction of the formal model itself, has particular relevance to the behaviour of the police. Sociologists, as Feeley (1976) and McBarnet (1976, 1979) have pointed out, have taken it for granted that the law on criminal procedure embodies the notion of legality. The law is merely assumed to incorporate real rights and a great deal of empirical effort has been directed towards demonstrating that, in the everyday work of the police and also in the courtroom, these rights become largely irrelevant. This assumption has been challenged with considerable force in recent years by McBarnet, who argues that the important question is not whether individuals deviate from the legal rules but how far such deviation is institutionalized in the law itself.[4] In discussing police behaviour (1979), she concludes:

> Any gap between how the police should behave according to democratic principles and how they do is not simply a by-product of informal abuse and non-legal motivations among the police themselves, the administrators of justice; it exists in the law as defined in court decisions and statutes ... Deviation from legality is institutionalized in the law itself. The law does not need to change to remove

[2] Thus, for example, Blumberg (1967) saw heavy case-loads as the primary factor which led to plea settlements and the avoidance of contested trials, whereas it is now clear that bargaining occurs in courts which do not experience heavy case-loads. Cole (1970) prefers to see exchange dealings not as reflections of case pressure but in terms of long-term interaction and relationships between the different groups in question. See our earlier discussion at pp. 7–10 on these perspectives.

[3] On this, see the useful discussion in Bottomley (1973) at pp. 217–28.

[4] See the discussion of McBarnet's work given above at pp. 16–17.

hamstrings on the police: they exist only in the unrealized rhetoric. (p. 39.)

McBarnet's analysis acts as a timely corrective to the assumptions underlying both exposé and interactionist research, and she demonstrates that apparently deviant behaviour may in fact be licensed by the activities of those concerned with the enforcement of the criminal law and the administration of justice in the criminal courts and, more generally, that greater heed must be paid to the formal structure of the system within which the various participants operate.

In the following discussion, we shall set out the conclusions at which we have arrived from our research into the English criminal justice system. Though we have emphasized in earlier chapters the limitations of this research, it is worth repeating here that this study has been confined to the higher criminal courts and to cases that have been heard there in Birmingham and London. Some of the findings appear to have equal relevance to cases disposed of in the magistrates' courts, and other studies of higher courts demonstrate that in many respects the same picture applies in other regions. It would nevertheless be wrong to suggest that the detailed analysis we have presented necessarily obtains elsewhere in England. Equally, however, our main concern is not with minor differences from area to area but with institutional arrangements that have relevance to all courts and to all regions. Thus, for instance, the fact that in some parts of the country the police employ private practitioners to prepare cases for prosecution and in others instruct professional prosecuting solicitors is something that must be taken into account in making sense of working practices and working relationships, but this should not blind us to the deeper and more significant institutional similarities shared by each region. Our basic conclusion, which is unaffected by local variations of this kind, is that criminal procedures in England are structured to produce convictions, within a framework of uncertain protections, confused and ill-defined responsibility, in which informal and even unlawful behaviour of various participants is directly or indirectly legitimated.

STRUCTURAL COMPLIANCE

One point which emerges from the results presented in this book (and which is not found by researchers in the United States) is the centrality of the police role in the prosecution process in England. The police dominate the process, they take most of the key decisions, and their work is a major factor in understanding the operation of the system. It was not always so:[5] in earlier times, the organization and management of prosecutions were in the hands of other bodies. At first, grand juries (made up of people from the neighbourhood who were expected to know the facts of the case) had the responsibility for naming suspects, but, as jurors began to act upon evidence rather than upon their own knowledge, justices came to investigate crime. Towards the middle of the nineteenth century, justices too had developed into a judicial body and the tasks they formerly carried out gradually devolved on the police. Although Lord Devlin (1960) has characterized these developments as showing 'a constant drift, always in the same direction, from unfettered administrative action to regulated judicial proceeding' (p. 10), it is by no means clear that this generalization applies to the police. As they have absorbed the justices' former responsibilities, the police have been able to establish a considerable measure of autonomy and independence.[6] There is, in practice, no real judicial supervision of their activities and they are accountable only in a remote sense. One of the last formal controls, albeit an ineffective control, was removed in 1967 when full committal proceedings were replaced by paper committals. It is true that the new simplified committal procedure was not designed to remove a check on the police, but that is how it has worked out in practice. This does not mean that the police are completely autonomous and free of any control, but such controls as exist are weak or distant or both.

The result is that, for practical purposes, it is the task of the police to discover whether and by whom a crime has been committed and to decide whether to institute a charge and for which offence. The police assemble the evidence, control its content, select, authenticate, and validate it. They interrogate the suspect on their own territory and on their own terms, and their record of the encounter is virtually unchallengeable and

[5] A concise summary of earlier developments is given in Williams (1955) and in Devlin (1960) pp. 1 25.

[6] It must be remembered that, within the police service, effective power and authority rest to a considerable extent with the lower ranks: see Barnard (1968); and Holdaway (1979).

for the most part unchallenged. For the overwhelming majority of cases, police investigations produce not merely the raw material of the criminal process but the final result itself. Police investigations are decisive in most cases, and the characteristic feature of the criminal justice system in England, as in the United States, is not public adjudication of responsibility but public proclamation of guilt. The dominant role of the police, both in the investigation of crime and in the decision to prosecute, may involve an overlap of functions that ought to be independent and it may produce conflicts and tensions.

It would be naive to imagine that the police always adopt a non-partisan approach in performing these functions. Indeed, under the adversarial system, they are not asked to seek out the truth: they are required to present evidence which points to the guilt of the person standing trial. A primary interest of the police, therefore, is to obtain convictions. This is not, of course, to say that for the police the truth is irrelevant. Rather it means that, once a police officer is satisfied that he knows who is the guilty party, his main concern is likely to lie in assembling a case that has good prospects of standing up in court. We have argued in chapter 9 that police officers, convinced of the guilt of an individual, may sometimes disregard explanations put forward by the suspect, reject versions of events that conflict with the view that they have already formed, and turn their backs on other lines of enquiry. A classic illustration of this—and there are many other *causes célèbres*—is provided by Sir Henry Fisher's (1977) inquiry into the Confait case. In that case, three boys made confessions to the police, two to killing the victim Confait, and all three to setting fire to the house in which he lived to destroy the evidence. They were convicted, but three years later their convictions were quashed by the Court of Appeal. Parts of the confessions were certainly false, and one of the boys had an unshakeable alibi which placed him elsewhere at the time death probably occurred. Why, then, did the prosecution take the course it did? Some of the answers are provided in Sir Henry Fisher's report. Once the confessions had been made, said Fisher, the police 'to all intents and purposes closed down the investigation into the murder and arson [and thereafter] enquiries continued only to strengthen the evidence against them' (p. 203). Fisher provided a list of matters which should have alerted the police, including the lack of supporting evidence, the fact that the police knew of others who might have had a motive to kill Confait and who had no alibi at the relevant time, and the apparent discrepancy between time of death and the sequence of events described in the statements, all of which 'cried out for further enquiry' (p. 204). It would be foolish to set much store by the outcome of a single case, notwithstanding its many disquieting features, but it is worth citing Fisher's more general observation regarding the police role in the investigation of crime. He concluded that

> the police do not at present see it as their duty to initiate enquiries which might point to the fact that they had got the wrong man, or that for some other reason the prosecution should fail. And there is nobody outside the police who regards it as his duty to spur the police on to question the case and to follow lines of enquiry which might be inconsistent with it. (p. 20.)

The point is not that the police are slapdash in conducting their investigations nor even that individual officers develop a psychological commitment to the prosecution which blunts their judgment and blinds them to alternative and no less credible hypotheses. Rather it is the responsibility for prosecution that requires the police to present the strongest possible case, and encourages all those concerned with the prosecution to reinforce the picture presented and to ignore doubts they may entertain. The police, for their part, may well feel that, if they are justified in arresting, they are justified in charging and that the case must be made as firm as possible in order to avoid the criticism of their conduct that they may think an acquittal would imply. In the Confait case, disturbing instances of a sort of *esprit de corps* among different members of the prosecution side were evident. Thus, when an expert witness realized that the time of death was crucial, he did not communicate the worries he held about his own evidence to the police. Indeed, those concerned with the investigation and prosecution made every effort to keep the time of death as vague as possible, and the pathologist was led by questions put to him by counsel to express views which made it possible for the judge to instruct the jury in the way that he did. It is hard to resist the conclusion of McBarnet (1978c) that conviction in this case, based as it was upon an inaccurate rendering of events, was no accident or freak, but 'exactly what was aimed at and exactly what one would expect to be aimed at in a system based on adversary investigation and advocacy' (p. 456). The extraordinary feature of the Confait case was not that it happened at all but that so much of what was done came to light: it is simply a well-documented illustration of a process that overlooks, and even legitimates, misconstruction, one-sided investigation, and partisan selectivity.

But more than selectivity may be involved. The need to build up the strongest case against the defendant requires the police to obtain the best evidence and it is understandable if they wish to do so in the least time-consuming and most efficient way. From the police viewpoint, confessions are the most convenient means of gaining convictions. Police work is, therefore, heavily geared towards obtaining admissions from suspects. Research recently conducted in England by Softley (1980) and Irving (1980) demonstrated that detectives interviewing an uncooperative suspect were prepared to use the battery of available psychological techniques, whether persuading, threatening, cajoling, or befriending, in order to heighten his inclination to co-operate, to unsettle him, or else to increase his suggestibility. Persuasion may take the form of the offer of inducements, such as the granting of bail (what some authors have described as 'bail bargaining'[7]) or putting in a good word for the accused at his trial.[8] Alternatively the suspect may be subjected to extended periods of confinement, intimidatory tactics, and, more rarely, the use of actual violence. English researchers have found that, contrary to the rules, juveniles are sometimes interrogated in the absence of their parents, and that it is general police practice for suspects to be kept in isolation away from family, friends, and legal advisers. It is not sufficient merely to castigate police officers for the adoption of such techniques and practices. Attention should be directed towards the rules that exist to regulate the conduct of interrogations and towards the hierarchical structure of the police organization itself. As Mr Justice Kirby (1979), Chairman of the Australian Law Reform Commission,[9] has observed:

[7] On this practice, see particularly Bottoms and McClean (1976) at pp. 199 204.

[8] This emerged clearly from the research conducted by Dell (1971), and Laurie (1972).

[9] Mr Justice Kirby's article contains a very useful discussion of the findings of various enquiries into police behaviour in Australia.

it must be conceded that the police function in an authoritarian, disciplined, hierarchically organised and cohesive unit. This work environment inevitably stimulates an attitude to authority and a concern about lawlessness which is inclined to regard the protections of individual rights as an obstacle course: impediments to be overcome in the fight against crime. (p. 633.)

Other practices became apparent to us in the course of our research. It became clear, for example, that police officers were on occasion prepared to go to extraordinary lengths to secure a conviction, even to buttress weak or inconclusive evidence against a suspect with manufactured verbal admissions. Public denials of this practice are unconvincing, but the private justifications advanced by the police (that innocent people are never put at risk and that police officers always know whether the suspect committed the offence) cannot be discarded as specious rationalizations. They can be properly understood only in the context of a system which requires the police to produce hard evidence implicating the accused and which permits the police to carry out their work with the firm knowledge that they will only rarely have to account for their behaviour and then in an environment—the courtroom—in which the dice are heavily loaded in their favour.

THE GUILTY PLEA SYSTEM

The common result is that defendants who want to fight their case in court face obstacles that often seem to them insuperable. The weak, the inadequate, and those with little resilience accordingly cut their losses and plead guilty. The more determined, who want to press on to trial, are likely to encounter considerable additional disincentives. Some of these derive from the informal behaviour patterns of those handling their case, others are institutionalized in the system itself. It is a characteristic of all organizations that informal norms may have a greater influence on individual and group behaviour than the formal rules,[10] and the court organization is no exception. This

[10] As Blau and Scott (1963) express it:

In every formal organization there arise informal organizations. The constituent groups of the organization, like all groups, develop their own practices, values, norms, and social relations as their members live and work together ... Official rules must be general to have sufficient scope to cover the multitude of situations that may arise. But the application of these general rules to particular cases often poses problems of judgment, and informal practices tend to emerge that provide solutions for these problems. (p. 6.)

brings us back to the subject on which we dwelt in chapter 1—the essence of criminal procedure as a guilty-plea system, in which the pressures militate strongly against confrontation and adversary proceedings and operate in favour of non-trial dispositions. Blumberg (1970), adopting an organizational framework, observes: 'the rational component of formal organization avoids the fortuitous, the random, and the contingent, such as the jury trial' (p. 61). The emphasis is upon co-operation, compliance, and negotiation, and these are most effectively achieved through the guilty plea, in which routinized justice is the order of the day.[11] Conflict damages personal relationships, interferes with work routines and practices, upsets the smooth functioning of the process and, if persistent, may bring into the open personal failings of the actors themselves.[12] By obtaining guilty pleas, the police and prosecutor save time in trial preparation, limit the number of court appearances, maximize the number of convictions, and avoid the uncertainties of a contest. As some writers have pointed out, more than time and efficiency may be involved: conviction may depend upon a guilty plea where the evidence is inherently weak, the police work sloppy, or the prosecution misguided or incompetent.[13] By delivering a guilty plea, defence lawyers can cultivate good relations with the prosecutor (thereby facilitating long-term access to helpful information), increase their credibility with both prosecutor and judge (thereby strengthening their hand in the occasional contested case), and benefit financially from a rapid turnover of cases. The co-operative norms may be informal, but they may be enforced as effectively as any formal rules. Even the radical lawyer may find it extremely difficult not to be co-opted into this informal system,[14] for an unwilling-

[11] As we saw in chapter 1, some writers have overplayed the importance of the administrative strains under which the courts operate (heavy case-loads, lack of time, resources, and personnel), and a more fashionable emphasis is upon the development of long-term relationships among those working within the criminal justice system. Cole (1970), for example, in his analysis of the defence/prosecutor relationships in Seattle, found that there were financial and career incentives which promoted co-operation which he characterized as 'exchange relationships'.

[12] Buckle and Buckle (1977) and Cole (1979) make the point that neither the judge, prosecutor, nor defence counsel wants to be caught looking unprepared in court.

[13] See, for instance, McBarnet (1976) at p. 180, and McDonald (1979) at p. 38.

[14] On this, see Grosman (1969); Battle (1971); and Oppenheimer (1973). Blumberg (1970) expresses the point as follows: 'The deviant or even maverick individual who predicates his official conduct on accepted notions of due process, or chooses possibilities

ness to settle cases outside the courtroom with the prosecution and judge will render much of his work ineffective and result only in his clients being penalized.

It is hardly surprising that defendants find this network of intimate relationships baffling and alien. Some are so bewildered by the guilty plea procedure that they view the advice they receive uncritically, they are scarcely aware of having made any decision to plead guilty, and often blindly do whatever their lawyers tell them.[15] Other defendants, their expectations confounded, find it difficult to decide whose side their lawyer is on, though, as Casper (1972) says, if a defendant thinks of his lawyer as one of 'them' rather than as someone on his side, he is, in an organizational sense, probably right. The more discerning defendant realizes his status as an outsider. As one defendant in our sample put it:

> the barrister who's defending and the one who's prosecuting have got it pretty nearly sewn up. They're in the law courts every day and they know what's going on. They brow-beat many people [into pleading guilty]. Where they've got a long indictment, they talk between themselves like a couple of carpenters saying 'We'll cut that piece to that length'. It's just a job for them.

Though they may be cynical and though they may feel alienated from the process in which they are central figures, defendants are generally powerless in this situation, and few can resist the blandishments and subtler pressures brought to bear upon them. Most comply and plead guilty.

It hardly needs to be re-emphasized that the whole guilty plea procedure is one that is covert and informal. In these essentially private dealings, judges, prosecutors, and defence lawyers have advantages other than territorial familiarity and a knowledge of the personnel, organization, and courtroom subcultures. The legal structure itself provides them with a strong arsenal of weapons. An adversarial system, founded upon conflict, might be expected to contain rules acknowledging the desirability of contested trials. It would seem inconsistent to trumpet the virtues of jury trial and at the same time punish

---

of action which run counter to normatively established routines, is quickly isolated, neutralized, or re-socialized.' (p. 61.)

[15] See Bottoms and McClean (1976); Carlen (1976); and Baldwin and McConville (1977a).

those who put the prosecution to the proof. And at first sight, it might appear that the English system protects the right of defendants to opt for trial by jury. For instance, it is well established that the way in which the defence is conducted at trial does not justify any increase in sentence above what is appropriate for the offence. Thus, in *Thomas and Whittle*,[16] the Court of Appeal said:

> It is no doubt deplorable to make an unjustifiable attack on the honesty of any witness but it is not a criminal offence in itself and it is not a matter that can be taken into consideration so as to add anything to the sentence ... The appropriate sentence cannot be increased by an attack that may be made on the credibility of any witness.

Though the rhetoric may be clear, there is no effective mechanism for enforcing it and, as is increasingly evident, it disguises actual practice.[17] Defence lawyers are only too ready to point out to defendants—and they would be failing in their duty if they did not do so—that certain defences (particularly those involving attacks upon police witnesses) are likely to incur the hostility of the judge and lead to a heavier sentence. Since judges do not have to give reasons for imposing a particular sentence, they can, by threatening an increased sentence for certain defences, exercise considerable control over lawyers and indirectly over defendants.

There is, in addition, a general rule that a sentence must not be increased merely because the defendant has pleaded not guilty, attached to which is the companion provision that the defendant may be rewarded if he has shown contrition and remorse. On its face, this rule is not incompatible with adversarial principles: the contested trial is taken to be the best method of adjudication and should be used to decide disputed issues. But if there are no such issues, and if the defendant has acknowledged guilt and shown signs of contrition, this should be reflected in a reduced sentence. In reality, the rule provides a mere façade for the underlying non-adversarial thrust of the system, as occasional judicial pronouncements and general sentencing practice demonstrate. Increasingly, judges are abandoning the pretence that they are rewarding defendants for showing

[16] Unreported (1967) 741/67: see also *Regan* [1959] Crim. L.R. 529; *Claxton* [1965] Crim. L.R. 737; and *Dunbar* (1966) 51 Cr. App. R. 57.

[17] See McCabe and Purves (1972a) and Baldwin and McConville (1978b).

remorse, and they are acknowledging instead that administrative and related concerns are uppermost in their minds. A couple of recent judicial pronouncements make this point clearly:

> it was trite to say that a plea of guilty would generally attract a somewhat lighter sentence than a plea of not guilty after a full dress-contest on the issue. Everybody knew that it was so, and there was no doubt about it. Any accused person who did not know about it should know it. The sooner he knew the better. (*Cain* [1976] Crim. L.R. 464.)

> It is counsel's duty, if the facts in his view justify it, to give firm and forceful advice to clients that, though the ultimate decision must be theirs, it may be to their advantage to anticipate the almost inevitable verdict of guilty by tendering the appropriate plea, knowing that in all probability credit will be given for saving public time and money by that plea of guilty. (*Phillips* (1976) Unreported 12459/B/75.)

The primacy of administrative considerations has been evident in a number of other statements emanating from the Court of Appeal.[18] The inducement of a more lenient sentence (or, what amounts to the same thing, the threat of a heavier one) is a powerful factor in persuading defendants that they will be better off pleading guilty. In an earlier study (Baldwin and McConville (1978b)), we attempted to measure the magnitude of sentencing differentials according to plea by comparing the sentences imposed on three different samples of defendants. The first sample comprised 150 defendants who had pleaded not guilty at trial and had been convicted; the second of 150 defendants who had pleaded guilty at trial; and the third of 150 defendants who had changed their plea to guilty only minutes before their trial was due to start in court, often as a result of some negotiated plea settlement.[19] The defendants in the three samples had been 'matched' according to criteria (such as sex, age, type of offence, prior criminal record) that we believed might have some bearing on the final sentence imposed. In other words, the three samples consisted of defendants as similar as possible in terms of criminal and social characteristics, and

[18] Some of these cases are discussed in Baldwin and McConville (1979b) at pp. 212–13. The traditional formulation of the rule relating to remorse requires that a guilty plea may only reduce a sentence and not change its form, but the Court of Appeal now appears to be going back on this: see *Hollyman* [1980] Crim. L.R. 60, and *McPhee* [1980] Crim. L.R. 445.

[19] For further details of these negotiated pleas, see Baldwin and McConville (1977a).

we postulated that any variations in the sentences they received were attributable to the pleas they had tendered at trial. Table 10 presents the results that emerged from this exercise.

TABLE 10
Sentences imposed on defendants

	Not guilty pleas (n=150) (%)		*Guilty pleas* (n=150) (%)		*Late plea-changes* (n=150) (%)	
Absolute or conditional discharge	4.0	30.7%	5.3	50.0%	10.0	57.4%
Fine	6.7		9.3		10.7	
Probation	2.7		11.4		12.0	
Suspended sentence	17.3		24.0		24.7	
Prison	57.3	69.3%	44.7	50.0%	35.9	42.6%
Other custodial sentence (e.g. Borstal)	12.0		5.3		6.7	
	100.0		100.0		100.0	

The differences in sentence for the three groups of defendants shown in Table 10 are statistically highly significant ($p<.001$), and indicate that there is no fixed discount (of, say, a quarter or a third) for a guilty plea but that the defendant who unsuccessfully contests his case at court is likely to suffer a very considerable penalty as a result. It might be argued that there is a perfectly sound legal rationale for imposing more lenient sentences in that it recognizes and rewards contrition. But this is very shallow reasoning, for contrition is not what motivates the great mass of defendants who plead guilty.[20] As one writer puts it, it is naive to expect 'this sort of spiritual awakening'.[21] Most defendants are, it seems, much more often confused,

[20] Nor do courts as a rule make any careful enquiry to establish the existence of contrition: see Baldwin and McConville (1978d).

[21] Rosett (1967) at p. 75. He continues: 'the guilty plea process looks more like the purchase of a rug in a Lebanese bazaar than like the confrontation between a man and his soul'.

cynical, or angry about what they have experienced than remorseful about the offences of which they have been convicted.[22]

We can conclude that, despite the rhetoric that surrounds an Englishman's right to be tried by jury and the lip service paid to the principle by the Court of Appeal, it is clear from the results set out in Table 10 that it is a right to which is attached a serious penalty clause. That most defendants, faced with the option of being tried by jury, fight shy and plead guilty comes as no surprise. Their decision represents in the circumstances a realistic appraisal of a system that is structured to produce precisely that result.

RIGHTS AND RESPONSIBILITIES

None of the foregoing should be taken to imply that criminal suspects or defendants are unable to enforce their rights or that practices adopted by the police, prosecution lawyers, or defence lawyers subvert rights enshrined in the formal law. It has usually been assumed by researchers that the practices uncovered are deviations from the legal provisions. Recently, however, this notion has been challenged by McBarnet (1976, 1979) who poses the question as follows:

> If police behaviour deviates from the rhetoric of legality . . . we cannot just assume it does so despite the law; we must also investigate how far the law incorporates its own rhetoric. Is deviation from the standards of legality merely a product of informalities and unintended consequences at the level of petty officials, or is it also institutionalized in the formal law of the state? (1979, p. 28.)

The answer she gives, based upon court observation and an examination of judicial rulings, is that the law does not encourage standing on one's right to freedom from arbitrary arrest, that vaguely defined offences (such as breach of the peace, loitering with intent, and possessing articles for use in crime) formally allocate wide discretion to the police, and that holding charges, far from being informal subversions of due process, constitute due process as defined by the courts. In short, she contends that the law on criminal procedure, rather than setting a standard of legality from which the police deviate, actually provides a licence to ignore it.

[22] On this, see Dell (1971); Carlen (1976); Bottoms and McClean (1976); and Baldwin and McConville (1977a).

McBarnet's argument, however, confuses two issues that ought to be kept distinct. The first relates to those instances in which the law appears or purports to confer certain rights but does not do so in fact; the second to cases in which the law does give the suspect rights, albeit ones that are not enforced. Whilst it is true to say that the law often fails to incorporate its own rhetoric, it is also true that it does sometimes give rights, and in this latter situation it is meaningful to speak of breaches. Suspects have, for example, a general right not to have led in evidence statements of admission which have been extracted by pressure, inducement, or coercion; they have a right not to be beaten during interrogation; and they have a right not to face inaccurate or fabricated evidence at trial. If, therefore, suspects are coerced, assaulted, 'verballed', or 'fitted up', their rights have been breached. And the important point to determine is whether those rights are breached or unenforced because (i) there is no effective mechanism to ensure compliance, or (ii) the courts choose not to enforce them. This distinction is important because the first alternative concerns the structure of the system and the process of rule-formulation, and the second gives insights into the ideology of the courts.

The criminal process seems to be structured in part to give rights which are unenforceable and in part to give rights which are in some measure enforceable but not enforced. Included in the unenforceable rights category is the right not to be coerced and the right not to be 'verballed'.[23] These rights are unenforceable, on the one hand, because the suspect is powerless to assert and enforce them in a situation controlled by those from whom the rules are designed to provide protection and, on the other, because the courts will rarely be satisfied (in the absence of contemporaneous scrutiny) that any breach of the rules did occur. In consequence, most defendants plead guilty and those who do not, unable as a rule to establish the fact of a breach, are left without protection. Although this means that, for practical purposes, suspects do not have rights in these respects, it is the organization and operation of the criminal process which produces this situation, not the formal law. There are, in

[23] Another example is the provision in section 62, Criminal Law Act, 1977, that an arrested person is entitled to have one reasonably named person informed of his arrest. Its enforcement is in the hands of the police and no sanction is provided for non-compliance.

contrast, other rights given to suspects which under existing arrangements are in some measure enforceable and their wholesale non-enforcement is only partially attributable to under-cutting provisions within the law itself. A good illustration, deriving from the Judges' Rules, is the right of a person in custody to consult a solicitor. As we have seen earlier in this book, the right is a qualified one and applies only when its exercise would cause 'no unreasonable delay or hindrance ... to the processes of investigation or the administration of justice'. This proviso cannot possibly justify withholding legal advice from the overwhelming majority of suspects, and the fact that so few are allowed to see a solicitor[24] demonstrates that the right is generally breached. It is no answer to say that there is no right because the Judges' Rules do not represent law and have only the status of administrative directions, for the courts treat the Rules as declaratory of the rights they set out. Nor is it sufficient to point out that all the difficulties of asserting the right and establishing breach are present. The point is that courts are not predisposed to enforce the right even where a breach is clear. Thus, in *Lemsatef* [1977] 2 All E.R. 835, customs officers had on improper grounds refused to allow the defendant to contact a solicitor, and the Court of Appeal asserted that:

> It is one of the principles of practice that if a man in custody wants to consult a solicitor he can do so. He is entitled to do so at an early stage of the investigation ... If detaining or arresting officers are going to refuse to allow solicitors to advise a man under detention or arrest, it is no use their mouthing the words of the Judges' Rules: they must be prepared, if asked, to justify what they are doing.

The Court of Appeal, however, went on to endorse the admission of evidence obtained in these circumstances *not* because the suspect had no right to consult a solicitor but because the breach was outweighed by what they saw as the greater interests of the administration of justice, specifically that investigating officers 'should have ample opportunity of finding out where the imported drugs are going to go' and that 'interference' in the investigations might lead to receivers escaping justice.

We shall return to this issue later, but it is important to note here that what emerges is not a simple picture of formal law

[24] See Zander (1972); Bottoms and McClean (1976); and Baldwin and McConville (1979d).

taking away with one hand what it has given with the other. Rights that the rhetoric of the law proclaims and, more so, rights that people believe it confers, often turn out upon examination to be emptied of all meaning by qualifications, provisos, and other under-cutting devices. Equally, however, it must be recognized that suspects are accorded certain rights and that their inability to enforce them may result from structural factors or from more immediate ideological preferences. If we are to understand the criminal justice system, these distinctions must be appreciated even if we are led to conclude that, for one reason or another, it is almost meaningless to speak of suspects' rights in the actual operation of the law.

Moreover, the under-enforcement or total non-enforcement of these rights is made the more intelligible since other groups and individuals with diffuse and unclear responsibilities are involved in a setting in which a variety of structural pressures are placed upon defendants. But it is not simply that responsibilities are unclear: the judicial process as a whole is fashioned to cloud vital issues and to invite rationalization and buck-passing. Divisions of interest, discrete obligations, and chains of accountability are not characteristics of the English system. Nowhere is this more clearly demonstrated than in the prosecution of defendants against whom there is insufficient evidence. Adversarial principles require that only those against whom there is at least a *prima facie* case be charged but, as we have seen in chapters 3–5, policy reasons or the perceived needs of crime control may in practice be given greater precedence. Thus, in order to put up the strongest possible case against A (against whom there is substantial evidence), the police might think it also necessary to charge B (against whom there is little), with the intention of preventing A from putting all the blame on B or in the hope that B's evidence will incriminate A. Prosecutions of this kind are, of course, more likely because the principles on which they purport to be based are legal principles—the rhetoric of the evidentiary sufficiency rule—but most decisions to prosecute are taken by police officers who may pay greater attention to non-legal considerations. Responsibility for this state of affairs is, however, thereafter unclear. The police may claim that all cases which reach the Crown Court have been through the hands of lawyers and that it is lawyers who must take final responsibility. Prosecuting solicitors point out that, once the police charge a man, the case must go to court and that, in any event, the final decision must rest with prosecuting counsel whose duty it is to present the case in court. On the defence side, solicitors say that it is the prosecution's responsibility not to charge unless there is a *prima facie* case, that it is defence counsel's duty to test the validity of each prosecution, and that, since defence counsel is rarely present at committal proceedings, there is little justification for objecting to committal and delaying the progress of the case.

Given the organization of the system, such explanations are not only expected but credible, and, where prosecutions are based in essence upon non-legal considerations, the procedures employed at court, the lack of inquiry, and the imperfect allocation of responsibility, provide an effective barrier to scrutiny. But the difficulties are not confined to weak cases. In our earlier study of pre-trial settlements of plea (Baldwin and McConville (1977a)), we found that representation by both solicitor and barrister, far from safeguarding the defendant's interest, could sometimes constitute a threat to it. Early in the proceedings, solicitors often gave advice which reinforced the defendant's determination to plead not guilty. On the day of trial, however, the solicitor himself rarely attended, sending an assistant or trainee instead. At this point the defendant encountered the barrister, usually for the first time, and, deprived of the support of his solicitor, was readily susceptible to any pressure the barrister cared to exert to persuade him to plead guilty. In this sense, rights accorded by the formal law may be easily subverted in a process which gives little consideration to the institutional allocation of duties and responsibilities and rests instead upon assumed professional standards and informal codes of conduct.

THE PROCESS OF LEGITIMATION

It is necessary at this point to reiterate that the behaviour of individuals and groups is only a factor in the equation, and, if one wishes to understand how the criminal process in England operates, it is necessary to examine the legal framework within which this behaviour takes place. Informal behaviour is not idiosyncratic and unpatterned: the formal rules and procedures may not have a close or direct bearing on what members of the organization do but the behaviour of members is related to the formal rules and the overall institutional structure. Some practices thought to be unfair, undesirable, or illicit may actually be within the rules; some, though not necessarily within the rules, thrive in conditions created by formal rules; and others, though contrary to the law, are countenanced or endorsed by the courts. Each of these possibilities will be considered briefly.

It cannot be taken for granted that legal rules embody accepted or perceived notions of legality. Detention for questioning, for example, is not a deviation from legality but, as McBarnet (1976, 1979) has demonstrated, a police power. The law of search has expanded so much that seizure without a warrant of legitimately possessed goods is perfectly lawful,[25] and goods may be taken not only from one thought to be implicated in a crime but also from someone who is wholly innocent of any connection with it.[26] Similarly, although every suspect has a right to remain silent during interrogation (and must be informed or reminded of this right by the police), its exercise may result in the judge making adverse comments to the jury.[27] Again, the rhetoric of the law enjoins that every defendant must be free from pressure when deciding how to plead, but the courts operate a differential sentencing practice which is calculated to place the defendant under a measure of lawful compulsion. These few examples support McBarnet's (1978c) contention that the law is not such a 'tightknit network of safeguards for the accused as the rhetoric of justice may suggest' (p. 460).

In some instances, however, informal practices are inconsistent with, and not directly sanctioned by, the formal rules, yet they continue unabated. A good demonstration of the way this can happen is provided by negotiated plea settlements, in which defendants plead guilty in return for offers of more lenient sentences. The legal rules which regulate pre-trial discussions about plea were laid down by the Court of Appeal in *Turner*, (1970) 54 Cr. App. R. 352. On their face, these rules encompass principles which represent the embodiment of the adversary model: the complete freedom of choice over plea that each defendant must enjoy; the complete freedom to do his duty that defence counsel must have; and the complete independence and

[25] *Chic Fashions Ltd.* v. *Jones* [1968] 2 Q.B. 299.
[26] *Ghani* v. *Jones* [1970] 1 Q.B. 693.
[27] *Ryan* (1966) 50 Cr. App. R. 144.

impartiality that must be exercised by the judge.[28] In practice, things turn out very differently, and pleas are negotiated with considerable frequency in the Crown Court in England, defendants and counsel are subjected to pressure, and judges readily drop the mask of impartiality.[29] How does this come about? One factor, already discussed, is the practice of awarding a lower sentence for a guilty plea, a practice which compromises defendants and counsel alike. Defendants cannot have freedom of choice and counsel cannot be free to do his duty where a penalty is routinely imposed on those who plead not guilty. A second factor is that the rules endorse the principle that there be freedom of access between judge and counsel. This means that defence counsel, before giving final advice to his client, may discuss the case privately with the judge. It is clear from the spate of cases which have reached the Court of Appeal in the last few years[30] that, whatever the pretext of the meeting, the private discussions can easily descend into bartering sessions in which judges have been prepared to indicate the difference in sentence that a guilty plea will make, thereby magnifying the force of the advice that counsel can then offer his client. And it is not just the defendant who loses his freedom of choice in this situation. The dynamics of the private discussion enable the judge, if he so desires, to use his position and authority to browbeat counsel. Thus, for, for instance, in *Cain* ([1976] Crim. L.R. 464), the trial judge sent for prosecution and defence counsel, told them that the defendant had no defence at all, that if he persisted in his plea of not guilty he would get 'a very severe sentence indeed', but that a plea of guilty was bound to make a considerable difference. The judge's intervention, said the Court of Appeal, 'embarrassed' the defence, and counsel felt he had no alternative but to tell the defendant exactly what the judge had said. Again, in *Inns* (1975) 60 Cr. App. R. 231, counsel was summoned to see the judge before trial in a case involving theft of some railway cable. The defence would have been that the cable was believed to be abandoned

[28] According to *Turner*, the judge's role in plea negotiation is very narrowly circumscribed. He must never indicate the sentence he intends to impose for a guilty plea unless he can say that, whatever the plea, the sentence will or will not take a particular form.

[29] See the discussion in Baldwin and McConville (1977a, 1979b).

[30] These cases are analysed in some detail in Baldwin and McConville (1979b).

property. In the privacy of the judge's chambers, the following extraordinary conversation was reported by counsel to have taken place:

Judge:	I understand there is some doubt as to whether your clients are pleading guilty.
Defence Counsel:	My client will be pleading not guilty.
Judge:	What is his defence?
Defence Counsel:	He says he was not dishonest; he thought the wire was abandoned.
Judge:	This was presumably signalling wire?
Prosecution Counsel:	Yes.
Judge:	If these men are asking the jury to believe that they thought they could just go and take railway property, one of them used to be an employee of the railway. If that is what they are saying, if they are convicted, they will go to detention centre. That is quite certain.
Defence Counsel:	I was sceptical myself when I read the papers, but if you look at the wire—it is in court—it looks as though it could have been abandoned—lots of pieces just thrown together.
Judge:	I was virtually standing counsel to the railways for about twenty years at the Bar—I know all about signalling wire. I take a very dim view indeed of going on to railway property and stealing things. If they are convicted they will be going away. If they plead [guilty] now, I may be able to take a more lenient course.

Defence counsel, his freedom to do his duty restricted and his independence compromised, relayed all this to the defendant, but the defendant said that he still wished to plead not guilty. Counsel returned to the judge's room, told the judge of the defendant's decision and asked for trial before a different judge. When this request was refused, counsel again saw his client who thereupon 'crumpled' and pleaded guilty. Such judicial behaviour must be examined in the context of the formal rules. But the formal rules serve other purposes. By mere repetition, appellate courts can characterize standard practice as deviant, thereby reinforcing the image that the rules direct, control, and describe actual behaviour, and at the same time explain away much of what is done as inadvertent, non-coercive, and unpatterned.[31]

The final category concerns those practices which are contrary to the formal rules but condoned, endorsed, or adopted by the courts. We are concerned here not with instances in which the courts translate what took place into terms which render the events consistent with controlling provisions, but with occasions on which there is no attempt to deny or to misinterpret what occurred. This may happen in a number of distinct ways. In the first place, courts may take the view that illegal or improper behaviour by the police or prosecuting authorities is simply not relevant to criminal trials. This view found forceful expression in *Sang*,[32] where Lord Diplock said:

> It is no part of a judge's function to exercise disciplinary powers over the police or prosecution as respects the way in which evidence to be used at the trial is obtained by them. If it was obtained illegally, there will be a remedy in civil law; if it was obtained legally but in breach of the rules of conduct for the police, this is a matter for the appropriate disciplinary authority to deal with. (p. 1230.)

Secondly, the courts may recognize the impropriety involved, condemn it in the abstract, but do nothing more about it. In *Lemsatef* ([1977] 2 All E.R. 835), the Court of Appeal went further and supplied a verbal formulation that would disguise reality but satisfy judges in the future. There the appellant had not been allowed to see his solicitor because, according to the investigating officer, the solicitor 'could be asked by [the suspect] to contact someone else and possibly something of evidential value might be lost' (p. 839). This was no doubt the reason that access to a solicitor was denied, but it does not constitute

[31] Thus, in *Atkinson* [1978] 2 All E.R. 460, where the judge said that for a guilty plea the defendant would be 'out in the sunshine' but sentenced him to six months' imprisonment after he had contested the case, the Court of Appeal said: 'Of course the trial judge was not striking any bargain with the defence. He was indicating the difference in sentence that a man can on occasion secure in his favour by a plea of guilty.' And in *Llewellyn* (1978) 67 Cr. App. R. 49, where the trial judge told counsel in private that he would look favourably upon a guilty plea, the Court of Appeal asserted that 'this is not a plea bargaining case'. Only rarely does the Court get trapped by its own logic, as in *Grice* [1977] 66 Cr. App. R. 167, where it remarked: 'We find it quite astonishing that any [Judge] should characterize what he is doing as "plea bargaining" but even more so when it clearly was "plea bargaining".'

[32] [1979] 2 All E.R. 1222. And see *Kuruma* [1955] 1 All E.R. 236; *Callis* v. *Gunn* [1964] 1 Q.B. 495; and *Jeffrey* v. *Black* [1978] 1 All E.R. 555.

in law a proper reason. The Court of Appeal nevertheless dealt with it in this way:

We do not consider that the answer [given] was a sufficiently good reason for refusing to allow the appellant to consult his solicitor. The answer should have been that solicitors could not reasonably be expected to turn up until ordinary business hours and that delaying interrogation till then might have caused unreasonable delay.

The suggested answer would square with the proviso in the Judges' Rules, even if it did not fit the facts. A third device has been to recognize unlawful practice and to excuse it without, however, attempting to reconcile it with the formal rules. A good example of this approach is found in *Ghani* v. *Jones* ([1970] 1 Q.B. 693), in which Lord Denning, MR, commenting on the fact that the police could not obtain search warrants for murder, said:

The police have to get the consent of the householder to enter if they can: or, if not, do it by stealth or by force. Somehow they seem to manage. No decent person refuses them permission. If he does, he is probably implicated in some way or other. So the police risk an action for trespass. It is not much risk. (p. 705.)

A final method has been to recognize behaviour as improper and then to redefine it as proper by amending the formal rules. This is what happened, for instance, with the law relating to the collaboration of police officers in preparing notes of an interrogation. It used to be the rule that such notes be written up by each officer independently and without consultation, thereby ensuring that courts would receive all versions of what happened and draw their own conclusions if discrepancies occurred. In the event of collaboration, police officers who denied it were forced to give perjured testimony to hide the truth. The Court of Criminal Appeal in *Bass*,[33] whilst recognizing the implications, adopted the practice:

This court has observed that police officers nearly always deny that they have collaborated in the making of notes, and we cannot help wondering why they are the only class of society who do not collaborate in such a matter. It seems to us that nothing could be more natural or proper when two persons have been present at an interview with a third person that they should afterwards make sure that they

[33] [1953] 1 Q.B. 680. See also *Stephen King*, discussed at p. 159, where the court also re-wrote the rules to accord with informal practice.

have a correct version of what was said. Collaboration would appear to be a better explanation of almost identical notes than the possession of a superhuman memory. (p. 686.)

This brief discussion demonstrates how complex is the relationship between the formal legal rules and the behaviour of individuals within the system. Unfair or illegal practices do not exist independently of the structure within which they operate and that structure may in various ways contribute to, and reinforce, improprieties. The historical record of English criminal courts shows that they are not well suited to settling rights and allocating responsibilities[34] and much of their effort is directed towards legitimizing informal practices. Part of the explanation may be that, when courts are asked to adjudicate on unlawful searches, oppressive interrogation techniques, improper refusal of access to a solicitor, and the like, they are almost invariably faced with searches and interrogations that have proved to be successful in producing incriminating evidence. Had they proved abortive, no more would have been heard of them. But this 'proof of the pudding' explanation can be no more than partial. The persistent exercise of 'discretion' in favour of the prosecution, the forced and one-sided interpretation of rules, the failure to condemn illegality, and the hostile attitude in informal discussions surrounding guilty pleas, create a strong impression of an ideological commitment to the prosecution and a predeliction, in the words of Krislov (1979), to have the defendant 'roll over and expose his jugular'. The final comment on this approach is appropriately left to a judge in a recent civil case,[35] in which Mr Justice Griffiths pertinently observed: 'If a judge knew that defendants were acting unlawfully but refused to interfere, and allowed the unlawful action to continue, what respect would such a cowardly course command for the law?'

CONCLUSION

We began by drawing attention to the essentially reformist tradition of social scientific research in England and cautioning

[34] On this, see the discussion in Griffith (1977) at pp. 79–106, 187–216.

[35] *Express Newspapers Ltd and Another* v. *Keys and Others*, *The Times* 9 May 1980. In this case, the plaintiffs were granted an injunction (instead of being left to pursue a remedy in damages) where the defendant trade union had sent out documents inciting their members to break their contracts of employment.

against this approach. The proposals for changing the judicial process that have become fashionable (the introduction of an independent prosecutor, extending access to legal advice, amending the rules of evidence, and the like) have to be looked at with circumspection, if not scepticism.[36] Altering the rules will not necessarily have any impact on behaviour and certainly will not lead to predictable or uniform change.[37] The very fact that current practices do not in many respects correspond to the formal rules should make this point obvious enough. No significant advances will be made until some of the central features of the present system are abandoned. What must be removed, as we see it, is the power of various groups to determine the outcome of cases without recourse to trial: in particular, the ability of the police to decide the fate of the suspect in conditions that they alone control, and the power of judges to strip formal protections of any meaning, to manoeuvre defendants into a position of compliance,and to persuade counsel to adopt norms of behaviour that often bear little relation to legal prescriptions and serve only to amplify the inherent institutional pressures.

The organization of criminal procedure away from trial and towards guilty pleas provides in fact a powerful argument in favour of trial by jury. Although our research into the workings of juries (Baldwin and McConville (1979c)) produced evidence of misunderstandings and unpredictability on the part of juries, we nevertheless see the jury as providing a necessary

[36] See the excellent account of reform approaches in Nimmer (1978) pp. 48-62.

[37] One recent change to the rules of criminal procedure, introduced by section 62 of the Criminal Law Act 1977, was neutralized by administrative action. Section 62 gives an arrested person who is held at a police station the right to have the fact of his arrest and the place at which he is being held notified to 'one person reasonably named by him ... without delay or, where some delay is necessary in the interest of the investigation or prevention of crime or the apprehension of offenders, with no more delay than is necessary'. The operation of the section is monitored by means of monthly returns which Chief Police Officers are required to make to the Home Office. Despite the provisions of the section, however, the police are presently being required by the Home Office to record in their returns only those cases in which a suspect has been held for four hours or more without anyone being notified of this fact. Given the short duration of most interrogations, this administrative device enables the police to continue to hold suspects *incommunicado* and, at the same time, permits the Home Office to present to Parliament statistics which hide the reality. Thus, for example, it was disclosed in the returns for the period June-November 1978 that only 870 out of over 500,000 persons had been held for over four hours without the notification procedure being observed: *Hansard*, Written Answers, 24 January 1979. The withholding of the right of notification is thus effectively hidden, and the Home Office instructions render the provision of the Act quite meaningless.

independent check on oppressive prosecutions and unfair treatment of defendants. Within the trial setting, the hold the police have over the prosecution case cannot be effectively challenged and courts are taking away rights that suspects have hitherto enjoyed. That juries may occasionally disregard the law for inexplicable reasons, that they may sometimes allow free rein to their prejudices, and that they are not in themselves a sufficient protection against arbitrary government is only now coming to be realized. But for all their imperfections, they represent one final control on behaviour and practices lawyers are too ready to overlook or condone.

We would argue that procedural protections need to be entrenched within the system and that the discretion to ignore or endorse breaches which the criminal courts are apt to exercise should be removed. Criminal procedure, though having many of the trappings associated with confrontation and contest, is neither adversarial in theory nor adversarial in fact. Some weaknesses of the system are no doubt attributable to errors of judgment and human failings, the 'aberrational' factors of which Kipnis (1978) has spoken. A police officer might, for instance, misunderstand the suspect or genuinely feel that the evidence is overwhelming when in reality it is weak and inconclusive. Or a defence lawyer may think the prosecution case is strong and feel that it is not in the defendant's interest to contest the case before a particular judge. Alternatively, a prosecuting solicitor may think that there is a *prima facie* case where there is none, and a judge may feel that there is no defence where there is a good one. All these things do happen and it would be much better if they did not. But in any system they will continue to happen and, if only because human abilities are limited, they are unavoidable. More important than these, however, are 'systemic' failings which result not from human error but from structural flaws within the system itself. Included here are such matters as selective investigation, inaccurate recording of evidence, prosecutions instituted for non-evidentiary reasons, imperfect screening of weak cases, indistinct and ambiguous allocation of responsibilities between different groups, pressures placed upon defendants and lawyers, and the denial or emasculation of rights. These are not accidental features of an otherwise sound system, a system framed to avoid such shortcomings: they constitute the system itself. The present organization of the criminal process makes these weaknesses both possible and inevitable, and the existing system works in the way it does because of these features not despite them. At present, beneath the quiet and reassuring hum of the machine, the pistons deliver a sharp knock to any sense of equity and fairness. A criminal justice process which works badly is unfortunate; one that works badly because its design is faulty is a blot on our system of jurisprudence.

BIBLIOGRAPHY

C. ALLEN 'The Report of the Departmental Committee on Proceedings Before Examining Justices' *Criminal Law Review* (1958) pp. 647–53.

A. W. ALSCHULER 'The Prosecutor's Role in Plea Bargaining' *University of Chicago Law Review* vol. 36 (1968) pp. 50–112.

P. ARMITAGE 'Tests for Linear Trends in Proportions and Frequencies' *Biometrics* vol. 11 (1955) pp. 375–86.

A. J. ASHWORTH 'Some Blueprints for Criminal Investigation' *Criminal Law Review* (1976) pp. 594–609.

Association of Chief Police Officers 'Trial by Jury' *New Law Journal* vol. 116 (1966) pp. 928–9.

Association of Chief Police Officers 'The Investigative Process Preceding Criminal Trials' Evidence submitted to the Royal Commission on Criminal Procedure (1978).

Association of Chief Police Officers 'The Prosecution Process' Evidence submitted to the Royal Commission on Criminal Procedure (1979).

J. BALDWIN and A. E. BOTTOMS *The Urban Criminal* London: Tavistock (1976).

J. BALDWIN and M. MCCONVILLE *Negotiated Justice* London: Martin Robertson (1977a).

J. BALDWIN and M. MCCONVILLE 'Patterns of Involvement Amongst Lawyers in Contested Trials in the Crown Court' *New Law Journal* vol. 127 (1977b) pp. 1040–1.

J. BALDWIN and M. MCCONVILLE 'Plea Bargaining: Legal Carve-Up and Legal Cover-Up' *British Journal of Law and Society* vol. 5 (1978a) pp. 228–35.

J. BALDWIN and M. MCCONVILLE 'The Influence of the Sentencing Discount in Inducing Guilty Pleas' in J. BALDWIN and A. K. BOTTOMLEY (ed.) *Criminal Justice: Selected Readings* London: Martin Robertson (1978b) pp. 116–28.

J. BALDWIN and M. MCCONVILLE 'The New Home Office Figures on Pleas and Acquittals—What Sense Do They Make?' *Criminal Law Review* (1978c) pp. 196–201.

J. BALDWIN and M. MCCONVILLE 'Sentencing Problems Raised by Guilty Pleas: An Analysis of Negotiated Pleas in the Birmingham Crown Court' *Modern Law Review* vol. 41 (1978d) pp. 544–58.

J. BALDWIN and M. MCCONVILLE 'Plea Bargaining and the

Research Dilemma' *Law and Policy Quarterly* vol. 1 (1979a) pp. 223–33.

J. Baldwin and M. McConville 'Plea Bargaining and the Court of Appeal' *British Journal of Law and Society* vol. 6 (1979b) pp. 200–18.

J. Baldwin and M. McConville *Jury Trials* London: Oxford University Press (1979c).

J. Baldwin and M. McConville 'Police Interrogation and the Right to See a Solicitor' *Criminal Law Review* (1979d) pp. 145–52.

J. Baldwin and M. McConville *Confessions in Crown Court Trials* Royal Commission on Criminal Procedure, Research Study, No 5, London: H.M.S.O. (1980).

Z. Bankowski and G. Mungham *Images of Law* London: Routledge and Kegan Paul (1976).

J. P. Barber and P. R. Bates 'Videotape in Criminal Proceedings' *Hastings Law Journal* vol. 25 (1974) pp. 1017–42.

C. Barnard *The Functions of the Executive* Harvard: Harvard University Press (1968).

J. A. Barnes *Who Should Know What? Social Science, Privacy and Ethics* Harmondsworth: Penguin (1979).

P. Barnes 'The Office of the Director of Public Prosecutions' in *The Prosecution Process* Institute of Judicial Administration, University of Birmingham Monograph (1975) pp. 22–35.

J. B. Battle 'In Search of the Adversary System—The Co-operative Practices of Private Defence Attorneys' *Texas Law Review* vol. 50 (1971) pp. 60–118.

H. S. Becker and I. L. Horowitz 'Radical Politics and Sociological Research: Observations on Methodology and Ideology' *American Journal of Sociology* vol. 78 (1972) pp. 48–66.

B. Berelson *Content Analysis in Communication Research* Glencoe, Illinois: The Free Press (1952).

P. L. Berger and T. Luckmann *The Social Construction of Reality* Harmondsworth: Penguin (1967).

A. D. Biderman 'Social-Psychological Needs and "Involuntary Behaviour as Illustrated by Compliance in Interrogation' *Sociometry* vol. 23 (1960) pp. 120–47.

E. Bittner 'The Police on Skid-Row: A Study of Peace Keeping' *American Sociological Review* vol. 32 (1967) pp. 699–715.

D. J. Black 'Production of Crime Rates' *American Sociological Review* vol. 35 (1970) pp. 733–48.

D. J. Black 'The Social Organization of Arrest' *Stanford Law Review* vol. 23 (1971) pp. 1087–111.

P. M. Blau *The Dynamics of Bureaucracy* Chicago: University of Chicago Press (1955).

P. M. BLAU and W. R. SCOTT *Formal Organizations* London: Routledge and Kegan Paul (1963).

A. S. BLUMBERG 'The Practice of Law as Confidence Game: Organizational Co-optation of a Profession' *Law and Society Review* vol. 1 (1967) pp. 15–39.

A. S. BLUMBERG *Criminal Justice* Chicago: Quadrangle Books (1970).

E. M. BORCHARD *Convicting the Innocent* New York: Plenum (1970).

A. K. BOTTOMLEY *Decisions in the Penal Process* London: Martin Robertson (1973).

A. K. BOTTOMLEY *Criminology in Focus* Oxford: Martin Robertson (1979).

A. K. BOTTOMLEY and C. COLEMAN 'Criminal Statistics: The Police Role in the Discovery and Detection of Crime' *International Journal of Criminology and Penology* vol. 4 (1976) pp. 33–58.

A. E. BOTTOMS and J. D. MCCLEAN *Defendants in the Criminal Process* London: Routledge and Kegan Paul (1976).

S. BOX *Deviance, Reality and Society* London: Holt, Rinehart and Winston (1971).

R. BRANDON and C. DAVIES *Wrongful Imprisonment: Mistaken Convictions and their Consequences* London: Allen and Unwin (1973).

S. BROWN 'The Role of Counsel for the Crown' in *The Prosecution Process* Institute of Judicial Administration, University of Birmingham Monograph (1975) pp. 1–12.

S. R. T. BUCKLE and L. G. BUCKLE *Bargaining for Justice: Case Disposition and Reform in the Criminal Courts* New York: Praeger (1977).

E. BURNEY *JP, Magistrate, Court and Community* London: Hutchinson (1979).

C. M. CAMPBELL and P. WILES 'The Study of Law in Society in Britain' *Law and Society Review* vol. 10 (1976) pp. 547–78.

C. CAMPBELL and P. WILES *Law and Society: Readings in the Sociology of Law* Oxford: Martin Robertson (1979).

P. CARLEN *Magistrates' Justice* London: Martin Robertson (1976).

M. CARLISLE 'The Criminal Justice Act 1967—Its Procedures and Practices' *Criminal Law Review* (1967) pp. 613–21.

J. D. CASPER *American Criminal Justice: The Defendant's Perspective* Englewood Cliffs, N.J.: Prentice-Hall (1972).

W. E. CAVENAGH *Juvenile Courts, the Child and the Law* Harmondsworth: Penguin (1967).

W. J. CHAMBLISS 'A Sociological Analysis of the Law of Vagrancy' *Social Problems* vol. 12 (1964) pp. 67–77.

W. J. CHAMBLISS (ed.) *Crime and the Legal Process* New York: McGraw-Hill (1969).

W. J. CHAMBLISS and R. B. SEIDMAN *Law, Order, and Power* Massachusetts: Addison-Wesley (1971).

M. CHATTERTON 'Police in Social Control' in J. F. S. KING (ed.)

Control Without Custody Cambridge: Cambridge Institute of Criminology (1976) pp. 104–122.

A. V. CICOUREL *Method and Measurement in Sociology* New York: The Free Press (1964).

A. V. CICOUREL *The Social Organization of Juvenile Justice* New York: Wiley (1968).

R. V. G. CLARKE 'Penal Policy-Making and Research in the Home Office' in N. WALKER (ed.) *Penal Policy-Making in England* Cambridge: Cambridge Institute of Criminology (1977) pp. 115–26.

G. F. COLE 'The Decision to Prosecute' *Law and Society Review* vol. 4 (1970) pp. 331–45.

G. F. COLE *The American System of Criminal Justice* California: Duxbury (1979).

R. K. COOKE 'A Police Officer's Notes' *Criminal Law Review* (1954) pp. 833–5.

B. COX *Civil Liberties in Britain* Harmondsworth: Penguin (1975).

B. COX, J. SHIRLEY, and M. SHORT *The Fall of Scotland Yard* Harmondsworth: Penguin (1977).

Criminal Law Revision Committee *Evidence (General) 11th Report 1972* Cmnd. 4991, London: H.M.S.O.

SIR RUPERT CROSS 'A Very Wicked Animal Defends the 11th Report of the Criminal Law Revision Committee' *Criminal Law Review* (1973) pp. 329–40.

SIR RUPERT CROSS *Evidence* (5th edition) London: Butterworths (1979).

P. K. L. DANKS 'The Prosecuting Solicitor' in *The Prosecution Process* Institute of Judicial Administration, University of Birmingham Monograph (1975) pp. 64–73.

HIS HONOUR JUDGE DAVID 'In the Crown Court' *The Magistrate* vol. 34 (1978) pp. 74–5.

P. DEELEY *Beyond Breaking Point: A Study of Techniques of Interrogation* London: Arthur Barker (1971).

S. DELL *Silent in Court* London: Bell (1971).

LORD DEVLIN *The Criminal Prosecution in England* London: Oxford University Press (1960).

LORD DEVLIN 'The Police in a Changing Society' *Journal of Criminal Law, Criminology and Police Science* vol. 57 (1966) pp. 123–9.

LORD DEVLIN 'The Practice of Judging' *The Listener* vol. 101 (1979a) pp. 441–2.

LORD DEVLIN *The Judge* Oxford: Oxford University Press (1979b).

DIRECTOR OF PUBLIC PROSECUTIONS Written Evidence to the Royal Commission on Criminal Procedure (1978).

J. DITCHFIELD 'Police Questioning of Suspects: A Pilot Study' *Police Review* (1979) pp. 208–9.

J. D. Douglas *The American Social Order* New York: The Free Press (1971).

E. D. Driver 'Confessions and the Social Psychology of Coercion' *Harvard Law Review* vol. 82 (1968) pp. 42-61.

E. Durkheim *Divisions of Labour in Society* New York: Macmillan (1933).

J. Eisenstein and H. Jacob *Felony Justice: An Organizational Analysis of Criminal Courts* Boston: Little, Brown (1977).

D. H. Eisman 'Videotaped Court Proceedings and Computerized Justice Information Systems—Technological Contributions to the American Justice System' *International Bar Journal* (1977) pp. 26-34.

K. T. Erikson *Wayward Puritans: A Study in the Sociology of Deviance* New York: Wiley (1966).

M. A. Feeley 'Two Models of the Criminal Justice System: An Organizational Perspective' *Law and Society Review* vol. 7 (1973) pp. 407-25.

M. A. Feeley 'The Concept of Laws in Social Science: A Critique and Notes on an Expanded View' *Law and Society Review* vol. 10 (1976) pp. 497-523.

R. H. Field 'The Right to Silence: A Rejoinder to Professor Cross' *Journal of the S.P.T.L.* vol. 11 (1970) pp. 76-80.

Sir Henry Fisher *Report of an Inquiry into the circumstances leading to the trial of three persons on charges arising out of the death of Maxwell Confait 1977*) London: H.M.S.O.

C. Foote 'Vagrancy-type Law and its Administration' *University of Pennsylvania Law Review* vol. 104 (1956) pp. 603-50.

L. M. Friedman 'Plea Bargaining in Historical Perspective' *Law and Society Review* vol. 13 (1979) pp. 247-59.

J. F. Galliher and J. L. McCartney 'The Influence of Funding Agencies on Juvenile Delinquency Research' *Social Problems* vol. 21 (1973) pp. 77-90.

J. Galtung *Theory and Methods of Social Research* London: Allen and Unwin (1967).

E. Gardner and M. Carlisle 'The Case for Reform' *Criminal Law Review* (1966) pp. 498-502.

H. Garfinkel 'Conditions of Successful Degradation Ceremonies' *American Journal of Sociology* vol. 61 (1956) pp. 420-4.

R. H. Gebhardt 'Video Tape in Criminal Cases' *F.B.I. Law Enforcement Bulletin* (1975) pp. 6-10.

General Council of the Bar *Evidence in Criminal Cases* Memorandum on the Eleventh Report of the Criminal Law Revision Committee (1973).

E. Goldrein 'Proposals to Expedite Criminal Trials: Some Comments' *Criminal Law Review* (1959) pp. 273-4.

J. Gorecki 'Miranda and Beyond—The Fifth Amendment Reconsidered' *University of Illinois Law Forum* (1975) pp. 295-312.

J. Gorecki *A Theory of Criminal Justice* New York: Columbia University Press (1979).

K. Greenawalt 'Perspectives on the Right to Silence' in R. Hood (ed.) *Crime, Criminology and Public Policy* London: Heinemann (1974) pp. 235–68.

P. W. Greenwood, J. M. Chaiken, and J. Petersilia *The Criminal Investigation Process* Lexington: Heath (1977).

J. A. G. Griffith *The Politics of the Judiciary* Glasgow: Fontana (1977).

J. Griffiths 'Ideology in Criminal Procedure or a Third "Model" of the Criminal Process' *Yale Law Journal* vol. 79 (1970) pp. 359–417.

J. Griffiths and R. E. Ayres 'A postscript to the Miranda Project: Interrogation of Draft Protestors' *Yale Law Journal* vol. 77 (1967) pp. 300–19.

B. A. Grosman *The Prosecutor: An Inquiry into the Exercise of Discretion* Toronto: University of Toronto Press (1969).

T. Hadden and S. Wright 'A Terrorist Trial in Crumlin Road' *New Society* vol. 48 (1979) pp. 770–1.

J. Hagan 'Extra-legal Attributes and Criminal Sentencing: An Assessment of a Sociological Viewpoint' *Law and Society Review* vol. 8 (1974) pp. 357–83.

P. Hain, D. Humphrey, and B. Rose *Policing the Police* London: Calder (1979).

J. Hall *Theft, Law and Society* Indianapolis: Bobbs-Merrill (1952).

C. Hampton *Criminal Procedure* (2nd edition) London: Sweet and Maxwell (1977).

O. Hansen 'Justice Delayed—Justice Denied' *Legal Action Group Bulletin* (1980) pp. 83–6.

B. F. Harrison 'Advocacy at Petty Sessions' *Criminal Law Review* (1955) pp. 153–8.

J. L. Heberling 'Conviction Without Trial' *Anglo-American Law Review* vol. 2 (1973) pp. 428–72.

M. Heumann 'A Note on Plea Bargaining and Case Pressure' *Law and Society Review* vol. 9 (1975) pp. 514–28.

M. Heumann *Plea Bargaining: The Experiences of Prosecutors, Judges, and Defence Attorneys* Chicago: University of Chicago Press (1978).

J. D. Heydon 'Obtaining Evidence versus Protecting the Accused: Two Conflicts' *Criminal Law Review* (1971) pp. 13–34.

J. D. Heydon 'Illegally Obtained Evidence' *Criminal Law Review* (1973) pp. 603–12; 690–9.

J. D. Heydon 'Confessions and Silence' *Sydney Law Review* vol. 7 (1976) pp. 375–93.

S. L. Hills *Crime, Power, and Morality* London: Chandler (1971).

S. Holdaway (ed.) *The British Police* London: Arnold (1979).

Home Office *The Feasibility of an Experiment in the Tape-recording of Police Interrogations* Cmnd. 6630, London: H.M.S.O. (1976).

R. R. HOPKINS 'The Function of Committal Proceedings' *Justice of the Peace* vol. 140 (1976) pp. 287–8.

M. HOROWITZ 'The Psychology of Confession' *Journal of Criminal Law, Criminology and Police Science* vol. 47 (1956) pp. 197–204.

F. E. INBAU 'Democratic Restraints upon the Police' *Journal of Criminal Law, Criminology and Police Science* vol. 57 (1966) pp. 265–70.

F. E. INBAU 'Popular Misconceptions Regarding Police Interrogations of Criminal Suspects' *Buffalo Law Review* vol. 14 (1968) pp. 274–7.

F. E. INBAU and J. REID *Criminal Interrogations and Confessions* Baltimore: Williams and Wilkins (1967).

M. INMAN 'Convicting the Innocent Confessor—The Problem and its Avoidance' Memorandum of Evidence submitted to the Royal Commission on Criminal Procedure (1979).

B. IRVING and L. HILGENDORF *Police Interrogation: The Psychological Approach* Royal Commission on Criminal Procedure, Research Study No 1, London: H.M.S.O. (1980).

B. IRVING *Police Interrogation: A Case Study of Current Practice* Royal Commission on Criminal Procedure, Research Study No 2, London: H.M.S.O. (1980).

James' Committee *The Distribution of Criminal Business Between the Crown Court and the Magistrates' Court* Cmnd. 6323 London: H.M.S.O. (1975).

Note, Journal of Criminal Law, Criminology and Police Science 'Police Interrogation Privileges and Limitations under Foreign Law' *Journal of Criminal Law, Criminology and Police Science* vol. 52 (1961) pp. 47–73.

JUSTICE *The Interrogation of Suspects* London: Justice (1967).

JUSTICE 'The Prosecution Process in England and Wales' *Criminal Law Review* (1970) pp. 668–83.

JUSTICE *Memorandum on Eleventh Report of the Criminal Law Revision Committee* London: Justice (1972).

JUSTICE 'Pre-trial Criminal Procedure: Police Powers and the Prosecution Process' Evidence submitted to the Royal Commission on Criminal Procedure (1979).

A. M. P. KELLAM 'A Convincing False Confession' *New Law Journal* vol. 130 (1980) pp. 29–33.

H. C. KELMAN 'The Rights of the Subject in Social Research' *American Psychologist* vol. 27 (1972) pp. 989–1016.

M. KETTLE 'Trying to Make the Verdict Fit the Evidence' *New Society* vol. 48 (1979) pp. 440–2.

M. KING *Bail or Custody* London: Cobden Trust (1971).

K. KIPNIS 'Criminal Justice and the Negotiated Plea' in K. KIPNIS (ed.) *Philosophical Issues in Law* Englewood Cliffs, N.J.: Prentice-Hall (1978) pp. 304–18.

MR JUSTICE KIRBY 'Controls over Investigation of Offences and Pre-Trial Treatment of Suspects' *Australian Law Journal* vol. 53 (1979) pp. 626–47.

J. M. KRESS 'The Agnew Case: Policy, Prosecution and Plea Bargaining' *Criminal Law Bulletin* vol. 10 (1974) pp. 80–4.

S. KRISLOV 'Debating on Bargaining: Comments from a Synthesizer' *Law and Society Review* vol. 13 (1979) pp. 573–82.

R. H. KUH 'The "Rest of Us" in the "Policing the Police" Controversy' *Journal of Criminal Law, Criminology and Police Science* vol. 57 (1966) pp. 244–50.

W. R. LAFAVE and F. J. REMINGTON 'Controlling the Police: The Judge's Role in Making and Reviewing Law Enforcement Decisions' *Michigan Law Review* vol. 63 (1965) pp. 987–1012.

J. R. LAMBERT *Crime, Police, and Race Relations: A Study in Birmingham* London: Oxford University Press (1970).

J. H. LANGBEIN 'Understanding the Short History of Plea Bargaining' *Law and Society Review* vol. 13 (1979) pp. 261–72.

H. D. LASSWELL 'The Politically Significant Content of the Press: Coding Procedures' *Journalism Quarterly* vol. 19 (1942) pp. 12–23.

P. LAURIE *Scotland Yard* Harmondsworth: Penguin (1972).

Legal Action Group 'Legality in the Criminal Process' Evidence submitted to the Royal Commission on Criminal Procedure (1979).

L. H. LEIGH *Police Powers in England and Wales* London: Butterworths (1975).

L. S. LEIKEN 'Police Interrogation in Colorado: The Implementation of Miranda' *Denver Law Journal* vol. 47 (1970) pp. 1–53.

M. J. LIPETZ 'Routine and Deviations: The Strength of the Courtroom Workgroup in a Misdemeanour Court' *International Journal of the Sociology of Law* vol. 8 (1980) pp. 47–60.

LORD LLOYD OF HAMPSTEAD *Introduction to Jurisprudence* (4th edition) London: Stevens (1979).

C. LOW 'The Sociology of Criminal Justice: Progress and Prospects' in J. BALDWIN and A. K. BOTTOMLEY (ed.) *Criminal Justice: Selected Readings* London: Martin Robertson (1978) pp. 7–22.

D. J. MCBARNET 'Pre-trial Procedures and the Construction of Conviction' in P. CARLEN (ed.) *The Sociology of Law* Keele: University of Keele (1976) pp. 172–201.

D. J. MCBARNET 'False Dichotomies in Criminal Justice Research' in J. BALDWIN and A. K. BOTTOMLEY (ed.) *Criminal Justice: Selected Readings* London: Martin Robertson (1978a) pp. 23–40.

D. J. MCBARNET 'The Police, the Courts and the Right to Silence' A paper presented to the Socio-legal Conference on Judicial Reasoning and Procedure, University of Oxford (1978b).

D. J. McBarnet 'The Fisher Report on the Confait Case: Four Issues' *Modern Law Review* vol. 41 (1978c) pp. 455-63.

D. J. McBarnet 'Arrest: The Legal Context of Policing' in S. Holdaway (ed.) *The British Police* London: Arnold (1979) pp. 24-40.

S. McCabe and R. Purves *By-passing the Jury* Oxford University Penal Research Unit: Blackwell (1972a).

S. McCabe and R. Purves *The Jury at Work* Oxford University Penal Research Unit: Blackwell (1972b).

S. McCabe and F. Sutcliffe *Defining Crime* Oxford University Penal Research Unit: Blackwell (1978).

J. D. McClean and J. C. Wood *Criminal Justice and the Treatment of Offenders* London: Sweet and Maxwell (1969).

F. H. McClintock *Crimes of Violence* London: MacMillan (1963).

F. H. McClintock and N. H. Avison *Crime in England and Wales* London: Heinemann (1968).

J. McCluskey 'Prosecutions in Scotland' in *The Prosecution Process* Institute of Judicial Administration, University of Birmingham Monograph (1975) pp. 37-57.

W. F. McDonald (ed.) *The Prosecutor* Beverly Hills: Sage (1979).

D. M. McIntyre and D. Lippman 'Prosecutors and Early Dispositions of Felony Cases' *A.B.A. Journal* vol. 56 (1970) pp. 1154-9.

Sir Brian MacKenna 'Police Interrogation' *New Law Journal* vol. 120 (1970) pp. 665-9.

Sir Brian MacKenna 'Criminal Law Revision Committee's Eleventh Report: Some Comments' *Criminal Law Review* (1972) pp. 605-21.

J. A. Mack 'Full-time Major Criminals and the Courts' *Modern Law Review* vol. 39 (1976) pp. 241-67.

Sir Robert Mark *Minority Verdict* The 1973 Dimbleby Lecture, London: B.B.C. Publications (1973).

L. M. Mather *Plea Bargaining or Trial?* Lexington: Heath (1979).

R. Mawby *Policing The City* Farnborough: Saxon House (1979).

R. J. Medalie, L. Zeitz, and P. Alexander 'Custodial Police Interrogation in our Nation's Capital: The Attempt to Implement Miranda' *Michigan Law Review* vol. 66 (1968) pp. 1347-422.

R. K. Merton 'Bureaucratic Structure and Personality' *Social Forces* vol. 18 (1940) pp. 560-8.

R. K. Merton, A. Gray, B. Hockey, and H. C. Selvin (eds.) *Reader in Bureaucracy* Glencoe, Illinois: The Free Press (1952).

M. Mileski 'Courtroom Encounters: An Observation Study of a Lower Criminal Court' *Law and Society Review* vol. 5 (1971) pp. 473-538.

C. J. Miller 'Silence and Confessions—What are they worth?' *Criminal Law Review* (1973) pp. 343–55.

N. A. Milner *The Court and Local Law Enforcement: The Impact of Miranda* Beverley Hills: Sage (1971).

A. Morris 'Weeding out the Weak—A Comment on Examining Justices' *New Law Journal* vol. 126 (1976) pp. 883–4.

P. Morris *Police Interrogation: Review of Literature* Royal Commission on Criminal Procedure, Research Study No 3, London: H.M.S.O. (1980).

T. Morris 'Some Thoughts on the Politics of Criminology' *Times Literary Supplement* (26 September 1975).

J. Morton 'To Combat Verbals' *New Law Journal* vol. 125 (1975) pp. 830–1.

D. Napley 'The Case for Preliminary Inquiries' *Criminal Law Review* (1966) pp. 490–8.

P. F. Nardulli *The Courtroom Elite* Cambridge, Mass.: Ballinger Publishing Co. (1978).

P. F. Nardulli 'The Caseload Controversy and the Study of Criminal Courts' *Journal of Criminal Law and Criminology* vol. 70 (1979) pp. 89–101.

D. W. Neubauer 'Confessions in Prairie City: Some Causes and Effects' *Journal of Criminal Law and Criminology* vol. 65 (1974a) pp. 103–112.

D. W. Neubauer *Criminal Justice in Middle America* Morristown, N.J.: General Learning Press (1947b).

D. J. Newman 'Pleading Guilty for Considerations: A Study of Bargain Justice' *Journal of Criminal Law, Criminology, and Police Science* vol. 46 (1956) pp. 780–90.

D. J. Newman *Conviction: The Determination of Guilt or Innocence Without Trial* Boston: Little, Brown (1966).

D. J. Newman and E. C. NeMoyer 'Issues of Propriety in Negotiated Justice' *Denver Law Journal* vol. 47 (1970) pp. 367–407.

B. Niblett and J. Boreham 'Cluster Analysis in Court' *Criminal Law Review* (1976) pp. 175–80.

R. T. Nimmer *The Nature of System Change: Reform Impact in the Criminal Courts* Chicago: American Bar Foundation (1978).

D. H. Oaks 'Studying the Exclusionary Rule in Search and Seizure' *University of Chicago Law Review* vol. 37 (1970) pp. 665–757.

D. H. Oaks and W. Lehman 'Lawyers for the Poor' in A. S. Blumberg (ed.) *The Scales of Justice* Chicago: Aldine (1970) pp. 91–104.

C. E. O'Hara *Fundamentals of Criminal Investigation* Springfield, Illinois: Thomas (1970).

C. Oppenheimer 'Rebel With a Cause: The Movement Lawyer in the Criminal Courts' *American Journal of Criminal Law* vol. 2 (1973) pp. 146–86.

H. L. Packer *The Limits of the Criminal Sanction* Stanford: Stanford University Press (1968).

H. E. PEPINSKY 'A Theory of Police Reaction to Miranda v. Arizona' *Crime and Delinquency* vol. 16 (1970) pp. 379–92.

President's Commission on Law Enforcement and the Administration of Justice *Task Force Report: The Courts* Washington, D.C.: Government Printing Office (1967).

C. PRICE and J. CAPLAN *The Confait Confessions* London: Marion Boyars (1977).

Prosecuting Solicitors' Society Written Evidence to the Royal Commission on Criminal Procedure: Part II Policy (1979).

J. RAWLS *A Theory of Justice* London: Oxford University Press (1971).

T. REIK *The Compulsion to Confess: On the Psychoanalysis of Crime and Punishment* New York: Farrer, Strauss, and Codaby (1959).

A. J. REISS and D. J. BLACK 'Interrogation and the Criminal Process' *Annals of the American Academy of Political and Social Science* vol. 374 (1967) pp. 47–57.

A. J. REISS and D. J. BORDUA 'Environment and Organization: a perspective on the police' in D. J. BORDUA (ed.) *The Police: Six Sociological Essays* New York: Wiley (1967) pp. 25–55.

Release Lawyers' Group *Guilty Until Proved Innocent* London: Release (1973).

R. W. RENTON and H. H. BROWN *Criminal Procedure According to the Law of Scotland* (4th edition by G. H. GORDON) Edinburgh: Green (1972).

O. J. ROGGE 'Confessions and Self-Incrimination' in S. S. NAGEL (ed.) *The Rights of the Accused* Beverly Hills: Sage (1972) pp. 59–108.

D. E. ROSENTHAL *Lawyer and Client: Who's in Charge?* New Brunswick, N.J.: Transaction Books (1974).

A. ROSETT 'The Negotiated Guilty Plea' *Annals of the American Academy of Political and Social Science* vol. 374 (1967) pp. 70–81.

Royal Commission on the Police Cmnd. 1728 London: H.M.S.O. (1962).

E. SAGARIN 'The Research Setting and the Right not to be Researched' *Social Problems* vol. 21 (1973) pp. 52–64.

A. SAMUELS 'Criminal Justice Act' *Modern Law Review* vol. 31 (1968) pp. 16–39.

A. SAMUELS Commentary in *The Prosecution Process* Institute of Judicial Administration University of Birmingham Monograph (1975) pp. 74–8.

W. SARGANT *Battle for the Mind* London: Heinemann (1957).

M. SCAPARONE 'Police Interrogation in Italy' *Criminal Law Review* (1974) pp. 581–8.

W. J. SCHAFER *Confessions and Statements* Springfield, Illinois: Thomas (1968).

R. H. SEEBURGER and R. S. WETTICK 'Miranda in Pittsburgh—A Statistical Study' *University of Pittsburgh Law Review* vol. 29 (1967) pp. 1–26.

T. Sellin and M. E. Wolfgang *The Measurement of Delinquency* New York: Wiley (1964).

C. Selltiz, M. Jahoda, M. Deutsch, and S. W. Cook *Research Methods in Social Relations* London: Methuen (1965).

A. V. Sheehan *Criminal Procedure in Scotland and France* Edinburgh: H.M.S.O. (1975).

H. J. Shin 'Do Lesser Pleas Pay? Accommodations in the Sentencing and Parole Processes' *Journal of Criminal Justice* vol. 1 (1973) pp. 27–42.

C. E. Silberman *Criminal Violence, Criminal Justice* New York: Random House (1978).

J. H. Skolnick *Justice Without Trial* New York: Wiley (1966).

J. H. Skolnick 'Social Control in the Adversary System' *Journal of Conflict Resolution* vol. 11 (1967) pp. 52–70.

B. L. Smith, H. D. Lasswell, and R. D. Casey *Propaganda, Communication and Public Opinion* Princeton: Princeton University Press (1946).

P. Smith 'Social Workers and the Judges' Rules' *Journal of Social Welfare Law* (1979) pp. 155–61.

N. R. Sobel 'The Exclusionary Rules in the Law of Confessions: A Legal Perspective—A Practical Perspective' *New York Law Journal* vol. 154 (1965) pp. 1–5.

N. R. Sobel *The New Confession Standards: Miranda v. Arizona* New York: Gould Publications (1966).

P. Softley *Police Interrogation: An Observational Study in Four Police Stations* Royal Commission on Criminal Procedure, Research Study No 4, London: H.M.S.O. (1980).

T. Souris 'Stop and Frisk or Arrest and Search—The Use and Misuse of Euphemisms' *Journal of Criminal Law, Criminology and Police Science* vol. 57 (1966) pp. 251–64.

D. Steer *Uncovering Crime: The Police Role* Royal Commission on Criminal Procedure, Research Study No 7, London: H.M.S.O. (1980).

O. H. Stephens, R. L. Flanders, and J. L. Cannon 'Law Enforcement and the Supreme Court: Police Perceptions of the Miranda Requirements' *Tennessee Law Review* vol. 39 (1972) pp. 407–31.

O. H. Stephens *The Supreme Court and Confessions of Guilt* Knoxville: University of Tennessee Press (1973).

D. L. Sterling 'Police Interrogation and the Psychology of Confession' *Journal of Public Law* vol. 14 (1965) pp. 25–65.

J. Svartvik *The Evans Statements: A Case for Forensic Linguistics* Goteborg: Goteborgs Universitet (1968).

G. L. Teh 'The Criminal Suspect's Right to Silence: A Hallowed Shibboleth' *University of Tasmania Law Review* vol. 4 (1973) pp. 113–36.

D. A. Thomas *Principles of Sentencing* (2nd edition) London: Heinemann (1979).

P. A. Thomas and P. Smith 'The Fisher Report and the Judges' Rules' *New Law Journal* vol. 128 (1978) pp. 548–50.

E. P. Thompson *Whigs and Hunters: The Origins of the Black Act* London: Allen Lane (1975).

Thomson Committee *Criminal Procedure in Scotland (Second Report)* Cmnd. 6218, Edinburgh: H.M.S.O. (1975).

Tucker Committee *Report of the Departmental Committee on Proceedings before Examining Magistrates* Cmnd. 479, London: H.M.S.O. (1958).

P. J. Utz *Settling the Facts* Lexington: Heath (1978).

C. H. Van Meter *Principles of Police Interrogation* Springfield, Illinois: Thomas (1973).

J. Vennard *Contested Trials in Magistrates' Courts: The Case for the Prosecution* London: H.M.S.O. (1980).

Vera Institute 'Taping of Police Interrogations in the 20th Precinct' N.Y.P.D. Mimeo (1969).

Vera Institute *Felony Arrests: Their Prosecution and Disposition in New York City's Courts* New York: Vera Institute Monograph (1977).

D. R. Vetri 'Guilty Plea Bargaining: Compromises by Prosecutors to Secure Guilty Pleas' *University of Pennsylvania Law Review* vol. 112 (1964) pp. 865–908.

M. Wald, R. Ayres, D. W. Hess, M. Schantz, and T. H. Whitebread 'Interrogations in New Haven: The Impact of Miranda' *Yale Law Journal* vol. 76 (1967) pp. 1519–1648.

M. Weber *The Theory of Social and Economic Organization* London: Oxford University Press (1947 edition).

B. Whitaker *The Police* Harmondsworth: Penguin (1964).

S. White, M. Newark, and A. Samuels 'Offences Taken into Consideration' *Criminal Law Review* (1970) pp. 311–35.

J. H. Wigmore *Evidence (Chadbourn rev 1970)* Boston: Little, Brown (1970).

A. F. Wilcox *The Decision to Prosecute* London: Butterworths (1972).

A. F. Wilcox 'Changing the Rules—Will Professional Criminals Mind?' *New Law Journal* vol. 124 (1974) pp. 39–40.

P. Wiles 'Introduction: The New Criminologies' in P. Wiles (ed.) *The Sociology of Crime and Delinquency in Britain: Vol. 2* London: Martin Robertson (1976).

G. Williams 'The Power to Prosecute' *Criminal Law Review* (1955) pp. 600–5.

G. Williams 'Proposals to Expedite Criminal Trials' *Criminal Law Review* (1959) pp. 82–95.

G. Williams 'Questioning by the Police: Some Practical Considerations' *Criminal Law Review* (1960) pp. 325–46.

G. Williams 'The Authentication of Statements to the Police' *Criminal Law Review* (1979) pp. 6–23.

I. D. Willock 'Getting On with Sociologists' *British Journal of Law and Society* vol. 1 (1974) pp. 3–12.

J. W. Witt 'Non-coercive Interrogation and the Administration of Criminal Justice: the Impact of Miranda on Police Effectuality' *Journal of Criminal Law and Criminology* vol. 64 (1973) pp. 320–32.

M. E. Wolfgang *Patterns of Criminal Homicide* New York: Wiley (1958).

J. Young *The Drugtakers* London: Paladin (1972).

E. J. Younger 'Results of a Survey Conducted in the District Attorney's Office of Los Angeles County Regarding the Effect of the Miranda Decision upon the Prosecution of Felony Cases' *American Criminal Law Quarterly* vol. 5 (1966a) pp. 32–9.

E. J. Younger 'The Impact of the Miranda and Dorado Decisions' *Fordham Law Review* vol. 35 (1966b) pp. 255–62.

M. Zander 'Access to a Solicitor in the Police Station' *Criminal Law Review* (1972) pp. 342–50.

M. Zander 'Are Too Many Professional Criminals Avoiding Conviction?—A Study of Britain's Two Busiest Courts' *Modern Law Review* vol. 37 (1974a) pp. 28–61.

M. Zander 'The CLRC Evidence Report—A Survey of Reactions' *Law Society's Gazette* vol. 71 (1974b) pp. 954–5.

M. Zander 'The Legal Profession and Academic Researchers—A Plea for a Better Relationship' *Law Society's Gazette* vol. 74 (1977) pp. 1121–2.

M. Zander *Legal Services for the Community* London: Temple Smith (1978).

M. Zander 'The Investigation of Crime: A Study of Cases tried at the Old Bailey' *Criminal Law Review* (1979) pp. 203–19.

P. G. Zimbardo 'The Psychology of Police Confessions' *Psychology Today* vol. 1 (1967) pp. 17–27.

A. A. S. Zuckerman 'Criminal Law Revision Committee 11th Report, Right of Silence' *Modern Law Review* vol. 36 (1973) pp. 509–18.

Author Index

Subject Index